Peio Aguirre//Allora & Calzadilla//Domenick Ammirati//Margaret Atwood//J.G. Ballard//Jean Baudrillard//Christopher Bedford//Franco 'Bifo' Berardi//Janet Catherine Berlo//Rosi Braidotti// Ama Josephine Budge//Rachel Carson//Angela Chan//Dawn Chan//Ted Chiang//Neil Cummings// Jeffrey Deitch//T.J. Demos//Siân Ede//Helena Feder// Francesca Ferrando//Lisa Garforth//John Gill// Dominique Gonzalez-Foerster//Elizabeth C. Hamilton// Donna J. Haraway//Anya Harrison//N. Katherine Hayles//Jessica L. Horton//Wanuri Kahiu//Patrick Keiller//Josh Kline//Cathy Lane//Lee Bul//Marysia Lewandowska//Roger Luckhurst//Amna Malik//Tom McCarthy//Jessica Morgan//Timothy Morton//David Musgrave//Alondra Nelson//Benjamin Noys//Eduardo Paolozzi//Carrie Paterson//Michele Robecchi//Kim Stanley Robinson//Gwyneth Shanks//N.J. Stallard// Jamie Sutcliffe//Darko Suvin//Gilane Tawadros// Ana Teixeira Pinto//John Timberlake//Suzanne Treister// Jan Tumlir//Sherryl Vint//Frank Whitford//Gilda Williams

Science Fiction

Whitechapel Gallery
London
The MIT Press
Cambridge, Massachusetts

Edited by Dan Byrne-Smith

SCIE
NCE
FICT
ION

Documents of Contemporary Art

Co-published by Whitechapel Gallery
and The MIT Press

First published 2020

ISBN 978-0-85488-281-6 (Whitechapel Gallery)
ISBN 978-0-262-53885-5 (The MIT Press)

A catalogue record for this book is available from the British Library

Library of Congress Cataloging-in-Publication Data

Names: Byrne-Smith, Dan, editor.
Title: Science fiction / edited by Dan Byrne-Smith.
Description: London : Whitechapel Gallery ; Cambridge, Massachusetts : The MIT Press, 2020. | Series: Whitechapel: documents of contemporary art | Includes bibliographical references and index.
Identifiers: LCCN 2019049200 | ISBN 9780262538855 (paperback)
Subjects: LCSH: Science fiction--History and criticism. | Art and literature.
Classification: LCC PN3433.6 .S373 2020 | DDC 809.3/8762--dc23 LC record available at https://lccn.loc.gov/2019049200

Whitechapel Gallery 10 9 8 7 6 5 4 3 2 1
The MIT Press 10 9 8 7 6 5 4 3 2 1

Series Editor: Iwona Blazwick
Commissioning Editor: Anthony Iles
Project Editor: Francesca Vinter
Design by SMITH
Gemma Gerhard, Justine Hucker, Allon Kaye, Claudia Paladini
Printed and bound in China

Cover, Lee Bul, *Willing To Be Vulnerable* (2015–16). Installation view at the 20th Biennale of Sydney, 2016. Courtesy Studio Lee Bul and Lehmann Maupin, New York, Hong Kong, and Seoul. Photo: Algirdas Bakas

Whitechapel Gallery Ventures Limited
77–82 Whitechapel High Street
London, E1 7QX
whitechapelgallery.org

Distributed to the book trade (UK and Europe only) by Thames & Hudson
181a High Holborn
London, WC1V 7QX
+44 (0) 20 7845 5000
sales@thameshudson.co.uk

The MIT Press
Cambridge, MA 02142
mitpress.mit.edu

Whitechapel Gallery

Documents of Contemporary Art

In recent decades artists have progressively expanded the boundaries of art as they have sought to engage with an increasingly pluralistic environment. Teaching, curating and understanding of art and visual culture are likewise no longer grounded in traditional aesthetics but centred on significant ideas, topics and themes ranging from the everyday to the uncanny, the psychoanalytical to the political.

The Documents of Contemporary Art series emerges from this context. Each volume focuses on a specific subject or body of writing that has been of key influence in contemporary art internationally. Edited and introduced by a scholar, artist, critic or curator, each of these source books provides access to a plurality of voices and perspectives defining a significant theme or tendency.

For over a century the Whitechapel Gallery has offered a public platform for art and ideas. In the same spirit, each guest editor represents a distinct yet diverse approach – rather than one institutional position or school of thought – and has conceived each volume to address not only a professional audience but all interested readers.

THE POLITICAL
FUNCTION OF
SCIENCE FICTION
IS NOT MERELY TO
**FORECAST
THE DAY AFTER
TOMORROW,**
BUT TO MAKE US
AWARE ABOUT THE
PROBLEMS WE HAVE
IN IMAGINING IT

COGNITIVE ESTRANGEMENT

FUTURES

ECOLOGIES

IS IT EASIER TO IMAGINE **THE END** OF THE WORLD THAN **THE END** OF THE UNSUSTAINABLE MEGA-EXHIBITION?

T.J. Demos, 'Gardening Against the Apocalypse: The Case of dOCUMENTA (13)', 2016

Dan Byrne-Smith
Introduction//Sci-Fi

What makes science fiction so appealing to artists today? Why has this particular narrative form had such an influence on theoretical discourses around contemporary culture? It may be due to the ongoing integration of technologies into all aspects of life, as well as the continued acceleration of technological change experienced globally. It could also be due to the ability of science fiction narratives to reflect the increasing obviousness of climate change and the catastrophic implications. Or it may be the capacity to speculate on new forms of social relations and economic structures. Alternatively, science fiction might be used to explore the boundaries of what it means to be human when faced with the non-human. Whatever facets of the field that artists, writers, theorists or curators respond to, they are also responding to a sense of affinity between art and science fiction. In framing some aspects of this affinity, I hope to challenge the idea that science fiction can only be thought of as genre. Instead science fiction can be forms of practice, complex networks, or a set of sensibilities. It can be thought of as a field, a space of metaphor or a methodology. It resonates with ideas of change and uncertainty, as well as with the seemingly endless saturation of life by technology. It can also pertain to social unrest or new and darkening regimes of power. It speaks to those threats, anxieties and demands, providing opportunities to imagine new configurations. The importance of simple acts of imagining things as other than they seem cannot be overstated.

This collection responds to intensifications in engagements between art and science fiction in the early decades of the twenty-first century. This intensification in part reflects a seemingly exponential growth of science fiction as a global field. However, within the engagements brought together here is the recognition that it is a form capable of addressing politics, economics, social organisation, subjectivity and climate change. As artists have become increasingly open to incorporating tropes, themes and methodologies from science fiction in their own practices, discourses around contemporary art have kept pace. These emerging relationships have historical precedents. Reciprocal glances have long since been exchanged between the worlds of surrealism and science fiction. Despite André Breton's disdain for science fiction as a pulp genre, surrealism and science fiction are bound by an interest in fragmentation, a combining of tropes of documentary and narrative, as well as a shared concern with exploring limits and boundaries of consciousness.

Both have explored the hinterlands of logic, the collapse of the rational, and contradictions between the everyday and the unfamiliar.[1] In the 1950s, the Independent Group held up science fiction as a lens through which to observe post-war modernity. The exhibition 'This is Tomorrow', held at the Whitechapel Gallery in 1956, was subsequently an influence on the young writer J.G. Ballard, who saw in it an example of how the world can be perceived in new ways, as well as the ways it might be remade.[2] Ballard, who was to be one of the authors associated with the New Wave of science fiction in the 1960s, became a lifelong friend of artist Eduardo Paolozzi. Ballard and fellow New Wave writer Brian Aldiss shared a lifelong fascination with surrealist painting. In the late 1960s and early 70s Robert Smithson turned to the writings of Aldiss and Ballard to help formulate new kinds of spatial and temporal interventions.[3] Ballard also wrote about Smithson, an interest that subsequently led, in the later years of his life, to a correspondence with artist-filmmaker Tacita Dean.

The texts gathered here are arranged in four chapters: 'Cognitive Estrangement', 'Futures', 'Posthumanism' and 'Ecologies'. The first of these chapters unpacks the shared capacity of contemporary art and science fiction to make things strange. The notion of cognitive estrangement frames science fiction as a tool for reading and transforming the world. It reveals the potential for readers or audiences to rethink their surroundings. This is an idea developed by the literary critic Darko Suvin in his book *Metamorphosis and Science Fiction* (1979), an excerpt of which is included here as 'Strangeness and Cognition'. Suvin's influential work may appear already familiar to artists and their audiences. It relates to demands put upon art to generate meaningful and potentially transformative encounters, to engage beyond reductive notions of entertainment, consumption or the acquisition of cultural capital. Suvin privileges science fiction works that emphasise discontinuity, that rise above escapism towards a form of subversion. Here he sees a potential for the transformation of the world, rather than its reflection, taking the Brechtian idea of alienation and applying it to science fiction works that emphasise the construction of their reality, enabling social critique. Suvin argues that cognitive estrangement frames the world as constructed by human agency, revealing the potential for change. Suvin offers a useful and influential definition of what science fiction is – *the literature of cognitive estrangement* – as well as what it does. However, that is not to say that he resolves any possible uncertainty around how science fiction might be defined.[4]

Discussions around definition are present in this collection, for example in the excerpt from Margaret Atwood's *In Other Worlds* (2011). However, they are not resolved. To describe something in terms of science fiction is to change the way it is perceived, addressed and discussed. It is not necessarily an inherent or fixed set of properties, relating to immutable or obvious boundaries but, as Sherryl Vint usefully suggests in the text 'Cognitive Estrangement', science fiction can be thought of as a network of linked elements. These include motifs, themes, tropes and imagery. Science fiction's ability to operate between critical operations such as analogy or metaphor, to surrender to strangeness or the weird, is suggestive of techniques of distancing and substitution that resonate with contemporary art.[5] These processes might be devices or contrivances that can explore the familiar and re-present it in abstracted form. This method was used in the 2008 exhibition *The Martian Museum of Terrestrial Art*, held at the Barbican Gallery in London. Represented here by Tom McCarthy's inventive written piece for the catalogue essay, the exhibition's curators constructed a narrative contrivance that displayed the work as if it had been selected, presented and interpreted by anthropologists from another planet.

Running through the texts collected in this section chapter is the idea that estrangement is linked to the possibility of agency. However, the question of what forms this agency might actually take is difficult to answer. Nevertheless, appeals to agency through science fictional estrangement recur here as urgent and necessary. Estrangement does not necessarily negate hopelessness but it can facilitate the formulation of speculative problems in generative ways. This can apply to art that looks to science fiction but it is a property of science fiction, even in its most mainstream and popular forms.

Ted Chiang is perhaps best known for his novella 'Story of Your Life' (1998), which was used as the basis for the 2016 Hollywood film *Arrival*. Closing this chapter is his story 'The Great Silence', which he developed in collaboration with the artists Jennifer Allora and Guillermo Calzadilla. The text was incorporated into Allora & Calzadilla's video footage of the Arecibo Observatory in Puerto Rico and the parrots that live in the surrounding forest. In a simple act of estrangement, Chiang's text is written from the perspective of one of the parrots, who mournfully reflects on the limits of anthropocentric thinking.

The field of science fiction is a space for envisioning things to come and for future orientated speculation. 'Futures', the second chapter in the book, explores the embeddedness of these concepts and processes in science fiction. This is not to say that all science fiction is defined by the idea of futurity; but rather that preoccupations with the 'not yet' and 'what might be' have shaped the histories of science fiction. In turn, science fiction has been a means for both stimulating and questioning imaginary configurations of possible, desirable or disagreeable futures. The transition to an industrial and scientific modernity that included preoccupations with futurity was also, of course, largely coterminous with the formation of European modernism in visual art. However, science fiction has mirrored a broader sense of problematic cultural understanding of the future, which could be understood as a loss of confidence and belief in the very idea of futurity. It correlates to an impression that while for much of the twentieth century Western art was orientated towards newness and futurity as opposed to the past, contemporary art has lost a tangible sense of connection to the future. Artists seem to have got into a habit of addressing the idea of the future as something abandoned, approaching the future from critical, nostalgic or ironic positions. However, over the past two decades, some artists have become interested in imagined futures that look back to the present in order to defamiliarise the contemporary, a method employed by Kapwani Kiwanga in her ongoing *Afrogalactica* project (2012–). The character of Rosalind Brodsky, created as an alter ego by artist Suzanne Treister, claims to be a time traveller, uncovering historical networks of conspiracy and influence that have shaped the present. The future history offered in *Museum Futures* (2008) by Neil Cummings and Marysia Lewandowska presents a speculative genealogy for social, cultural, economic and technological developments, explored in an interview with the future director of Moderna Museet, Stockholm, in 2058.

Science fiction, particularly in its popular forms in the West, has a tendency to appear as an unending sequence of bad futures. These are generally referred to as dystopias, without qualifying or examining what such a term means, other than as shorthand for a future that is not particularly nice. However, dystopias, as tropes, are only genuinely useful if they enable people to grasp the concept of working towards futures beyond the present moment. The short text included here by Franco 'Bifo' Berardi, 'Future Exhaustion and Happy Frugality', addresses the collapse of constructive projections of the future, arguing that it is necessary to come to terms with death of the future, as an abandoning of the acceptance of the economic and social conditions of the present. Contemporary anxieties around technology, distortions of power and threats to subjectivity today can be found in the famous dystopias of Orwell and Huxley, and even more presciently in E.M. Forster's *The Machine Stops* (1909). This short story is the point of reference in N.J. Stallard's 'I Want to See You Not Through the Machine', a text originally written for a small group exhibition.[6] Stallard makes clear the uncanny prescience of Forster's story, which in turn acts as a prompt. The resulting group show explores experience as mediated through screen-based technologies; dystopia is mobilised to rethink relations in the present.

Many of the texts selected here engage with futures that move beyond Eurocentric, Western and white projections, building on the legacies of Afrofuturism in particular. Technological and cultural dimensions of futurity, as well as notions of time, change when opened up to a broader range of perspectives, struggles and traditions. Ana Teixeira Pinto presents an overview of contested and unevenly distributed futures. She unpacks relations between time and technology, aspects of privilege, social reality and the importance of Afrofuturisms and Sinofuturisms. Dawn Chan explores Asian futurisms, with an emphasis on the agency and representation of Asians in global/Westernised narratives, looking for generative images of Asian futures that move beyond techno-orientalism and racist cliché. Her ideas are referred to and built on in a text by Jamie Sutcliffe, who continues the task of unpacking recent trends in art and science fiction in relation to Asian Futurisms. These globalised concepts of futurity relate to the demands for new possibilities and propositions, made explicit by Ursula K. Le Guin in her acceptance speech at a National Book Awards ceremony in 2014. For Le Guin, science fiction is part of a duty towards hope and change, to begin now, to be carried out into the futurity of next week, next year or the next century.[7]

The texts collected in the next chapter explore different facets of posthumanism. The term is used in part to suggest future-orientated possibilities for how humans might be remade. Yet the idea of posthumanism is also rooted in historical considerations, in critical enquiries that explore the ways in which humans have been defined and linked to social, technological and cognitive changes. It is a set of ideas that reflect anxieties but can also be used to offer positive models. This is a field that charts the end of a coherent subject in Western thought and the emergence of new possibilities of being. The chapter brings together texts that consider the boundaries between the human and the non-human, that critique the rational human subject, open up discussions relating to non-human otherness, and that refer to transhumanist impulses towards a technological future for the species. The understanding of posthumanism here is built on a lineage of challenges to patriarchal Western essentialism, an essentialism that has been used to reproduce repressive ideological frameworks.[8] This is also a genealogy that maps a convergence of science fiction with theory as a network of generative exchanges, as demonstrated by Donna Haraway's profoundly influential writings on the figure of the cyborg, represented here by her 'Cyborg Manifesto', first published in 1985 and subsequently included in the book *Simians, Cyborgs and Women* in 1991.

Posthumanism can also be thought of as a field for exploring relations between technologies and identities. Through the science fictional lens of posthumanism, these are not discrete elements but interdependent. In foregrounding this interdependence, posthumanism offers insights and reconfigurations of social relations all too often assumed to be determined by nature.[9] As biotechnology continues to transform from an area of speculative and dramatic consideration to a growing and increasingly powerful industry, the need for science fiction to continue to address the moral and ethical implications also intensifies. The touring exhibition 'Post Human' (1992–3) was a significant moment in the establishment of science fiction as a relevant cultural force for artists, as well as in the establishing of the currency of the term itself. Curator Jeffrey Deitch brought together artists that documented a transition to an irrational, neurotic, increasingly technological futurity that challenged traditional constructions of embodied subjectivity. The essay Deitch wrote for the catalogue, included in this volume, was prescient in identifying themes that have retained a sense of urgency.[10] However, 'Post Human' also retains significance through acting as a kind of science-fictional argument. Deitch framed his selection of artists with a call for all artists to help shape these emergent futures rooted in the present. 'Post Human' was staged as a demand for new kinds of art that could shape future relationships with technologies and emergent social formations. The exhibition, comprised of practices that had emerged in the 1980s, also corresponded to an emergent conflation of science fictional ideas with critical writing, particularly through the influence of Jean Baudrillard and Haraway. Both writers explored different ways in which contemporary lived experience and notions of subjectivity were undergoing processes of reconfiguration, moving towards conditions that increasingly resembled certain forms of science fiction.

Rachel Carson's *Silent Spring*, originally published in 1962, warns of the devastating consequences of the misuse of chemicals on the natural world. Although *Silent Spring* is not a work of science fiction, her book begins with 'A Fable for Tomorrow', a speculative piece of writing that opens the 'Ecologies' chapter. Carson's warning, that disaster has already begun through chemical pollution, powerfully asserts that along with the possibility of human extinction through nuclear war, the material conditions of all life on the planet are under severe threat. Carson provides a worst-case scenario which makes for devastating reading. The emergence of environmental movements in the wake of *Silent Spring* has been accompanied by the efforts of science fiction writers to explore ecological challenges in relation to human activity. Carson's fable can be placed in a tradition of science fiction writing that looks towards catastrophe.[11]

Science fiction can be read as a literature of technological modernity, but also a literature of the end of humanity. Not only is the end of the world and after a recurrent theme but it is a theme that has helped to shape and popularise notions of ecology and a planetary environment, as well as the impact of human activity on the natural world. Science fiction also has a long history of suggesting alternative models of social organisation, despite a tendency to show many of those alternatives as undesirable. The kinds of stories that can be told in the field can often be understood as not only reflections of the spaces of culture in which they operate but also as forces in themselves that shape those spaces. With this recognition comes the possibility of imagining science fiction and science-fictional thought as having a power to influence possible futures. Images of alien worlds on screen could show strange ecologies with the potential to sensitise viewers to non-human life on their own planet. A story set in a future dominated by corporations rather than democratically elected governments offers audiences an opportunity to question current locations of power. Science fiction can operate as a shorthand, or a form of cultural currency, while on other occasions it is presented as a tool for shifting modes of thought in unexpected directions. It might, in certain forms, be read as escapist or compensatory but even in the most apparently simplistic guises, science fiction can often contain counter-narratives, alternatives, metaphorical elements, or a strangeness that disorientates.

1 Abigail Susik, 'Surrealism and Jules Verne: Depth of a Subtext in a Collage by Max Ernst', in *Surrealism, Science Fiction and Comics*, ed. Gavin Parkinson (Liverpool: Liverpool University Press, 2015) 16–39, 19.

2 J.G. Ballard and Hans Ulrich Obrist, 'Nothing is Real: Everything is Fake', published for Beck's Futures 2003 exhibition (London: ICA, 2003). Reprinted in *Extreme Metaphors: Selected Interviews with J.G. Ballard 1967–2008* (London: Fourth Estate, 2012) 383–95, 385.

3 The novel *Earthworks* (1965) by Brian Aldiss provided Smithson with the term that he would go on to use in describing artworks and actions situated in the landscape.

4 Science fiction is frustratingly difficult to define, even though it often appears obvious upon first engagement with it. See Adam Roberts, *Science Fiction: New Critical Idiom* (Abingdon and New York: Routledge, 2006) 1.

5 'Reveling in Genre: An Interview with China Miéville', *Science Fiction Studies*, vol. 30, no. 3 (2003) 355–73.

6 'The Machine Stops', Danielle Arnaud Gallery, London, 24 February–24 March, 2018.

7 Ursula K. Le Guin, 'National Book Award Medal for Distinguished Contribution to American Letters Acceptance Speech' (2014), in *Dreams Must Explain Themselves and Other Essays* 1972–2004 (London: Gollancz, 2018) 383–4.

8 See Neil Badmington (ed.), *Posthumanism: Readers in Cultural Criticism* (Basingstoke and London: Macmillan, 2000).

9 Science fiction has long since looked to biological sciences. *Frankenstein* is not only a worthy candidate for the first work of science fiction but also a candidate for the first work of modern posthumanism.

10 The 2014 exhibition 'Science Fiction: New Death' at FACT Liverpool is in many ways an urgent and updated return to the themes addressed in 'Post Human'.

11 Mary Shelley's *The Last Man* (1826), in which plague wipes out the human population, was preceded by Jean-Baptiste Cousin de Grainville's *Le Dernier Homme* (*The Last Man*, 1805), a Christian fantasy set in a distant future where the life of humanity as a species on Earth is damned by their sinful nature, but the planet itself is imbued with a kind of natural spirit. Narratives emerged in the twentieth century that explored disasters as explicitly caused by humans, such as John Cristopher's *The Death of Grass* (1956), whereas Frank Herbert's *Dune* (1965) can be seen as the originator of a type of work that maps out a planetary ecology. The novel reads as a drama of a dynastic power struggle but also addresses the idea of a planet as a fragile ecosystem at the centre of a complex process of narrative world building. In Joan Slonczewski's *A Door into Ocean* (1986), a complex ecosystem is described that presents the problem of a lack of adequate land and the fragility of a food chain.

It seems to me that so-called

SCIENCE FICTION

was defining our contemporary environment better than art

Suzanne Treister, 'In Conversation with Roger Luckhurst', 2013

COGNITIVE ESTRANGEMENT

Margaret Atwood
Is Science Fiction Going Out of Date?//2011

[...] Our earliest loves, like revenants, have a way of coming back in other forms; or, to paraphrase Wordsworth, the child is mother to the woman. To date, as what I am pleased to think of as an adult, I have written three full-length fictions that nobody would ever class as sociological realism: *The Handmaid's Tale*, *Oryx and Crake*, and *The Year of the Flood*. Are these books 'science fiction'? I am often asked. Though sometimes I am not asked, but told: I am a silly nit or a snob or a genre traitor for dodging the term because these books are as much 'science fiction' as *Nineteen Eighty-Four* is, whatever I might say. But is *Nineteen Eighty-Four* as much 'science fiction' as *The Martian Chronicles*? I might reply. I would answer not, and therein lies the distinction.

Much depends on your nomenclatural allegiances, or else on your system of literary taxonomy. Back in 2008, I was talking to a much younger person about 'science fiction'. I'd been asked by the magazine *New Scientist* to answer the question 'Is science fiction going out of date?' But then I realised that I couldn't make a stab at the answer because I didn't really grasp what the term science fiction meant anymore. Is this term a corral with real fences that separate what is clearly 'science fiction' from what is not, or is it merely a shelving aid, there to help workers in bookstores place the book in a semi-accurate or at least lucrative way? If you put skin-tight black or silver clothing on a book cover along with some jet-like flames and/or colourful planets, does that make the work 'science fiction'? What about dragons and manticores, or backgrounds that contain volcanoes or atomic clouds, or plants with tentacles, or landscapes reminiscent of Hieronymus Bosch? Does there have to be any actual science in such a book, or is the skin-tight clothing enough? These seemed to me to be open questions.

This much younger person, let's call him Randy, which was in fact his name – did not have a hard and fast definition of 'science fiction', but he knew it when he saw it, kind of. As I told *New Scientist*, 'For Randy – and I think he's representative – sci–fi does include other planets, which may or may not have dragons on them. It includes the wildly paranormal – not your aunt table-tilting or things going creak, but shape-shifters and people with red eyeballs and no pupils, and Things taking over your body.' Here I myself would include such items as Body Snatchers – if of extraterrestrial rather than folkloric provenance – and Pod People, and heads growing out of your armpits, though I'd exclude common and garden-variety devils, and demonic possession, and also vampires and werewolves, which have literary ancestries and categories all their own.

As I reported in my *New Scientist* article, for Randy sci-fi includes, as a matter of course, spaceships, and Mad Scientists, and Experiments Gone Awfully Wrong. Plain ordinary horror doesn't count – chainsaw murderers and such. Randy and I agreed that you might meet one of those walking along the street. It's what you definitely would not meet walking along the street that makes the grade. Randy judged such books in part by the space-scapes and leathery or silvery outfits on their covers, which means that my speculations about jacket images are not entirely irrelevant. As one friend's child put it: 'Looks like milk, tastes like milk – it IS milk!' Thus: looks like science fiction, has the tastes of science fiction – it IS science fiction!

Or more or less. Or kind of. For covers can be misleading. The earliest mass-market paperbacks of my first two novels, *The Edible Woman* and *Surfacing*, had pink covers with gold scrollwork designs on them and oval frames with a man's head and a woman's head silhouetted inside, just like Valentines. How many readers picked these books up, hoping to find a Harlequin Romance or reasonable facsimile, only to throw them down in tears because there are no weddings at the ends?

Then there was the case of the former Soviet Union. No sooner did the Wall come down in 1989 than pornography flooded across the former divide. Porn had hitherto been excluded in favour of endless editions of the classics and other supposed-to-be-good-for-you works, but forbidden fruit excites desire, and everyone had already read Tolstoy, a lot. Suddenly the publishers of serious literature were hard-pressed. Thus it was that *The Robber Bride* appeared in a number of Soviet-bloc countries with covers that might be described as, at best, deceptive and, at worst, as a Eurotrash slutfest *in flagrante*. How many men in raincoats purchased the *Robber Bride* edition sporting a black-satin-sheathed Zenia with colossal tits, hoping for a warm one-handed time in a back corner, only to heave it into the bin with a strangled *Foiled Again!* curse? For the Zenia in my book performs what we can only assume is her sexual witchery offstage.

Having thus misled readers twice – inadvertently – by dint of book covers and the genre categories implied by them, I would rather not do it again. I would like to have space creatures inside the books on offer at my word-wares booth, and I would if I could: they were, after all, my first childhood love. But, being unable to produce them, I don't want to lead the reader on, thus generating a frantic search within the pages – *Where are The Lizard Men of Xenor?* – that can only end in disappointment.

My desire to explore my relationship with the SF world, or worlds, has a proximate cause. In 2009, I published *The Year of the Flood*, the second work of fiction in a series exploring another kind of 'other world' – our own planet in a future. (I carefully say *a* future rather than *the* future because the future is an unknown: from the moment *now*, an infinite number of roads lead away to 'the future', each heading in a different direction.)

The Year of the Flood was reviewed, along with its sibling, *Oryx and Crake*, by one of the reigning monarchs of the SF and Fantasy forms, Ursula K. Le Guin. Her 2009 *Guardian* article began with a paragraph that has caused a certain amount of uproar in the skin-tight clothing and other-planetary communities – so much so that scarcely a question period goes by at my public readings without someone asking, usually in injured tones, why I have forsworn the term science fiction, as if I've sold my children to the salt mines.

Here are Le Guin's uproar-causing sentences:

> To my mind, *The Handmaid's Tale*, *Oryx and Crake* and now *The Year of the Flood* all exemplify one of the things science fiction does, which is to extrapolate imaginatively from current trends and events to a near-future that's half prediction, half satire. But Margaret Atwood doesn't want any of her books to be called science fiction. In her recent, brilliant essay collection, *Moving Targets*, she says that everything that happens in her novels is possible and may even have already happened, so they can't be science fiction, which is 'fiction in which things happen that are not possible today.' This arbitrarily restrictive definition seems designed to protect her novels from being relegated to a genre still shunned by hidebound readers, reviewers and prize-awarders. She doesn't want the literary bigots to shove her into the literary ghetto.

The motive imputed to me is not in fact my actual motive for requesting separate names. (If winning prizes were topmost on my list, and if writing such books would guarantee non-wins, my obvious move would be just to avoid writing them.) What I mean by 'science fiction' is those books that descend from H.G. Wells' *The War of the Worlds*, which treats of an invasion by tentacled, blood-sucking Martians shot to Earth in metal canisters – things that could not possibly happen – whereas, for me, 'speculative fiction' means plots that descend from Jules Verne's books about submarines and balloon travel and such – things that really could happen but just hadn't completely happened when the authors wrote the books. I would place my own books in this second category: no Martians. Not because I don't like Martians, I hasten to add: they just don't fall within my skill set. Any seriously intended Martian by me would be a very clumsy Martian indeed.

In a public discussion with Ursula K. Le Guin in the fall of 2010, however, I found that what she means by 'science fiction' is speculative fiction about things that really could happen, whereas things that really could not happen she classifies under 'fantasy'. Thus, for her – as for me – dragons would belong in fantasy, as would, I suppose, the film *Star Wars* and most of the TV series *Star Trek*. Mary Shelley's *Frankenstein* might squeeze into Le Guin's 'science fiction' because its author had grounds for believing that electricity actually might be able to reanimate dead flesh. And *The War of the Worlds*? Since people thought at the time that intelligent beings might live on Mars, and since space travel was believed to be possible in the imaginable future, this book might have to be filed under Le Guin's 'science fiction'. Or parts of it might. In short, what Le Guin means by 'science fiction' is what I mean by 'speculative fiction', and what she means by 'fantasy' would include some of what I mean by 'science fiction'. So that clears it all up, more or less. When it comes to genres, the borders are increasingly undefended, and things slip back and forth across them with insouciance.

Bendiness of terminology, literary gene-swapping, and inter-genre visiting has been going on in the SF world – loosely defined – for some time. For instance, in a 1989 essay called 'Slipstream', veteran SF author Bruce Sterling deplored the then-current state of science fiction and ticked off its writers and publishers for having turned it into a mere 'category' – a 'self-perpetuating commercial power-structure, which happens to be in possession of a traditional national territory: a portion of bookstore rack space.' A 'category', says Sterling, is distinct from a 'genre', which is 'a spectrum of work united by an inner identity, a coherent aesthetic, a set of conceptual guidelines, an ideology if you will.'

Sterling defines his term *slipstream* – so named, I suppose, because it is seen as making use of the air currents created by science fiction proper in this way:

> [...] I want to describe what seems to me to be a new, emergent 'genre', which has not yet become a 'category'. This genre is not 'category' SF; it is not even 'genre' SF. Instead, it is a contemporary kind of writing which has set its face against consensus reality. It is fantastic, surreal sometimes, speculative on occasion, but not rigorously so. It does not aim to provoke a 'sense of wonder' or to systematically extrapolate in the manner of classic science fiction. Instead, this is a kind of writing that simply makes you feel very strange; the way that living in the late twentieth century makes you feel, if you are a person of a certain sensibility.

His proposed list of slipstream fictions covers an astonishing ground, with works by a wide assortment of people, many of them considered to be 'serious' authors – from Kathy Acker and Martin Amis to Salman Rushdie, José Saramago and Kurt Vonnegut. What they have in common is that the kinds of events they recount are unlikely to *have actually taken place*. In an earlier era, these 'slipstream' books might all have been filed under the heading of 'traveller's yarn' – stories like, for example, Herodotus' accounts of monopods and giant ants or medieval legends about unicorns, dragons and mermaids. Later they might have turned up in other collections of the marvellous and uncanny, such as *Des Knaben Wunderhorn*, or, even later, the kind of You-won't-believe-this-hair-raiser to be found in assortments by M.R. James or H.P. Lovecraft or, occasionally, R.L. Stevenson.

But surely all draw from the same deep well: those imagined other worlds located somewhere apart from our everyday one: in another time, in another dimension, through a doorway into the spirit world, or on the other side of the threshold that divides the known from the unknown. Science Fiction, Speculative Fiction, Sword and Sorcery Fantasy, and Slipstream Fiction: all of them might be placed under the same large 'wonder tale' umbrella. [...]

Margaret Atwood, extract from 'Introduction', in *Other Worlds: SF and the Human Imagination* (London: Virago, 2011) 2–8.

Gilane Tawadros and John Gill
We Are the Martians//2006

[...] Articulating deep-seated fears about a rapidly changing world over which we exert little control, science fiction's narratives confront the apparent perils of the present seen through the prism of an imaginary future. Much has been written about the connection between science fiction cinema of the 1950s, 60s and the Cold War, where fears of invasion, Communism and nuclear war were played out in fictional films that reflected contemporary anxieties. More recently, many artists have similarly used science fiction and the trope of the alien as a way of exploring the fear of difference and a potent metaphor for the perceived threat of the outsider.

'Alien Nation' presents the work of twelve international artists all of whom explore themes of 'otherness' and 'difference' through the language and iconography of science fiction juxtaposed with original films and film posters from the 1950s and 60s. The artworks encompass film, sculpture, photography, multimedia installation and painting – and expose a disturbing contemporary narrative in which the media perpetuate a terror of 'invasion' from immigrants, asylum seekers (indeed any racial, cultural or ethnic 'other') and position such 'outsiders' as the dominant threat to both family and national stability. Often witty and irreverent, these artists have adopted the figure of the extraterrestrial and the alien(ated) landscape in order to comment upon the fantasies, fears and desires that lie, barely suppressed, beneath the surface of contemporary culture and society.

The storylines of 1950s and 60s science fiction films were restricted, for the most part, to a small number of narratives that were played out over and over again in stories that rehearse the dangers of infiltration and attack by alien invaders. Scenarios often involve the 'invisible' duplication and transformation of friends, family and associates into emotionless aliens (*Invasion of the Body Snatchers*; *It Came from Outer Space*); the breeding of life-threatening alien life forms that threaten to overwhelm and wipe out human life (*Invasion of the Body Snatchers*; *The Thing from Another World*; *The Day of the Triffids*); the fear of annihilation (*The Day the Earth Stood Still*; *The War of the Worlds*; *Forbidden Planet*); the threat of brainwashing and mind control (*Village of the Damned*; *Quatermass and the Pit*); and anxieties about miscegenation and racial impurity (*The Day the Earth Stood Still*; *Village of the Damned*).

In the aftermath of 9/11 and the bombings in London and Madrid in recent years, these narratives have been re-played once again, this time in both documentary and fictional media representations, emerging from a society which has displaced its fears and paranoias onto the figure of the migrant, the asylum seeker and the Islamic 'other'. Images of the asylum seeker who poses a criminal threat to the wider society, or the terrorist whose outward appearance does not betray his/her loyalties to an 'alien' ideological cause; the brainwashing and 'radicalisation' of young men, converting them to militant Islam; and the fear of attack from long-range chemical weapons or terrorist devices closer to home, have become the subject of our collective nightmares, frequently stoked and fired up by politicians and the media so that it becomes almost impossible to distinguish reality from nightmare. [...]

Robots and Aliens: the Good, the Bad and the Ugly

The aliens and robots that populate science fiction films of the 1950s are an assortment of the good, the bad and the ugly. The Frankenstein-like 'Thing' (James Arness) in *The Thing from Another World* is closer to the monsters dreamt up by Mary Shelley's nineteenth-century gothic imagination than any futuristic, advanced life form; while Klaatu's human appearance in *The Day the Earth Stood Still* belies his super-human capacity to resist disease and ageing. Other aliens are more distant from human form.

The aliens in *It Came from Outer Space* (1953) are forced to take on human appearance while they repair their damaged spaceship because their true alien form is too hideous and terrifying for human beings to behold and, by implication, to accept. These are peaceful aliens who simply want to be left alone to fix their ship and return home but they are well aware (as Klaatu is) of man's instinctively violent response not only to those who are different but also to their own race. The robot Gort (Lock Martin), who eventually descends from the spaceship in *The Day the Earth Stood Still* (after soldiers have shot at Klaatu having mistaken his gift for a weapon), is a massive metallic humanoid figure from a race of intergalactic policemen whose job it is to enforce peace and avert violence and conflict in the rest of the universe. Gort's immense destructive powers are triggered by the assaults on Klaatu in the same way that the visit to earth by these alien/robot visitors has been provoked by the threat of mankind's military expansionism.

In Forbidden Planet (1956), the sophisticated robot Robby has been programmed by his creator, the scientist Dr Morbius (a space-age Prospero played by actor Walter Pidgeon), in such a way as to make it impossible for him to kill or destroy human life. The mysterious and invisible alien life form that inhabits the planet Altair 4 and destroys the lives of innocent crew members turns out at the end of the film to be not an alien life form but rather the 'monstrous Id' of the scientist Dr Morbius, a horrific alter-ego that acts out his murderous and suppressed desires. Like *Quatermass*, which originated as a television series on the BBC in 1953, *Forbidden Planet* presented as the greatest threat to mankind its inner destructive nature rather than any extraterrestrial bent on the annihilation of the earth. As the scientist Quatermass pronounces at the conclusion of the television version of *Quatermass and the Pit* (1958–9): 'Every war, crisis, witch-hunt, race riot and purge, is a reminder and warning. We are the Martians. If we can not control the inheritance within us, this will be the second dead planet.'

Aliens and robots feature in the works of many of the artists in the 'Alien Nation' exhibition, although what is striking is how ambiguous and indeterminate these characters of contemporary art are both in appearance and morality. A reflection of the more equivocal times in which we live and also of the more open-ended structure of contemporary art by comparison with film narrative (which has a beginning, middle and end, and moves invariably towards a resolution of some kind), there are no clear-cut goodies and baddies, no positively good aliens or downright evil ones. Laylah Ali's bizarre humanoid figures are indeterminate beings that look alternately like children in extravagant dressing-up costumes or freakish genetic mutations, part-animal and part-human. In earlier works populated by Ali's 'Greenheads' and 'Blueheads', the physical indeterminacy of the figures – alien/human, male/female, black/white – reflected their ambiguous morality. [...] These strange creatures might be figments of a surreal imagination or discarded mutations of terrible scientific experiment.

The source for Hamad Butt's early video work *The Triffid* (part II of the *Transmission* installation) made in 1990 was a drawing of a triffid on an early Penguin edition of John Wyndham's *The Day of the Triffids*, first published in 1951. Possibly the 'outcome of a series of ingenious biological meddlings'[1] and cultivated on an industrial scale in order to extract its valuable oil, the triffids were tall, large-rooted plants whose venomous sting could blind its victims and feed on their decomposing human flesh. When the majority of people on earth are blinded as a result of witnessing an extraordinary comet display, the triffids are in a position to take over the planet. For Butt, the triffid was a metaphor for a contemporary and equally deadly epidemic that was capable of generating as much fear as Wyndham's toxic, walking plants. [...] The triffid embodied many of Butt's preoccupations as an artist – the intersection of art and science, the arcane (alchemy) and the popular (science fiction), sexuality and death. These themes permeate Butt's works, invoking the precariousness of human existence and the settled sense of security which is shattered so abruptly by the coming of the triffids in Wyndham's fiction and by AIDS in the contemporary world. [...]

In most of the science fiction narratives of the 1950s, the tension arises from the fear of the apocalypse that is yet to happen and the action takes place on the brink of this apocalyptic event. *The Day of the Triffids*, written at the height of the Cold War, imagines the aftermath of the apocalypse in a post-war world where the complete annihilation of the human race was seen as a distinct possibility. As Michael Beadley tells the sighted survivors in *Triffids*: 'From 6 August 1945, the margin of survival has narrowed appallingly. Indeed, two days ago it was narrower than it is at this moment... . In any single moment of the years since then the fatal slip might have been made. It is a miracle that it was not.'[2]

In the world of David Huffman's paintings, the trauma has already taken place many years earlier. Huffman creates an alternative universe that still bears the trauma of the past and present, carrying it forward into the future. In earlier paintings, from the late 1990s, Huffman conceived the Traumasmiles: black-faced minstrels that wear a perpetual grin, fixed in place permanently by the trauma of slavery and its repercussions through time. As Huffman explains, 'trauma was the subverted awareness of the trauma of slavery itself – the horrific holocaust that wasn't digested or dealt with in a mature way. So to me it was very traumatic to create characters with big smiles when that had actually occurred for so long. The smile was false, not a simple expression of joy or happiness, but a disguise that covered an internal anguish. Pain was subverted through that smiling face'.[3]

Alongside the race of Traumasmiles are their powerful robotic creations, the Traumabots, which are animated and powered by the Traumasmiles 'who get inside and become physically connected to them [...] it is a neurological connection in that they can feel everything that happens to the robots. They become one.'[4] In a reversal of the classic science fiction storyline where aliens occupy the bodies of human beings, here the Traumabots are inhabited by the Traumasmiles, endowing them with both a body and power. For Huffman, who grew up in the United States on a diet of television programmes like *Astroboy*, *Shogun Warriors*, *Transformers* and *Star Trek*, science fiction provided both intellectual and aesthetic source material whose storylines frequently dealt with the fear of difference: 'I've always been interested in the way 50s science fiction came out of McCarthyism and the idea that the Reds are here. The whole alien and UFO thing was mostly about other people, other cultures.'[5] In *It's All Over Now, Baby Blue* (2006) – Huffman's new three-panel screen work – the artist creates a world where extraterrestrial protagonists collide with recent events. References to conflicts (from Vietnam to Iraq), in which indigenous populations are overpowered by military might, are intermingled in Huffman's narrative paintings with references to the science fiction movie *Beneath the Planet of the Apes*, with its inverted evolutionary narrative in which apes evolve from humans: 'the Traumasmiles are shaped by contemporary socio-political minefields that are played out in my parallel universe of Traumanauts'.

Outer space provides an other-worldly place where earthly conflicts and tensions can be resolved and where new alliances can be forged. The crew of the Starship Enterprise in *Star Trek* (first aired in the early 1960s at the height of the Civil Rights Movement) presented an idealised interplanetary and ethnic alliance. The first interracial kiss on television, between Captain Kirk (William Shatner) and Lieutenant Uhura (Nichelle Nichols, whose character's name was inspired by *uhuru*, the Swahili word for freedom) in the 1968 episode 'Plato's Children', played out mixed-race relationships in the furthest reaches of the universe, that were still capable of inflaming violent racist passions and reprisals on our own planet.

Mario Ybarra Jr.'s mural, *Brown and Proud* (2006), imagines a very different alliance between rebels not only from different spaces/places but also from different planets. Ybarra, who himself combines a variety of roles including artist, educator, gallerist, social anthropologist and archivist, creates artworks and interventions that frequently involve constructing a platform for the meeting of different worlds that blend and cross in contemporary Chicano art culture: North American/Mexican; popular culture/Hollywood; science fiction/political reality. In this new work, Ybarra pictures a meeting between the hairy alien rebel Chewbacca (a giant fur-covered Wookie) and the Mexican revolutionary Zapata, both rebels engaged in battling against an awesome empire, whether galactic or earthly. In Ybarra's universe, the partnership between Chewbacca and Zapata also represents the coalition of political revolt and popular culture as a strategy for resistance against more conventional (and potentially alienating) political structures.

A different kind of displacement occurs in Yinka Shonibare's *Dysfunctional Family* (1999). A typical family group – mother, father and two kids – Shonibare's nuclear family are remarkable only in the sense that they obviously belong to another species from another planet and, perhaps, even from another universe. With their short bodies and disproportionately large heads, Shonibare's *Dysfunctional Family* is a witty and acerbic play on the fear of difference. Based on popular images of aliens, Shonibare's extraterrestrials are fashioned out of the batik cloth that has become the signature of many of the artist's works with its indeterminate status (Indonesian fabric exported to Africa that has come to be seen as traditional African fabric). This alien family is equally indeterminate. Conventional in every respect, other than its questionable outer space origin, Shonibare's *Dysfunctional Family* is a playful spin on the legal and social designation of the 'alien' as a marker of difference and the fears and fantasies that it ignites.

The term 'alien' was still being employed by the British government as late as 1970 to designate foreigners entering the country who were also obliged to register their presence at a police station. The Alien Act of 1793 had been enacted in Britain after the French Revolution had turned to terror and was designed to monitor and register all foreigners entering Britain, the information being sent to a central index at the Home Office. By 1800 the Alien Office had become 'the centre of Britain's spy network, watching subversives through the apprehending and copying of letters sent through the Post Office'.[6] Fifteen years later, the Federalists in the United States passed the Alien and Seditions Acts (1798) as a response to the recent influx of political refugees – French Jacobins, Irish rebels, English and Welsh radicals – who had become outspoken supporters of the Republican party.[7] To some radical screenwriters in the United States in the late 1940s, the mounting anti-Communist crusade bore a striking resemblance to the events that had taken place 150 years earlier. As the writer Philip Dunne wrote: 'Attempts to force conformity of opinion are nothing new in the United States. The Alien and Seditions Act of the first Adams administration, directed against the Jeffersonians who were thought to be too sympathetic to the French revolutionaries, afford what is almost a direct parallel to the anti-Communist proposals of today.'[8]

Alongside Shonibare's *Dysfunctional Family*, the floor of the gallery space is littered with strange metallic objects that could be extraterrestrial constructions or exquisite space debris, reclaimed as ornamental sculptures or oversized Christmas decorations. There is a kind of alchemy to the practice of the artist Marepe whose works frequently transform found, everyday objects into poetic and evocative artworks that invite both physical and social interactions. In earlier installations such as *The Itinerant Merchants* (1996) or *Cafezinho Pushcart* (1996), Marepe reproduces or else imports into the gallery space the mobile carts, suitcases and tables used by street vendors in the markets of El Salvador da Bahia in Brazil; or, as in *Embutido Renconcavo-Renconcavo embutido* (2003), reconstructs the simple, wooden dwellings of Bahia's poorer inhabitants in the contemporary art space. The process by which Marepe replicates and transforms the everyday into something that merits our care and attention is echoed in countless science fiction narratives in which the familiar and commonplace are disrupted or suspended by the arrival of aliens in our domestic landscape.

Alien Landscapes: Deserts, Cities and Suburbia

> No-one would have believed, in the last years of the nineteenth century, that this world was being watched keenly and closely by intelligences greater than man's and yet as mortal as his own; that as men busied themselves about their various concerns they were scrutinised and studied, perhaps almost as narrowly as a man with a microscope might scrutinise the transient creatures that swarm and multiply in a drop of water. With infinite complacency men went to and fro over this globe about their little affairs, serene in their assurance of their empire over matter.[9]

Alien spaceships can land just about anywhere: the Arizona desert, Antarctica, small-town America, Washington, DC. New Jersey is the site of the Martian invasion in the Mercury Theatre's 1938 production of Wells' *The War of the Worlds*. Sand Rock, Arizona is the setting for the 1953 movie *It Came from Outer Space*. The empty, uninhabited desert plains that stretch for miles around the small community of Sand Rock are reminiscent of the site where the testing of the atom bomb took place in the 1940s. Amateur astronomer John Putnam (Richard Carlson) has abandoned city living to relocate to Arizona and is watching the night sky through his telescope when he sees a spacecraft crash land in the desert. The spaceship has been damaged in its collision with the ground and needs urgent repair. The aliens then kidnap some of Sand Rock's inhabitants and assume their physical appearance so that they can go about their repairs undisturbed. Driving through the desert, Putnam and his fiancée Ellen (Barbara Rush) come across Frank and George (Joe Sawyer and Russell Johnson), two of the town's residents (significantly, their work involves repairing the telegraph/telephone communication lines) behaving strangely, very unlike their true selves. It is here that the aliens reveal what they are doing: 'Don't be afraid. It is within our power to look like you or anyone. For a time it will be necessary to do this.'

This is the moment that artists Ellen Gallagher and Edgar Cleijne elect to rework in one of the five 16mm projections that make up the film installation *Murmur* (2003–4). Scratching directly into the film emulsion, the artists create a parallel narrative that moves along and hijacks the already existing one. Set in the desert, a sheriff's office, an empty stretch of road at night, *Monster* takes place in elastic in-between space, where the aliens – the others – all appear monstrously white with blonde hair and sightless eyes that could not so easily 'pass' as human. While deep space offers alien life forms that can replicate human likeness, the deep sea is home to bizarre and unfamiliar species that skulk in the depths of the ocean. These antediluvian life forms are the inspiration for Gallagher's series of drawings *Watery Ecstatic* (2001–), which subsequently gave rise to the stop action film of the same name that also forms part of the *Murmur* installation. In *Blizzard of White*, a 'shoal of spiky white plasticine creatures [...] sink slowly toward the ocean floor against an inky graphite backdrop of underwater volcanoes',[10] while *Kabuki* features a 3D animation of a fractal, fragmented 'wiglady' slowly looping down into the ocean's unfathomable depths.

As the first thing one encounters when entering the space, *Suberboo* is both the coda and opening 'credit' of an installation that is thought through as a film. Constructed of already existing signs and data, *Suberboo* takes a drawing from Gallagher's *Ebony* series as a ground. In this animation the camera moves along the drawing to create a fight sequence with Bruce Lee and Jim Kelly. Adding to the layering of images and references that *Murmur* combines, the soundtrack is extracted from a Dizzee Rascal sample of Javanese gamelan music. *Murmur* sets the tone for a journey that gives history, myths, autobiographies and fictions a form that the artists describe as follows: 'The physical form of *Murmur* is a singular entity made up of several parts that, taken together, have the properties of expressive phrasing. The various forms within *Murmur* are modulated to create emphasis. This applies to *Murmur* as a whole as well as to the way forms are combined within the individual 16mm projections that make up *Murmur*.'

It is small-town America that is conjured up by Kori Newkirk's beaded landscapes. Newkirk's images of suburban America are constructed from beaded curtains that visualise fragments of small-town America that you might see speeding along a US highway: a telegraph pole (*Echo*, 2001) or one-storey houses viewed from a distance (*The World and the Way Things Are*, 2001). Newkirk's works quite literally fracture these icons of everyday American life, breaking up its seamless appearance. The world envisaged by Newkirk recalls the small Californian town of Santa Mira, the setting for Don Siegel's *Invasion of the Body Snatchers* (1956), which is irrevocably changed by the alien invasion that engulfs it. Nothing seems the same when Dr Miles Bennell (Kevin McCarthy) and his girlfriend Becky (Dana Wynter) return to Santa Mira: 'Everything looked the same but it wasn't. Something evil had taken possession of the town.' According to the local psychiatrist Dan Kauffman, 'an epidemic of mass hysteria' had taken over Santa Mira. Huge seed-pods are deposited at the homes of Santa Mira's residents, eventually bursting open to reveal the exact likenesses of their hosts. From the town centre, trucks are loaded up with pods to travel out through the whole country like 'a malignant disease'. The alien replicants hold out the promise of an untroubled, simple world where everyone is the same and where desire, ambition and faith have been eradicated. The film's penultimate scene pictures Bennell escaping from Santa Mira and trying desperately to get the attention of truck and car drivers on the freeway as trucks roll out of Santa Mira, loaded with hundreds of giant, alien pods: 'Listen to me... We're in danger... Help! Help! We're in danger. Listen to me. You fools, you're in danger. Listen to me. They're after you. They're after all of us. They're here already... .'

Henna Nadeem's exquisite collages, saturated in colour, picture the serene, idyllic English countryside through a lens of abstract patterns that obscure the landscape. The source material for her digitally-manipulated images are photographs of Britain, originally published by *Country Life* magazine from the 1930s to the 1970s in a series of popular publications entitled *The Picture Books of Britain*, which from 1957 turned to super-real colour reproduction. Overlain with elaborate, abstract designs, the familiar English landscape appears alien and strange, almost as if it were being seen for the first time by extraterrestrial visitors. Just as in *It Came from Outer Space*, where we see the planet from the perspective of the one-eyed, stout bubble-shaped creatures that arrive from another world, Nadeem's photographs present us with a familiar landscape that has been irreversibly altered.

Hew Locke's installation is fabricated from familiar objects and broken toys that have been assembled and re-configured by the artist to create a strange fleet of shimmering gold and silver vessels that invades the gallery space. It is difficult to work out the origins of this arresting but eerie flotilla. Locke's assemblage appears as a contemporary reworking of a baroque altarpiece, populated by gun-toting, menacing anatomical dolls. With their gold and silver swords and shields, their guns and bullet belts, Locke's sinister cherubs have lost all trace of innocence and offer up a dystopian vision of the future – conjured up from the past and the present – with its hints of colonial invasion and indiscriminate violence. For Locke, science fiction works in parallel to his own creative practice, opening up 'a doorway into a different reality that speaks to this reality'.[11]

Like Nadeem and Locke, many of the artists in 'Alien Nation' envision a world in which the familiar has been rendered strange, or vice versa, with the alien depicted as ordinary and everyday. The fears and paranoias that might have been projected onto an apocalyptic future or onto aliens from elsewhere have been accommodated into the present whose trajectory remains equivocal and open-ended. Perhaps, after all, the future has arrived and the aliens are already here.

1 [Footnote 6 in source] John Wyndham, *The Day of the Triffids* (1951) (London: Penguin, 2000) 28.

2 [9] *The Day of the Triffids*, op. cit., 96.

3 [10] David Huffman from an 'Interview with Patricia Sweetow', 30 May, 1999.

4 [11] Ibid.

5 [12] David Huffmann, quoted in Kenneth Baker in the *San Francisco Chronicle*, 5 September 2001.

6 [13] Clive Bloom, *Violent London: 2,000 Years of Riots, Rebels and Revolts* (London: Pan Books, 2004) 183.

7 [14] Maldwyn A. Jones, *The Limits of Liberty: American History*, 1607–1992 (Oxford and New York: Oxford University Press, 1995) 87.

8 [15] Larry Ceplair and Steven Englund, *The Inquisition in Hollywood: Politics in the Film Community, 1930–60* (Urbana and Chicago: University of Illinois Press, 2003) 245.

9 [16] H.G. Wells, *The War of the Worlds* (1898) (London: Penguin, 2005) 7.

10 [17] Caoimhín Mac Giolla Léith, *Ellen Gallagher: Orbus* (Edinburgh: Fruitmarket Gallery/Zurich: Hauser & Wirth, 2005).

11 [18] Hew Locke interviewed by Jens Hoffmann and quoted in Jens Hoffmann, 'The Truth is Out There', in *Alien Nation*, eds. John Gill, Gilane Tawadros and Jens Hoffmann (London: ICA and Iniva/ Osfildern: Hatje Cantz Verlag, 2006).

Gilane Tawadros and John Gill, extracts from 'We are the Martians…', in *Alien Nation*, eds. John Gill, Gilane Tawadros and Jens Hoffmann (London: ICA and Iniva/Osfildern: Hatje Cantz Verlag, 2006) 11–12, 15–27.

Darko Suvin
Estrangement and Cognition//1979

The importance of science fiction (SF) in our time is on the increase.[1] First, there are strong indications that its popularity in the leading industrial nations (United States, USSR, United Kingdom, Japan) has risen sharply over the last hundred years, despite all the local and short-range fluctuations. SF has particularly affected such key strata or groups of modern society as college graduates, young writers and the avant-garde of general readers appreciative of new sets of values. This is a significant cultural effect which goes beyond any merely quantitative census. Second, if one takes the minimal generic difference of SF the presence of a narrative *novum*[2] (the dramatis personae and/or their context) significantly different from what is the norm in 'naturalistic' or empiricist fiction, it will be found that SF has an interesting and close kinship with other literary subgenres that flourished at different times and places of literary history: the classical and medieval 'fortunate island' story, the 'fabulous voyage' story from antiquity on, the Renaissance and Baroque 'utopia' and 'planetary novel', the Enlightenment 'state [political] novel', the modern 'anticipation' and 'anti-utopia'. Moreover, although SF shares with myth, fantasy, fairy tale and pastoral an opposition to naturalistic or empiricist literary genres, it differs very significantly in approach and social function from such adjoining non-naturalistic or meta-empirical genres. Both these complementary aspects, the sociological and the methodological, are being vigorously debated by writers and critics in several countries, evidence of lively interest in a genre that should undergo scholarly discussion too. In this essay, I will argue for an understanding of SF as the *literature of cognitive estrangement*. This definition seems to possess the unique advantage of rendering justice to a literary tradition which is coherent through the ages and within itself, yet distinct from non-fictional utopianism, from naturalistic literature, and from other non-naturalistic fiction. It thus makes it possible to lay the basis for a coherent poetics of SF.

I want to begin by postulating a spectrum or spread of literary subject matter which extends from the ideal extreme of exact recreation of the author's empirical environment[3] to exclusive interest in a strange newness, a *novum*. From the eighteenth to the twentieth centuries, the literary mainstream of our civilisation has been nearer to the first of these two extremes. However, at the beginnings of a literature, the concern with a domestication of the amazing is very strong. Early tale-tellers relate amazing voyages into the next valley, where they found dog-headed people, also good rock salt which could be stolen or at the worst battered for. Their stories are a syncretic travelogue and *voyage imaginaire*, daydream and intelligence report. This implies a curiosity about the unknown beyond the next mountain range (sea, ocean, solar system), where the thrill of knowledge joined the thrill of adventure.

From Iambulus and Euhemerus through the classical utopia to Verne's island of Captain Nemo and Wells's island of Dr. Moreau, an island in the far-off ocean is the paradigm of the aesthetically most satisfying goal of the SF voyage. This is particularly true if we subsume under this the planetary island in the aether ocean – usually the Moon – which we encounter from Lucian through Cyrano to Swift's mini-Moon of Laputa, and on into the nineteenth century. Yet the parallel paradigm of the valley, 'over the range' (the subtitle of Butler's SF novel *Erewhon*) which shuts it in as a wall, is perhaps as revealing. It recurs almost as frequently, from the earliest folktales about the sparkling valley of Terrestrial Paradise and the dark valley of the Dead, both already in *Gilgamesh*. Eden is the mythological localisation of utopian longing, just as Wells' valley in 'The Country of the Blind' is still within the liberating tradition which contends that the world is not necessarily the way our present empirical valley happens to be, and that whoever thinks his valley is the world is blind. Whether island or valley, whether in space or (from the industrial and bourgeois revolutions on) in time, the new framework is correlative to the new inhabitants. The aliens – utopians, monsters, or simply differing Strangers – are a mirror to man just as the differing country is a mirror for his world. But the mirror is not only a reflecting one, it is also a transforming one, virgin womb and alchemical dynamo: the mirror is a crucible.

Thus it is not only the basic human and humanising curiosity that gives birth to SF. Beyond an undirected inquisitiveness, which makes for a semantic game without clear referent, this genre has always been wedded to a hope of finding in the unknown the ideal environment, tribe, state, intelligence, or other aspect of the Supreme Good (or to a fear of and revulsion from its contrary). At all events, the *possibility* of other strange, co-variant coordinate systems and semantic fields is assumed.

The approach to the imaginary locality, or localised daydream, practiced by the genre of SF is a supposedly factual one. Columbus' (technically or genealogically non-fictional) letter on the Eden he glimpsed beyond the Orinoco mouth, and Swift's (technically non-factual) voyage to Laputa, Balnibarbi, Glubbdubbdrib, Luggnagg, 'and Japan' represent two extremes in the constant intermingling of imaginary and empirical possibilities. Thus SF takes off from a fictional ('literary') hypothesis and develops it with totalising ('scientific') rigour – the specific difference between Columbus and Swift is smaller than their generic proximity. The effect of such factual reporting of fictions is one of confronting a set normative system – a Ptolemaic-type closed world picture – with a point of view or look implying a new set of norms; in literary theory this is known as the attitude of *estrangement*. This concept was first developed on non-naturalistic texts by the Russian Formalists (*'ostranenie'*, Viktor Shklovsky) and most successfully underpinned by an anthropological and historical approach in the work of Bertolt Brecht, who wanted to write 'plays for a scientific age.' While working on a play about the prototypical scientist, Galileo, he defined this attitude (*'Verfremdungseffekt'*) in his *Short Organon for the Theatre*: 'A representation which estranges is one which allows us to recognise its subject, but at the same time makes it seem unfamiliar.' And further: for somebody to see all normal happenings in a dubious light, 'he would need to develop that detached eye with which the great Galileo observed a swinging chandelier. He was amazed by that pendulum motion as if he had not expected it and could not understand its occurring, and this enabled him to come at the rules by which it was governed.' Thus, the look of estrangement is both cognitive and creative; and as Brecht goes on to say, 'one cannot simply exclaim that such an attitude pertains to science, but not to art. Why should not art, in its own way, try to serve the great social task of mastering Life?'[4] (Later, Brecht would note that it might be time to stop speaking in terms of masters and servants altogether.)

In SF the attitude of estrangement – used by Brecht in a different way, within a still predominantly 'realistic' context – has grown into *the formal framework of the genre*. [...]

1 The first version of this essay emerged from a lecture given in Spring 1968 in J.M. Holquist's seminar on fantastic literature in the Yale University Slavic Languages and Literatures Department. I have derived much profit from discussions with him, with the late Jacques Ehrmann, my UMass colleague David Porter, and my McGill colleagues Irwin and Myrna Gopnik [...]. The final version owes much to Stanislaw Lem's *Eztntastyka i futurologia* which considerably emboldened me in further pursuits within this protean field, even where I differed from some of Lem's emphases and conclusions. [...]

2 *Novum* (Latin for 'new thing') is the term, drawn from the early scientific work of Francis Bacon, Suvin uses to describe the scientifically plausible innovations used by science fiction narratives. The hypothetical 'new thing' which the story is about can be imagined to exist by scientific means rather than by magic, i.e., by the *factual reporting of fictions* and by relating them in a plausible way to reality, https://en.wikipedia.org/wiki/Novum. See also, Francis Bacon, *Novum Organum, sive indicia vera de Interpretationes Naturae* (1620).

3 [Footnote 1 in source] A benefit of discussing the seemingly peripheral subject of 'science fiction' is that one has to go back to first principles, one cannot really assume them as given. One must ask,

for example, what is literature? Usually, when discussing literature one determines what it says (its subject matter) and how it says what it says (the approach to its themes). If we are talking about literature in the sense of significant works possessing certain minimal aesthetic qualities rather than in the sociological sense of everything that gets published at a certain time or in the ideological sense of all the writings on certain themes, this principle can more precisely be formulated as a double question. First, epistemologically, what possibility for aesthetic qualities is offered by different thematic fields ('subjects')? The answer given by the aesthetics prevalent at the moment is: an absolutely equal possibility. With this answer the question is booted out of the field of aesthetics and into the lap of ideologists, who pick it up by our default and proceed to bungle it. Second, historically, how has such a possibility in fact been used? Once one begins with such considerations, one comes quickly up against the rather unclear concept of realism (not the prose literary movement in the nineteenth century but a meta-historical stylistic principle), since this genre is often pigeonholed as non-realistic. I would not object but would heartily welcome such labels if one had first persuasively defined what is 'real' and what is 'reality'. True, this genre raises basic philosophical issues, but it is perhaps not necessary to face them in an initial approach. Therefore I shall here substitute for 'reality' (whose existence independent of any observer or group of observers I do not at all doubt, in fact) the concept of 'the author's empirical environment', which seems as immediately clear as any.

4 [2] Viktor Shklovsky, 'Iskusstvo kak priem', in *Sborniki po teorii poeticheskogo iazyk*a, (Petrograd, 1917). In the translation 'Art as Technique', in Lee T. Lemon and Marion J. Reis (eds.), *Russian Formalist Criticism* (Lincoln, NE: University of Nebraska Press, 1965), *ostranenie* is rendered somewhat clumsily as 'defamiliarisation'. See also Victor Erlich's classical survey, *Russian Formalism* (New Haven: Yale University Press, 1955). Bertolt Brecht, 'Kleines Organon für das Theater', in his *Gesammelte Werke*, 16 (Frankfurt am Main, 1973), translated in John Willett (ed.), *Brecht On Theatre* (New York: Methuen, 1964). My quotations are from 192 and 196 of this translation, but I have changed Mr. Willett's translation of *Verfremdung* as 'alienation' into my 'estrangement', since 'alienation' evokes incorrect, indeed opposite, connotations: estrangement was for Brecht an approach militating directly against social and cognitive alienation. See Ernst Bloch, '*Entfremdung, Verfremdung*: Alienation, Estrangement', in Erika Munk (ed.), *Brecht* (New York: Bantam Books, 1972).

Darko Suvin, extract from 'Estrangement and Cognition' (1979), in *Metamorphoses of Science Fiction: On the Poetics and History of a Literary Genre* (Bern: Peter Lang, 2016) 15–19.

Sherryl Vint
Cognitive Estrangement//2014

[...] The version of sf that emerges from this discussion – the literature of technologically saturated societies – is one familiar to fans of the genre, especially those coming to it via print. Early academic discussions of sf, as I have noted, have their roots in fan communities, with many founding scholars of the field coming out of fan writing and organisation, such as Thomas Clareson and James Gunn.

The study of sf crept around the edges of respectable academia in the 1950s, and gained increased visibility when Clareson founded the journal *Extrapolation* (1959) and the Science Fiction Research Association (1970). Academic interest quickly moved into this new intellectual territory, and other speciality journals soon followed, the most prominent of which is *Science Fiction Studies* (*SFS*), co-founded by R.D. Mullen and Darko Suvin in 1973. *SFS* shifted the discussion away from a predominant focus on American pulp-and-paperback writers, drawing on European traditions of the fantastic and publishing work that theorised the genre's formal properties. Readers coming to the genre through academic study, then, encountered a different sense of sf and a different set of questions and concerns than those emerging from fan communities.

Darko Suvin's *Metamorphoses of Science Fiction* (1979), a study of the genre's poetics, has perhaps been the most significant influence on academic understanding. Suvin argues that sf is a literature premised upon radical discontinuity with the empirical world, yet one whose features are 'not impossible' in that world.[1] He feels that sf is 'allied to the rise of subversive social classes' and contrasts it to an 'opposed tendency toward mystifying escapism' that he associates with religious visions of otherworldly fulfilment and genre fantasy.[2] Yet Suvin sets himself a difficult challenge, dismissing as 'perishable' at least 90% of what was published under the label sf at the time, defining the genre not by its 'empirical realities' but according to its 'historical potentialities'.[3] He wants to discount most of pulp sf as a wrong turn in the genre's path, privileging instead texts by writers such as Ursula K. Le Guin, Stanislaw Lem and Philip K. Dick, authors whose work uses the techniques of the genre to present 'dynamic transformation' of the world rather than the 'static mirroring' he associates with realist fiction. Science fiction, in Suvin's view, is 'not only a reflecting of but also on reality'.[4]

Suvin defines sf as '*the literature of cognitive estrangement*', developing the concept from Bertolt Brecht's work on alienation in theatre, a quality of works that force the audience to realise that the setting is a construction of reality, not simply reality itself.[5] Suvin suggests cognitive is another word for science, although by 'science' he means something broader than experimental method; he insists that the difference between the text's world and our own be based on rational extrapolation, not mere fantasy. True sf for Suvin provides a socially transformative vision of a full social world, and he is suspicious of the limiting attitude of hard sf that demands that a tale conform to 'a "real possibility" – to that which is possible in the author's reality and/or according to the scientific paradigm of his culture'; Suvin prefers the more enabling 'ideal possibility', that is, 'any conceptual or thinkable possibility the premises and/or consequences of which are not internally contradictory'.[6] Cognition and estrangement interact dialectically in sf, allowing us to not only recognise the world of the story but also to see it as strange, prompting creative understanding and critical reflection about the difference between the text's world and our own.

Works of cognitive estrangement achieve this effect through a *novum*, a new thing introduced into the textual world that serves as the catalyst for the difference between the textual and the reader's worlds. For Suvin, the *novum* must 'be hegemonic in a narration in order that we may call it an SF narration'; that is, not only must the *novum* be something that is different between our world and the text's world, but the implications of this new thing must also be worked through in a totalising way.[7] The estranging effect must transform the fictional world, not serve as mere window dressing for a tale of adventure that might equally be set in an unchanged social world. The *novum* must be 'so central and significant that it determines the whole narrative logic – or at least the overriding narrative logic – regardless of any impurities that might be present'.[8] Suvin sought to link sf with an established tradition of utopian and dystopian writing, and thus he privileges an ideal of sf as social critique. Understanding a work as sf thus requires more than an inventory of certain settings, technologies or beings (such as aliens or robots); for Suvin, sf is defined by the skewed perspective it encourages us to take on both reality as experienced and reality as it is represented in realist fiction. Sf forces us to confront ideas and conventions that have been made to appear natural and inevitable, by giving us a world founded on other premises. The dialectical interaction between what is familiar and what is alien thus opens up a more critical understanding of the structures underlying and shaping the familiar world of daily experience. This movement back and forth between a normal world that begins to appear strange, a strange one that becomes more normalised as we immerse ourselves in the sf world, is the source of the genre's ability to be a reflection on reality as well as *of* it. [...]

1 Darko Suvin, *Metamorphoses of Science Fiction* (Oxford: Peter Lang, (1979) 2016) viii.

2 Ibid., ix.

3 Ibid., viii.

4 Ibid., 10.

5 Ibid., 4.

6 Ibid., 66.

7 Ibid., 63.

8 Ibid., 70.

Sherryl Vint, extract from 'Cognitive Estrangement', in *Science Fiction: A Guide for the Perplexed* (London and New York: Bloomsbury, 2014) 37–9.

Tom McCarthy
Letting it Be: A Red Paper on Terrestrial Art//2008

[...] Terrestrial Study has come to be considered a minor branch of the overall Tree of Knowledge: indeed, no more than a twig. For over a century now it has been assumed that all that lay to be discovered about our undistinguished, simple neighbour had already been brought to light. Its systems of governance were self-explanatory; its rituals crude; its military capacities negligible and entirely self-directed; its communication networks primitive. [...]

To infer from the brief handed to me late in Cycle 77305 that overall Alien Affairs Committee (AAC) thinking on the Terrestrial Question had shifted would be erroneous. On the contrary, the AAC's intention in commissioning this report was simply to confirm, as part of a wider Solar Systems Rationalisation Programme, Terra's diminutive status, so that it, like all other planets, could be assigned a policy label: colonisation, exploitation, destruction, cultivation as military/trade partner, etc. Martian agents already installed on Terra were recommending destruction. Before formally advocating this or any other course of action to the Council, though, the AAC, in their anxiety to avoid oversight, were keen to fill in the one gap in their knowledge of the Blue Planet: namely, an understanding of the category *Art*.

On no other known planet does such a category exist and, as it seems to serve such little purpose, no significance had until recently been attributed to its Terrestrial occurrence. The term itself, *Art*, is in most Terrestrial languages the root or basis of the term for artificial, fake, deceptive. Thus in German *Kunst* gives *künstlich*; in the Slavic languages *umelec* gives *umelecni*; and so on. This etymological happenstance, considered in conjunction with the fact that aerial reconnaissance of Terra has turned up from time to time such topographic anomalies as islands ringed with synthetic bands of colour, volcanic craters modified for no apparent reason or large areas of earth scraped over so as to bear simulacra of animals or geometric shapes, with subsequent intelligence from Martian agents confirming that these interventions are considered *artworks* – such instances have of late led the AAC to suspect that the term *Art* might in fact name a strategy of camouflage, a means of simultaneously hiding military or other installations and signalling their whereabouts to others. The fact that art occupies a symbolic stratum – and, moreover, does so with a rationale whose key or legend seems to elude both Martian and Terrestrial observers – has led to a suspicion that it forms a system of encryption that alone among Terrestrial codes has hitherto eluded deciphering. That it serves as both repository and index of the populace's desires, fantasies, terrors and so on suggests it as a potential field for mind control activities – yet one that must be mastered or, alternatively, neutralised by Martians lest it be directed against us. Overall, it was (in my opinion wisely) decided that art should be fully understood before any plan vis-à-vis Terra is executed, lest this one rogue element upset such project's efficacy.

A decision was thus taken: to insert a Martian agent – myself – into the art systems of Terra. Since at the time of the mission's inception the metropolis of London was viewed by most Terrestrial commentators as such systems' primary node and locus, it was decided that I should centre my activities there. My brief was simple: to infiltrate the networks concomitant upon these systems, and to report back to Mars and the AAC. [...]

The Method

In all, I spent two cycles, or seven Terrestrial 'years', in London, with the odd excursion to Berlin, Kassel, Basel, Miami, Venice and New York. Reconnaissance of the systems and mechanisms at play in the domain of art had led to the decision taken before I was conscripted, that I should be inserted at a relatively junior level and, by rising through art's institutions, come to know and comprehend them. I was thus enrolled, with the help of agents *in situ* on Terra, in an instructional course at one of London's many artist training camps. The importance of this move cannot be overestimated. Not only did my presence at the camp enable me to forge the webs of acquaintance and allegiance that would support my subsequent ascendance, but it also equipped me with a fundamental understanding of the way in which art's vectors and control lines operate.

These, stated simply, follow two rules: any operative, or 'artist', is required both to possess an extensive knowledge of the history of his or her own discipline (much as the followers of Fulcrology, for example, are expected to be able to recite the names, dates and formulas of all the Hierophants) *and* to supplement this history with iterations that, presented to observers, at once reprise and mutate it.[1] [...]

In addition to the formal history of art that they recycle and reactivate, operatives are, to a degree that's lesser but still worthy of mention, expected to engage the histories of other disciplines, most notably those of Terrestrial Philosophy and Letters. This 'third' rule of engagement (in reality a sub-rule of the first and second), in its playing out, brought to my attention a paradox that was most illuminating, and proved instrumental to my subsequent ascendancy. To any Martian with even the most cursory acquaintance with the aforementioned disciplines, it would be immediately evident that the instructors' – and, consequently, operatives' – knowledge of these fields was scant. Yet this fact made no material difference, as the issue was not to *understand* the fields but rather to link to and cite them at a level one degree above that of one's audience and interlocutors, thus deploying them as currency. Once this fact was appreciated, one could profit from this currency almost at will.

This I did. Before I'd even graduated from the training camp, I had amassed a certain status through a simple application of the two rules of engagement.[2] Having ascertained my co-trainees' level of acquaintance with a given body of aesthetic or epistemological information, I would set my citational pointers one notch higher. By setting them two or three notches higher, I was able to extend my operational field beyond the confines of the training camp. [...]

A few words about art's governing bodies would be appropriate at this point. [...] The extent to which corruption has taken hold of this sector of the system cannot be overstated. It is endemic, more the rule than the exception. Indeed, were the same criteria used to regulate the (by no means pristine) financial institutions of Terra to be applied to those of art, I find myself hard pressed to think of a single Administrator or Selector I encountered in my two cycles there who would not be incarcerated in one of London's many penitentiary houses for 'insider trading', 'failure to disclose an interest' or a dozen other misdemeanours one could mention. Needless to say, once I'd understood the ways in which such practices operate, I exploited them systematically, to my great advantage. [...]

Within a year of graduating I was, with the help of five full-time assistants, producing ten or more high-profile iterations each terrestrial year. As my status grew, I forged links with Terrestrial celebrities not directly associated with the world of art but whose profiles in their own fields helped shore up my own.[3]

With my production facilities becoming increasingly self-operating, I was able to pass more and more time dining with contacts, attending social functions and conducting sexual research, all the while alternately bathing these activities in Terrestrial alcohol and powdering them with Terrestrial cocaine.[4]

Findings (1)

Taking stock of my situation half-way through the second cycle of my Terrestrial sojourn, I found that I'd accumulated: large amounts of wealth; a media profile above and beyond the one I enjoyed in the publications attendant on art networks; thanks to this profile, a degree of access to public debate and, consequently, political opinion forming; and even some access, by dint of both my profile and connections, to major politicians themselves. [...] As far as the question of political influence was concerned, it will be well known to the AAC that we have numerous politicians, both Terrestrial and Martian, on our books. What need, then, of an artist to relay directives to them?

Considering these facts, I turned my efforts to investigating art's potential for camouflage and encryption, as touched on above. While simulacra are habitually deployed in military situations in the Terrestrial field just as in the Martian, these could not be said to constitute art in its true sense as they publicly neither reference nor mutate previous iterations, and I can report with confidence that the camouflage line of enquiry is a *faux piste*. The question of encryption is a bit more complex. While art certainly deploys encryption, it does so with little end. Despite the popularity among uneducated Terrestrials of fables speculating that the iterations of past operatives contain coded messages about the nature or identity of Terrestrial divinities, art in practice seems to encrypt in such a way as to preclude the information entered producing a single message or instruction which could later be retrieved to useful purpose. Thus that second line of enquiry, while more tantalising, is for practical ends ultimately no less fruitless.

I then began to explore the potential of art for harnessing the third field outlined in my introduction: that of fantasies, desires and terrors. Since the capacity of art for sexual suggestiveness had long been surpassed by that of the more popular media by the time I was producing iterations, I hired people to enact sequences and gestures that tapped into anxieties: instructing, for example, Asiatic assistants to mumble aggressively while fiddling with backpacks on the transport networks, or unshaven Caucasian ones to leer at children outside schools and playgrounds. These and other iterations, it must be admitted, produced an effect – especially when they declined, in the first instance, to announce themselves as 'art'. Again, though, this effect was minor when compared to that produced when, for example, real bombs are detonated, or, indeed, by governments' own calculated overstatement of the likelihood of such eventualities. Terrestrials have no need of art to live in states of fear.

Having exhausted these and other lines of enquiry too minor to warrant mention in these pages, I prepared, in the third phase of the second cycle of my mission, to pen my report. I intended at that point to concur with the *in situ* agents advocating destruction, or at least not to oppose their recommendation. I deemed both art and Terra utterly devoid of any imaginable value to the Council's overall project for the advancement of Martian concerns. I missed Mars, and longed for repatriation.

Findings (2)

Then a strange thing happened. Committee members will forgive my turn of phrase – but that's how it was. I was relaxing on a sofa in the back room of my operational headquarters one afternoon, recovering from a particularly demanding session of status and network consolidation on the previous night, when something caught my eye. It was an object with which I was familiar: a case for housing sunglasses, the ones that I habitually wore when out in public irrespective of the brightness or otherwise of my environment. When I'd returned some hours before, the case had fallen from the pocket of my jacket, with some force: enough to burst it open and disgorge its contents when it hit the ground. Thus case and glasses both lay on the floor a few feet from the sofa and each other. And I, from my sofa, stared at them.

As I did so, I found myself overcome by a sense of the two objects' import. The way the case lay on its side, open about its hinges like a clam, exposed to the atmosphere of the headquarters, the atmosphere in general – as though waiting to receive this, in the manner of a net or radio antenna; then the sunglasses themselves, reflecting the space around them as they bent the headquarter's surfaces into a mild parabola before absorbing them in patches from which no light issued back, little black holes – and hinged as well, just like the case. The objects seemed to institute a set of correspondences – not just between each other and the room, but between all other sunglasses and cases and all other rooms, all clams and radio antennae and carpets and black holes.

Observing them, I felt a surge inside my chest, as though we – these objects and I – were standing on the brink of some great cataclysm, a disaster in which space itself would simply implode under the weight of its own fullness, dragging time down with it. I felt it was happening already, without happening: that lying on my sofa motionless I was already falling away, contracting, and these objects were already gone, leaving, like a delayed, convex reflection, an after-impression that was passing itself off as consciousness. I was, at that moment, utterly convinced that it was only by dint of my looking at the sunglasses and case that everything was allowed to persist: not just the room or afternoon, but the whole universe – and that if I stopped, the consequences would be unthinkable. The sensation was so strong that I involuntarily began to moan, as though from the strain of holding it all together, and to secrete from my nasal glands.

I felt that something should be done, that an event of this magnitude should somehow be captured, or at least marked. Performing a quick scan of my memory, I identified several instances within the history of art to which this moment, in its formal aspects, corresponded; and a number of ways suggested themselves in which these instances could be cited and mutated with a view to accommodating and transforming the experience I was undergoing into an iteration. But this process, with which I was by now so familiar and at which so adept, seemed inadequate to the demand being issued from my headquarters' floor – both inadequate and unnecessary. The sheer presence of these objects, marshalling the space around them, returning space to itself and to me even as it appeared to collapse; and my enabling, through observing the objects, of all spaces, all time: this event already seemed to far surpass the significance that any iteration might have produced. And so I simply lay on the sofa looking at the case and glasses, moaning and secreting. I did this for several hours. The next day I underwent a similar experience. I was making my way by foot to a luncheon meeting, pausing on the side of the pavement as I waited to safely cross the street.[5] A noise above me drew my attention upwards and I saw, perched on scaffolding around a building that was being restored, a man winching a bucket from the ground towards the fifth or sixth floor outside which he stood. Above him, an aeroplane passed by, leaving a vapour trail that repeated – or, rather, half-repeated, at an offset angle – the horizontal lines of the scaffolding's grid. The man's movements as he gathered the rope upwards, hand over hand, possessed a certain regularity, a rhythm – one that, like the line, was almost, but not quite, reprised by the footsteps of a woman passing between the scaffolding and me, cutting the plane on which I stood in two. The woman strode towards a letterbox, posted a letter, then departed the plane on a diagonal. The tarmac over which she'd passed was ingrained with discarded masticatory plastic, or 'chewing gum', hundreds of flecks that formed large constellations. A train moved underground, making the street's surface shudder; as I ran my eye on down it, the buildings rising on either side seemed to crowd the street in and funnel it away, until it rushed, then vanished, with the train.

Once more I felt a surge run up my torso. It seemed to me that I was standing at the very edge of pure catastrophe, into whose empty chasm all lines, angles and movements were being funnelled; or even that I'd gone beyond this edge, entered the chasm already, rushed away and vanished with them – and yet that against this cataclysm I was held back by a geometric and kinetic configuration so intense that it contained the essence of geometry and force themselves, of balance and proportion. This small island of structure and activity in interstellar space was, against all universal logic, being allowed to remain – and being given leave to do so, I was absolutely sure, because I was standing in its midst, observing it. Once more, the responsibility seemed overwhelming; involuntarily, I started moaning; and once more my nasal glands secreted copiously.

I felt, with great conviction, that this episode, like the sunglass-and-case one of the previous day, needed – cried out for – somehow *attending to*. When I'd recovered, some hours later, to the point that I could move on from the spot to which I'd become rooted, I staggered to my headquarters with the intention of instructing my employees to go back and photograph the street, record its sounds and diagram its distances; and I identified immediately several past iterations that could be cited and mutated in a bid to capture the experience I'd had when occupying it. But, by the time I'd arrived there, I had realised, once more, that this act would be anathema: what lay behind its motivation had already taken place. The starred tarmac, the repeating lines, the transit vectors and the red post box: these things had cited and mutated space itself; and my contemplation of them had, as it were, *guaranteed* all locales – Terrestrial, Martian or otherwise – as one guarantees a loan or line of credit, and thus underwritten and secured the sum of all events that might take place in them, their ordering, expansions and contractions, their defiance of impossibility.

Did this mean that we were conducting art, the street and I: autonomously, independent of all formal measures, of all iteration? No. And yes. And no again. What I had experienced was, I came to realise over the next few days, *akin* to art – or, rather, it was art that had permitted the experience to come across me, strike me down. And yet it had done so *in absentia*. And it continued so to do: episodes of this type started occurring regularly. I would become arrested by the most insignificant of objects – bottles, tubes of lip balm, traffic lights – fall abject in front of them, moan and nasally secrete as the world ran away and then returned over passages of time in which a minute stretched into a thousand cycles, and a thousand cycles shrunk down to an instant so minute and insignificant it had no designation even in sub-nanos of the finest Martian physics. Objects became simulacra of themselves – or, more precisely, openings, incisions, rips through which every imaginable object, and matter itself in all its unformed denseness, jutted. Gasballs spanning galaxies from end to end were played out in a single breath; the arcs described by crane arms as they swung above the ground measured planetary ellipses. Markings on basketball and netball courts, the ventilator grids of car-parks underground, the rise and fall of lifts, the rhythmic chop of helicopters whose location up above the rooftops one couldn't quite pinpoint: these contained and incubated moments and events perhaps light-cycles away, letting them grow inside them then spill out again as their shapes and boundaries ruptured while somehow staying intact, pronouncing universal ruin without ever executing it – thus sparing both the universe and me by virtue of the fact that I was contemplating it.

As Committee members will be well aware, I soon became quite incapable of continuing my placement, and was recalled a phase before due time.

Conclusion

I have had half a cycle now to assess the phenomena I was simultaneously so exhilarated and disabled by, and have concluded that they were the effects, not of art per se, but of a process an appreciation and comprehension of which can only be approached by recourse to the category *Art*.

My reason for concluding this is twofold: firstly, it was through immersion in the field of art that I became susceptible to these occurrences, no matter how tangential they may seem to be to the formal activities I conducted in this field; and secondly, their nature was structurally identical to that of art as presencing, observation and persistence. The world, or portions of it, were made present to me; I observed them; we persisted. In this, my role differed from my role as an art operative in that, earlier, I had been the generator of the product whereas, now, I was its consumer. 'Product' and 'consumer' are, as terms, inadequate to convey my relation to these episodes: I did not 'consume' the glasses, street or car-park ventilator shafts in the sense of using them up or swallowing them physically, intellectually or otherwise; nor could spontaneously occurring experiences be designated 'products' in the same sense as art iterations are. And yet, in instituting correspondences between themselves and other episodes, experiences and stages, they performed the role of citation and mutation that art iterations perform. And in so doing, they issued a demand, to be attended to, preserved against oblivion and, through my offices whose role they, in turn, guaranteed, to simply be.

The implications of these conclusions are enormous. If I am correct, what we have hitherto regarded as an oddity occurring on a planet blocking (as it were) the exit to our driveway turns out to in fact constitute the underlying structure of the very well-being not just of Mars, but of the entire network of Amalgamated Solar Systems. Art may not name this structure in a word, but it at the very least points to the process by which space and time, constantly erupting and collapsing, are allowed to come into their own and, momentarily ignoring the death sentence already passed on them, to endure – and for us, as Martians (or indeed, Cassiopeans, Andromedans or others), to endure with them by dint of consciousness, or what passes itself off as this against the void.

I therefore recommend, in the strongest manner possible, the following: that we treat Terra, not as a work of art, but in the manner of an artist lying on a couch or on a stroll between appointments – that is, that we contemplate it, let it be. I urge this with great passion. I suspect that our continuing survival might depend upon this course of action.

I remain, Committee members, your obedient agent
083TOM33MCC5THY.

1 Iterations can take almost any form, from images to three-dimensional shapes to sounds (recorded or live), enactment of some process or event, even simply designating some other object, scene or situation as an iteration. The aim in this report is not to describe individual iterations, nor to provide an overall taxonomy, but rather to tease out the logic underlying their generation.

2 It might be wondered why, if my coevals were applying the same rules of engagement, my ascent was more rapid than their own. The obvious answer – my superior Martian intelligence – does not explain the situation full. It should be understood that the rules of engagement were never stated as such. Rather, trainee operatives were instilled with a Terrestrial ideology of 'craft' and 'self-expression' that, besides being regressive even by Terrestrial standards, was at odds with the reality of their practice.

3 [Footnote 5 in source] Their willingness to be seen in public, combined with their lack of intelligence, makes dramatic Actors most propitious for this purpose.

4 [6] Cocaine is the drug of choice among art networks, and with reason. It induces a strong sense of belief in the importance of a given statement, liaison or persona, combined with a financial profligacy that is most conducive to the trading of iterations.

5 [7] Transportation technology is one of the largest causes of death on Terra. In metropolises, this is largely due to collisions between vehicles and foot-bound Terrestrials; on the larger transportation vectors, be they ground-, sea- or air-based, vehicle-on-vehicle impact is more frequent. So prominent are such disasters that a number of the more striking iterations and fables of recent Terrestrial cycles have used them as a point of reference.

Tom McCarthy, extracts from 'Letting it Be: A Red Paper on Terrestrial Art', in *Martian Museum of Terrestrial Art*, eds. Francesco Manacorda & Lydia Yee (exh. cat) (London: Barbican, 2008) 17–32.

Jean Baudrillard
Simulacra and Science Fiction//1991

There are three orders of simulacra:

1. natural, naturalistic simulacra: based on image, imitation, and counterfeiting. They are harmonious, optimistic, and aim at the reconstitution, or the ideal institution, of a nature in God's image.
2. productive, productionist simulacra: based on energy and force, materialised by the machine and the entire system of production. Their aim is Promethean: worldwide application, continuous expansion, liberation of indeterminate energy (desire is part of the utopias belonging to this order of simulacra).
3. simulation simulacra: based on information, the model, cybernetic play. Their aim is maximum operationality, hyperreality, total control.

To the first order corresponds the imaginary of the utopia. To the second, SF in the strict sense. To the third... is there yet an imaginary domain which corresponds to this order? The probable answer is that the 'good old' SF imagination is dead, and that something else is beginning to emerge (and not only in fiction, but also in theory). Both traditional SF and theory are destined to the same fate: flux and imprecision are putting an end to them as specific genres.

There is no real and no imaginary except at a certain distance. What happens when this distance, even the one separating the real from the imaginary, begins to disappear and to be absorbed by the model alone? Currently, from one order of simulacra to the next, we are witnessing the reduction and absorption of this distance, of this separation which permits a space for ideal or critical projection.

It is at a maximum in utopias, where a transcendent world, a radically different universe, is portrayed (its most individualised form remains the Romantic dream, wherein transcendence is represented in all its depth, even unto its subconscious structure; but, in all cases, the separation from the real world is maximal – it is the utopian island in contrast to the continent of the real).

It is diminished considerably in SF: SF only being, most often, an extravagant *projection* of, but qualitatively not different from, the real world of production. Extrapolations of mechanics or energy, velocities or powers approaching infinity – SF's fundamental patterns and scenarios are those of mechanics, of metallurgy, and so forth. Projective hypostasis of the robot. (In the limited universe of the pre-industrial era, utopias *counterposed* an ideal alternative world. In the potentially limitless universe of the production era, SF *adds* by multiplying the world's own possibilities.)

It is totally reduced in the implosive era of models. Models no longer constitute an imaginary domain with reference to the real; they are, themselves, an apprehension of the real, and thus leave no room for any fictional extrapolation – they are immanent, and therefore leave no room for any kind of transcendentalism. The stage is now set for simulation, in the cybernetic sense of the word – that is to say, for all kinds of manipulation of these models (hypothetical scenarios, the creation of simulated situations, etc.), but now *nothing distinguishes this management-manipulation from the real itself: there is no more fiction*.

Reality was able to surpass fiction, the surest sign that the imaginary has possibly been outpaced. But the real could never surpass the model, for the real is only a pretext of the model.

The imaginary was a pretext of the real in a world dominated by the reality principle. Today, it is the real which has become the pretext of the model in a world governed by the principle of simulation. And, paradoxically, it is the real which has become our true utopia – but a utopia that is no longer a possibility, a utopia we can do no more than dream about, like a lost object.

Perhaps the SF of this era of cybernetics and hyperreality will only be able to attempt to 'artificially' resurrect the 'historical' worlds of the past, trying to reconstruct *in vitro* and down to its tiniest details the various episodes of bygone days: events, persons, defunct ideologies – all now empty of meaning and of their original essence, but hypnotic with retrospective truth. Like the Civil War in Philip K. Dick's *The Simulacra*; like a gigantic hologram in three dimensions, where fiction will never again be a mirror held to the future, but rather a desperate rehallucinating of the past.

We can no longer imagine other universes; and the gift of transcendence has been taken from us as well. Classic SF was one of expanding universes: it found its calling in narratives of space exploration, coupled with more terrestrial forms of exploration and colonisation indigenous to the nineteenth and twentieth centuries. There is no cause-effect relationship to be seen here. Not simply because, today, terrestrial space has been virtually completely encoded, mapped, inventoried, saturated; has in some sense been shrunk by globalisation; has become a collective marketplace not only for products but also for values, signs, and models, thereby leaving no room any more for the imaginary. It is not exactly because of all this that the exploratory universe (technical, mental, cosmic) of SF has also stopped functioning. But the two phenomena are closely linked, and they are two aspects of the same general evolutionary process: a period of implosion, after centuries of explosion and expansion. When a system reaches its limits, its own saturation point, a reversal begins to take place. And something happens also to the imagination.

Until now, we have always had large reserves of the imaginary, because the coefficient of reality is proportional to the imaginary, which provides the former with its specific gravity. This is also true of geographical and space exploration: when there is no more virgin ground left to the imagination, *when the map covers all the territory, something like the reality principle disappears.* The conquest of space constitutes, in this sense, an irreversible threshold which effects the loss of terrestrial coordinates and referentiality. Reality, as an internally coherent and limited universe, begins to haemorrhage when its limits are stretched to infinity. The conquest of space, following the conquest of the planet, promotes either the de-realising of human space, or the reversion of it into a simulated hyperreality. Witness, for example, the two-room apartment with kitchen and bath launched into orbit with the last Moon capsule (raised to the power of space, one might say); the perceived ordinariness of a terrestrial habitat then assumes the values of the cosmic and its hypostasis in Space, the satellisation of the real in the transcendence of Space – it is the end of metaphysics, the end of fantasy, the end of SF. The era of hyperreality has begun.

[...] It is no longer possible to manufacture the unreal from the real, to create the imaginary from the data of reality. The process will be rather the reverse: to put in place 'decentred' situations, models of simulation, and then to strive to give them the colours of the real, the banal, the lived; to reinvent the real as fiction, precisely because the real has disappeared from our lives. A hallucination of the real, of the lived, of the everyday – but reconstituted, sometimes even unto its most disconcertingly unusual details, recreated like an animal park or a botanical garden, presented with transparent precision, but totally lacking substance, having been de-realised and hyperrealised.

True SF, in this case, would not be fiction in expansion, with all the freedom and 'naiveté' which gave it a certain charm of discovery. It would, rather, evolve implosively, in the same way as our image of the universe. It would seek to revitalise, to reactualise, to re-banalise fragments of simulation – fragments of this universal simulation which our presumed 'real' world has now become for us.

But where can one find fictional works which already incorporate this condition of reversion? Clearly, the short stories of Philip K. Dick 'gravitate', one might say, in this new space (although it can no longer be expressed as such because, in fact, this new universe is 'anti-gravitational', or, if it still gravitates, it does so around the *hole* of the real, around the *hole* of the imaginary). [...]

Perhaps an even more convincing example would be Ballard and his fictional evolution from his earliest 'fantasmagorical' short stories – poetic, dream-like, alienating – to *Crash*, which (even more than *High Rise* or *Concrete Island*) constitutes without doubt the contemporary model for this SF which is no longer SF. *Crash* is our world, nothing is really 'invented' therein, everything is hyper-functional: traffic and accidents, technology and death, sex and the camera eye. Everything is like a huge simulated and synchronous machine; an acceleration of our own models, of all the models which surround us, all mixed together and hyper-operationalised in the void. What distinguishes *Crash* from almost all other SF, which still seem to revolve around the old (mechanical/mechanistic) duo of function vs. dysfunction, is that it projects into the future along the same lines of force and the same finalities as those of the 'normal' universe. Fiction can go beyond reality (or inversely, which is more subtle), but according to the same rules of the game. But in *Crash*, there is neither fiction nor reality – a kind of hyperreality has abolished both. And therein lies the defining character, if there is one, of our contemporary SF. [...]

Jean Baudrillard, extracts from 'Simulacra and Science Fiction', trans. Arthur B. Evans, *Science Fiction Studies*, vol. 18, no. 3 (1991) 309–13.

Suzanne Treister
In Conversation with Roger Luckhurst//2013

Suzanne Treister was born in London, daughter of a Jewish-Polish exile. She trained at St Martin's School of Art (1978–81) and Chelsea School of Art (1981–2). She lives in London, but has spent time in Berlin, the United States and Australia. She was a pioneering digital artist, always interested in the science-fictional possibilities of computers and computing, and in 1995 she developed an avatar called Rosalind Brodsky, named after her grandmother. Brodsky was a time traveller who worked at the Institute of Militronics and Advanced Time Interventionality (IMATI) sometime in the mid twenty-first century. Brodsky investigated the traumatic history of the twentieth century, travelling to its pivotal moments. This passage through time was partly driven by an openly autobiographical attempt to 'rescue' Treister's grandparents, who had been killed in the genocide of Polish Jewry during the Second World War. As a patient possibly suffering from obsessional delusional fantasies, Rosalind Brodsky was apparently treated by Sigmund Freud in 1886 and 1928, by Carl Jung in 1958, by Jacques Lacan in 1970, and by Melanie Klein in 2058 (after Klein had been transported into the future), all of whom left case notes on Brodsky. Installations, artworks, case histories, a book, a website, and an interactive CD-ROM emerged from this project. The last Brodsky project was *HEXEN 2039*, which appeared in 2006 as an internet site, a movie, a series of exhibitions, and interventions into places like the Science Museum, London, as well as a book. In a style that sometimes echoes the obsessional mapping and drawing associated with 'outsider art', *HEXEN* unravelled a host of links between military research, occult ritual, and mass popular culture. The diagrams included in the work make frenetic links between Second World War American rocket research, the smuggling of Nazi technicians, the black magic occultism of Aleister Crowley and other self-proclaimed masters of the dark arts, weird physical research experiments, science fiction, *The Wizard of Oz*, and the Jewish kabbala. Since *HEXEN*, Treister has explored the NATO codification system (the military numbering system that categorises every object that exists in the world into a four-number code, even including category 9999, 'items which cannot conceivably be classified in any existing classes'). *MTB (Military Training Base)* explores the use of virtual-reality technology to train American soldiers for conditions in Iraq and Afghanistan, and extends her manic mappings of hidden connections to epic scale (the exhibition centred on a diagram over seventeen feet long). These projects are all offered in a deadpan style, leaving one uncertain about the level of irony evident in the conspiracy theories and density of interconnections that are being mapped out. That some of the connections made in the pieces are true is unnerving, for it is now well established that the American security services have often invested time and money in psychical and occult research programmes (projects that have become the basis for popular culture like the *X-Files* television series). Where, though, does Treister leave documented history and enter the realms of paranoia, fantasy, or aesthetic transformation? [...] In the era of the internet, Treister's combination of interests in the history of technology, the military-industrial complex, and magical thinking about occult interconnectedness makes her work an important reflection on our weird and wired condition of being. Most of Treister's work is accessible in online form at www.suzannetreister.net.

Roger Luckhurst Like Thomas Pynchon in *Gravity's Rainbow* (1973) or Stewart Home's use of the occult in his avant-garde provocations, your work leaves the viewer uncertain about where fact stops and fiction starts, or just how ironic the sketching of these intricate connections really is.

Suzanne Treister [...] [F]irstly, there is the issue of how informed the audience is, how able they are to distinguish between what might be actual and what might be invented, and because my work contains a lot of information unfamiliar to many people there are varying degrees of slippage, and that is interesting in itself.

With the *HEXEN* project hardly anyone in the art world seemed familiar with the material I was referencing. Most of the reviewers assumed that I'd invented the whole thing, which I clearly hadn't. There really were men in the basement of Stanford Research Institute (SRI) and at Fort Meade in Maryland carrying out experiments with 'remote viewing' for a military programme, and there is no question that MKULTRA took place, and that it involved all kinds of experiments with drugs and the paranormal.[1] They used the facilities of many US universities, there are records to prove it, and the links between rocket scientists and the Ordo Templi Orientis have become public knowledge in books about the rocket scientist and occultist Jack Parsons. You'd have to be incredibly imaginative to invent all this stuff. Jon Ronson's book *The Men Who Stare at Goats* (2004) was one of the more interesting sources for the project because he was one of the only guys who'd interviewed people in the US military who were doing the occult-based research. His work validates much of the so-called 'conspiracy theory': these are real people doing real research. The American military have been interested in psychical warfare for a long time, since the Second World War at least. Some of those guys believe in it and others don't, but one of the reasons they do it is in case the other side are doing it.

I read pretty widely on the history of military-occult relationships, from the druids, through Rasputin, Dr John Dee, the Soviet experiments, and up to the present day, and a lot of that material is in *HEXEN 2039*. It was just a matter of threading it together with the other areas I was investigating for the project, like current neuroscientific research, and coming up with my own theory of potential future technologies and objectives within this strand of military research, and where that might take us. What happens in the gaps is the art bit.

Luckhurst The other difficulty of reading the work is that it's often filtered through a persona, so these are actually the researches of Rosalind Brodsky, rather than of Suzanne Treister. It's another level of mediation or ironic displacement: Brodsky sets up another screen in front of the information.

Treister The fiction and also the twist in *HEXEN 2039*, made possible through the Brodsky/IMATI construct, is the idea that this research into the military's (actual) historical involvement in the occult and alternative belief systems is itself part of a British military operation called *HEXEN 2039*, which takes place in the future and whose outcome is the development of new mind-control technologies, which enable the military, in turn, to remotely (at a distance) alter belief patterns in the subject, whether military or civilian.

HEXEN 2039 was the last Brodsky project of many, and in this instance she was somewhat in the background. But it's important to know how the work has developed because it's a sort of unfolding narrative. If you read Brodsky's diary, which I wrote back in the 1990s, and navigated the CD-ROM of her time travels, you'd know what the Institute of Militronics was about, and something of the nature of its research. It's kind of like an imaginary SRI International of the UK. IMATI is based in the near future, and the more recent projects focus on the programmes of the Institute rather than the life of Brodsky. So the work is like a vast diagram or web that you have to follow. The whole thing is a sci-fi construct, like a series of novels set in the future but drawing upon the past.

Luckhurst How would you characterise your relationship to this material: ambivalent?

Treister In terms of the military material and focus it's not really about ambivalence but more about ideas of complicity. My father ran a defence spares business, and, combined with my family's wartime history, I developed a love-hate relationship with things associated with the military, which is different from ambivalence. And there is the issue of science fiction writers who imagine new military technologies and whose ideas may in turn contribute to the military's research, which may or may not have been their intention.[...] I'm interested in difficult complicities, collusion, ideas of responsibility and accountability, and knowledge.

Luckhurst And does this position extend to your use of the occult? You have not only documented the military's use of the occult but in *HEXEN* you have experimented with it yourself... .

Treister I'm not completely about suspending the question of belief in my work. I have no fixed beliefs. I don't believe in binaries like normal-paranormal. We are all chameleons and we have moving, shifting parts, and that includes our brains. About three times a year in synagogue I can feel like a total Jew; I can even believe in God. For a few seconds I am tuned into a different level of understanding. Then, on other occasions, when for example I made my own remote-viewing experiments for *HEXEN 2039*, I experienced a hit; the first time I visualised the target so accurately it blew my socks off. I've heard that's common, and then you apparently have to undergo training [laughs]. Other times I am a total cynic, but days later I may feel the world is a place of strange paranormal forces and fantastical mysteries.

Luckhurst I get the sense that you want to fully investigate the *practices* of what might be called 'subjugated knowledges' – whether it's remote viewing, or using the kabbalah, or the manic drawing methods typical of 'outsider art'.

Treister I want to appropriate them. Yes, I want to use these methods myself; I'm not a hands-off person. [...] When it comes to 'manic drawing methods', these come about quite naturally when you have to include so much information and you are doing it by hand on a plain sheet of paper. Unless of course you mean the drawings where I have appropriated existing alchemical drawings as a structural/conceptual device.

Luckhurst In *Alchemy* and *A Time Line for Science Fiction Inventions*, for example, did you do deep research or do you just appropriate these alchemical and kabbalistic structures aesthetically?

Treister *A Time Line for Science Fiction Inventions* uses the kabbalah's tree of life. I know what it's about. I had to make the decision to use it; it's part of the work. But some of the source material for the *Alchemy* project comes from a book of alchemical drawings by Alexander Roob that I bought when I was living in Berlin and it's in German, which means I can't understand each caption fully. So when I chose which alchemical drawing to use in conjunction with information from a specific newspaper I was deliberately half in the dark. I've read widely on alchemy, but this semi-random way of choosing specific drawings made the process more exciting and opened up each work to additional, undetermined readings.

Luckhurst Do you have any responses from people who claim to know the magical tradition, who praise or complain about your uses of it?

Treister I haven't had any complaints from religious or spiritualist groups, but I do get a lot of interest from people who write blogs and various types of conspiracy-theory websites. Many of them have copied my images onto their pages, and in some cases have made links from their own sites to the *HEXEN* site, in order to substantiate their data. In most cases I don't think they realise it's an art project. For some of them it isn't: it's an information site similar to theirs. But then again, some of their sites look like other people's art projects. I keep a record of these blogs and what they're saying. There was a long review on one of them which was incredibly interesting. Someone like that is so well informed about the subject matter, compared to an average art critic, that they could discuss it at great length, so this guy wrote a really rigorous and critical review of the material without any sense of it being art whatsoever. Once when I was doing a public gallery talk on *HEXEN 2039* in a regional museum there was an elderly couple who looked really angry throughout the talk. During question time they erupted and demanded to know why I hadn't included so-and-so or referred to such-and-such. They were infuriated. According to them, I had edited various people out of history. I enjoy this kind of interaction because it becomes part of the work. If you work on webs of information and especially if you put them online, then you can't control the boundaries of whether it is perceived as art or not. That said, the same thing could go for an FBI agent looking at my work as for a conspiracy-theory blogger. [...]

Luckhurst Let's talk about your family background. Rosalind Brodsky is named in memory of your grandmother who died in the Holocaust in Poland. Your father got out, fought in the French Resistance, and after the war went on to set up an arms dealership.

Treister Yes, after the French Resistance my father escaped to the UK to join the Polish Army in Scotland and then the Polish Government in Exile in London. After the war, in the UK, he couldn't immediately use his qualifications in law and political sciences [...] so he went into business selling equipment left over from the Second World War. It was supposed to be a temporary measure. [...]

My father had me when he was quite old and I sometimes feel like I'm out of sync with my generation in terms of historical events. When my friends talk about the Second World War, they're usually talking about their grandparents' time. My school friends came from settled, middle-class families; their parents all seemed to work for the BBC. Some were hippies (albeit of the 1960s Hampstead variety), while my dad was this authoritarian Polish aristocrat who didn't want to read any more books, had a drawer full of Holocaust photos, and traded in spare parts for military equipment.

Luckhurst And the Brodsky project shows you're very aware of psychoanalytic ideas about transmission, the idea that the children of Holocaust survivors have the trauma passed on, what's sometimes called 'transgenerational haunting'.

Treister Yes, I know. It is all true. I can confirm it. In the past, some people have become angry when I've mentioned the war, and accused me of trying to get some sort of mileage out of it, but they don't understand that it's real. I think it's had an effect on a lot of decisions I've made in my life, good, bad, and in between. [...]

The *NATO* project came directly out of making the company website [for my father] because that's where I came cross the codification system. It's totally surreal: it's like a Borges novel. I mean, NATO probably have no idea how odd it looks, from the outside; they think they're being logical and business-like, but, to me, the idea of giving a four-digit military group classification number to everything from works of art to live animals is disturbing. Apparently it's becoming a universal system.

Luckhurst Not *HEXEN* then?

Treister Not specifically. That comes out of the Rosalind Brodsky and the Institute of Militronics project, which I began in 1995, and which came out of the broader family experiences you were talking about. For five years, I was working on: Brodsky's biography, the book, and the CD-ROM, which came out in 1999. During that time I was living in Australia, and being a long way from Europe, roots became very much more important. It was during this period that I went to Ukraine (in the area that was part of south-east Poland before 1939) with my brother to try and find my father's village.

In 2000, while I was moving more frequently between Australia and Europe and the Brodsky CD-ROM was finished, I decided it would be interesting to try and expand on the hypothetical and supposedly controversial activities of the Institute. Back in Australia I developed a couple of early research projects of the Institute, one of which was *Golem/Loew: Artificial Life*, and then, when I moved to Berlin in 2003, *Operation Swanlake*.

While living in Berlin I became obsessed with the weird underbelly of German culture. [...] There's something about Berlin that is horrifyingly stimulating because of its weight of history; everything is in your face, not only the Holocaust but the DDR period (Deutsche Demokratische Republik), and also much older histories and aspects of the culture. I became fascinated by the history of witchcraft in Germany. I decided in Berlin that I wanted to do a project on the occult, and I came across a lot of interesting material in the flea markets. Although to some extent the *Golem/Loew* and *Operation Swanlake* projects had touched on the occult, it wasn't until 2005 that I decided to make a project that encompassed it more fully. Before that, I'd say that science fiction and history were the main interest. The occult stuff really only began to make sense in Germany. You might say it was an evasion tactic, away fromthe historical political realities, and into the belly of the beast, and it was when I first went to the Harz Mountains, which has a huge witchcraft tradition linked to it, that I decided to go back with my video camera for Walpurgisnacht the following April.

While gathering material for what was to become *HEXEN 2039* I was simultaneously developing the narrative, which, due to the nature of the Institute, had to have a military imperative. And then, once I'd decided that *HEXEN* was to be set in 2039, it was a matter of working out a hypothetical future military research project that could potentially develop out of the material I was investigating. I had been interested in ideas of the occult as a teenager, but it was really being in Germany that brought it back out. For a long time, I think, my interest in science and technology substituted for it, because science and technology are always moving towards things we don't understand.

Luckhurst Your work seems to very consciously move with technological developments. You've worked on CD-ROMs, designed computer animations, were involved in digital arts very early on, and your website is now a crucial part of your practice.

Treister I actually got into computers because I became fascinated by the idea of video games. I've talked about that a lot in other interviews. As soon as I could afford to get a computer that could do graphics I got one. That was in 1991. But it was much more analytical at that stage; I was interested in a cultural commentary on computer games and new technologies. I got my first computer, an Amiga, while I was reading William Gibson's *Neuromancer* (1984). The thing about Gibson is that it's not just science fiction but was about defining our contemporary environment. It seemed to me that so-called science fiction was doing this better than art. When I went to Australia, I couldn't take the computer with me, so I backtracked a little and returned to painting. I made a series of software boxes, hypothetical software packages that might exist in the future. In a way, at the time, this seemed more interesting than anything that computers could actually do, since they were quite limited back then.

Luckhurst So, by *HEXEN*, had the technology caught up with the idea?

Treister Well, to turn that around a little, the future of technology that *HEXEN 2039* hypothesises may not be that far away, according to a scientist I met at a conference in 2007. Apparently it's being researched in Maryland.

But the thing about the current tech world, which unlike twenty years ago, is the world most of us are now immersed in, is that it's so much about being at the cutting edge of the latest gizmo, and the latest gizmo is more and more about government and corporate control of content and information, and so I got less interested in taking part in that. I'm interested in technology as a phenomenon, an ongoing trajectory into the future, but not necessarily in using the latest technology itself to make art. Nor am I a net activist or part of the open source movement, although I'm for both of these in principle. I felt it was more important to stand outside of these environments, not end up incorporated into them.

I like the idea of going back to old technologies to think about new technologies. This is why *HEXEN 2039* and *MTB* (*Military Training Base*) use drawing, sketching out networks and links in pencil, making a physical work outside of the internet, something that can't be deleted by the flick of a switch. These projects have related websites with remote links to other sites and so on, but I want them to end up as books too; I'd be very depressed if there wasn't some outcome in book form. The process is like writing a book, a graphic novel, a piece of science fiction. Science fiction is full of these meta-commentaries and info-dumps, and I love that capacity. So they're on the internet, but also it was very important that *HEXEN* existed in the old technology of the book. One day in the future, if the planet survives, or let's say the Unabomber gets out of his prison cell in Colorado and destroys the complete worldwide technological infrastructure, maybe someone will pick up *HEXEN* in a second-hand bookshop, if such things remain, and wonder 'What the hell was that? Is that all true?'

Luckhurst Every modern technology seems to have an occult double – the telegraph and spirits, the tape deck and voices of the dead, the internet and its deities and ghosts. Is there something intrinsically spooky about technology?

Treister I think one of my future software boxes had 'Spooky' written on it... .

Well, by its very nature technology is spooky: it preserves the dead, in film and video, on tape, on CD, on the internet. Every day, millions of dead people or 'ghosts' are walking around doing things: shopping, chatting, having coffee, going on holiday, discussing the meaning of life. In the same film, one of the players may be dead and another alive; there is nothing in the technology of video, for example, to differentiate, to tell us which is which, whereas online a site can be updated to reflect changes. Perhaps in this sense the internet is not as intrinsically spooky as film or video or audio recordings. But in another sense it's spookier, especially now that we have the idea of the all-encompassing cloud to look forward to, a massive techno space where all our data could end up under government lock and key, with corporations like YouTube co-owning everyone's home movies. You only have to use your imagination to wonder what may become of all this stuff one day. The future is getting weirder. There doesn't need to be a master plan for it to happen.

There is something spooky for us about technology because it transcends the human body. The whole idea of virtual reality is spooky. I used to go to the Trocadero in Piccadilly Circus and play on all the state-of-the-art VR [virtual reality] games they had there in the 1980s. In video games you die time and again in a virtual space but you remain alive in the real world. And now the US military are training soldiers using the multi-user computer games inspired DARWARS Program, 'allowing continuous on-demand training anywhere, anytime, for everyone'. That sounds pretty spooky to me.[2]

Luckhurst I suppose the big claim about your work would be that it's all an attempt to understand the trajectory of post-war history: its personal, familial, and national consequences; its military and domestic technologies; and the rise of the military-industrial complex. Perhaps the only way to tell aspects of this hidden history is to go to the occult or other kinds of marginal knowledges, because it is a means of getting outside the official history, the record of the victors.

Treister That's a big question. But as I've said earlier, in terms of the military, the occult is now an acknowledged part of the official history. Anything you can do, they can do better.

I guess when I started working with new technologies they were a marginal knowledge, and I thought I was going to discover something about where they were taking us, while trying to control and make use of them myself. The first text I wrote about the Brodsky project in 1995 contained this paragraph: 'Rosalind Brodsky comes from a mixed background, part Eastern European Jewish. Brodsky fetishises history. She becomes a necrophiliac invader of spaces containing the deaths of her ancestors, through the privileged violence of technology'. That was very much 1990s techno-speak but I think it means something quite real.

Since I was a teenager I always wanted to change the world, but then some people say maybe the world doesn't want to be changed. And we all know one man's utopia is another man's hell. When I explored the whole fantasy through Brodsky of travelling back in history to rescue my grandparents from the Holocaust, it was a fantasy intervention into history. There are things both in the past and in the future which you can't change. As you say, you can just try and get a better understanding of them, and knowledge can be empowering, but it can also be depressing.

With the *HEXEN* project, and the sequel, *HEXEN 2.0*, it's on one level about trying to imagine a worst-case scenario of what the military-industrial-academic-scientific-media complex might do to attempt to alter the course of history. I was told as a child that people went to the gas chambers like sheep, and since the age of five I've been planning how not to be a sheep. Maybe I *am* a paranoid conspiracy theorist. For example, I refuse to join any social networking sites, as that would implicate my friends in my activities. For most people this isn't a problem. But for me, the fact is that the National Socialists *did* come and get my grandparents. If, for example, the political situation in the UK changed significantly, it would be quite possible to find yourself in a category that some people didn't want to have around. [...]

Luckhurst So you take a dystopian view of the future? That techno-culture is an ever-encroaching, inhuman totality.

Treister It's obvious. Ultimately, the larger the weapon, the greater the threat. That doesn't mean a lot of people aren't going to benefit in all kinds of ways before we get there or something else gets there first.

Luckhurst Are we back to ambivalence then? About never being sure about the epistemological status of the knowledges you map, whether it's true or false?

Treister True or false is not the point. All the information in my work is on one level or another true. There is no invention, just re-presentation. There is so much recent art commentary rhetoricising this supposedly fascinating blurry area between fact and fiction. These people are missing the point. It's an academic fence-sitter position. There is no fence. Nowhere is a fence. There is only exposure of the horror and the joy, and the bits in between but there are no fences.

1 Stanford Research Institute (SRI) was an independent scientific research institute whose clients included government agencies, commercial businesses, and other types of organisations. The SRI used to be part of Stanford University until the time of the Vietnam War, when there was a lot of protest from people within the university who felt that the part of its work that was funded by the US military (through the Defense Advanced Research Projects Agency, DARPA) was co-opting the university into military-industrial complex. For more details about the SRI International, see www.sri.com/about.

2 DARWARS Program: wwwdarpa.mil/dso/archives/darwars/index.html

Suzanne Treister, extracts from 'What Happens in the Gaps: An Interview with Roger Luckhurst', in *The Machine and The Ghost: Technology and Spiritualism in Nineteenth- to Twenty-First-Century Art and Culture*, eds. Sas Mays & Neil Matheson (Manchester and New York: Manchester University Press, 2013) 140–57.

Patrick Keiller
Robinson//2012

[...] During ten months of 2008, I had photographed about four hours of 35mm negative of landscape and similar subjects encountered mostly in a slow, elliptical progress through part of southern England, intending to arrange the edited footage as the document of a journey by someone who had set out in the belief that, by making it, he or she would bring about some kind of transformation. To begin with, the film had not necessarily involved anyone called Robinson, but when I began to write its script, in March 2009, I decided that it would, and that I would call it *Robinson in Ruins*. [...]

The journey evolved in an exploratory manner, so that a camera subject was often determined by a chance encounter, sometimes only after having visited its predecessor. After ten months, the camera had mapped out an approximately elliptical, anti-clockwise progress.

The ruins were of four kinds: architectural, in that a surprising number of the locations encountered were, in one way or another, ruins; personal, in that, by then, Robinson seemed physically depleted, if not actually a ghost; ecological, in that, in the narrative, he is enlisted by non-human intelligences anxious to preserve a long-term future for the biosphere; and economic, in that the film had been photographed during 2008, the year of long-awaited neoliberal crisis [...].

Quatermass II was the second of Nigel Kneale's BBC *Quatermass* television series, broadcast in six episodes at 8 o'clock on Saturday nights in October and November 1955. It was adapted for the cinema as *Quatermass 2,* a feature film produced by Hammer Films, released in 1957.[1] In both versions, Professor Bernard Quatermass is the director of a team developing a nuclear-powered rocket with the aim of establishing permanent bases on the moon. His project is under threat of cancellation by a seemingly cost-conscious government, following a nuclear accident at the rocket project's testing range in Australia. At another UK location, 'Winnerden Flats', meteorite-research establishment, supposedly developing the production of synthetic food. Anyone who picks up one of the fallen projectiles is liable to be taken over by an alien life-form, briefly visible as an ectoplasm-like sliver when the projectile shatters, which leaves a mark at the point it enters the host, usually on the face. Most of the civil servants in the relevant ministry have already succumbed, so that Quatermass' efforts to reveal and repel the invasion are, initially, frustrated. In both the television series and the film, the Shell Haven refinery near Stanford-le-Hope in Essex, on the Thames estuary, represents the synthetic food establishment, inside which is an enormous, malevolent organism. In the film, the location that represents the temporary settlement where the research establishment's not yet body-snatched but compliant construction workers live was at or near the new town Hemel Hempstead, then under construction. Early in the Hammer film, Quatermass and a colleague set out from the rocket base to drive to Winnerden Flats. In the car, the colleague reads a map, telling Quatermass: 'You take the Carlisle road'. Turning off what appears to be a recently constructed road, perhaps somewhere in Essex, or Hemel Hempstead, they pass a sign 'Carlisle and the North', put there, presumably, by the film crew. There had been no mention of Carlisle, about twenty miles from Spadeadam, in the original television series.

Given the effort and expense involved, one wonders why these set-ups were added to the story already established by the television series. Perhaps they were intended merely to associate Quatermass' fictional rocket site with the actual test facility that would have been known, by the time of the film, to be under construction. [...]

1 [Footnote 18 in source] The first and third series were *The Quatermass Experiment*, broadcast in six episodes (of which only two survive) on Saturday evenings between 18 July and 22 August 1953 and *Quatermass and the Pit*, broadcast in six episodes on Monday nights between 22 December 1958 and 26 January 1959. By the end of the latter. BBC audience research indicated 11 million viewers. Hammer also produced feature-film adaptations of these series: *The Quatermass Xperiment* (1955) and *Quatermass and the Pit* (1967).

Patrick Keiller, extracts from 'Robinson', in *The Possibility of Life's Survival on the Planet* (London: Tate Publishing, 2012) 5, 10, 24–5.

Carrie Paterson
How to Build a Universe...//2007

'I have a secret love of chaos', confessed Philip K. Dick. The kill-your-TV excerpt from the master-craftsman of science fiction provides the title – 'How To Build A Universe that Doesn't Fall Apart Two Days Later' – for the newest exhibition at CCA's Wattis Institute, which is located in San Francisco's soon-to-be-gentrified industrial district. Dick's vision of building universes so that his characters can struggle as they fall apart is a prescient metaphor for the trials of urban growth, collapse and regeneration.

This aspect of Dick's essay ricochets off several notable works. Duelling avatars – a brain and a sword – continually circumscribe and disintegrate their virtual spaces in hilarious psychedelic contests (Nate Boyce). A photographic installation by Gitte Villesen features scrapper-cum-artist Kenn Dunn in the futuristic (as in *Blade Runner*, 1982) Creative Reuse Warehouse in Chicago. Bonnie Sherk's *Crossroads Community*, photographed and documented between 1974–81, is a slice of ingenuity and survivalism: the working farm occupied spaces peripheral to a raised freeway and was an educational as well as nutritional centre.

1970's paintings of space-station suburbia and celestial cities by Rick Guidice, in the collection of NASA, still make a delicious sales brochure. Meanwhile the spatial architectural rendering of maximal urban fabric (Lebbeus Woods) is almost a better deconstruction because it was immaterial at the show.

Tehran 1380 (2002) by Solmaz Shahbazi, films everyday Iranians, a few journalists and one tourist discussing rapid changes in the city and Iran's image in the West. The new architecture exemplifies these struggles – modern, cold and some opine 'against Islam' because people can see into each other's homes. The Western-looking urban moment in developments such as Ekbatan, 'a postmodern socialist experiment', and mega-structure Navvab pits apartment life against house and tradition. One architect for Navvab insists: 'Our role is forcing people to get used to new living conditions.' But the new structures only line the freeways – a 'facelift' for visitors rather than deep change. 'Reality is that which, when you stop believing in it, doesn't go away.' (Dick) Tehran's sudden growth from immigration has left some even living inside the city's new crop of billboards – just enough room for a bed and kettle. Here curator Bradley's omissions of the humorous apocalyptic Christianity in Dick's title essay would have spoken best to Shahbazi's contribution: Dick relates that when his God-character Ubik says 'I am the word', the German translation interprets 'I am the brand name'. What could be better tribute to the original paranoid genius who taught us the poetry of coincidences?

Carrie Paterson, 'How to Build a Universe... CCA Wattis Institute, San Francisco', *Flash Art* (March/April 2007) 75.

Jan Tumlir
The Time Machine in Contemporary Art from Los Angeles//2007

The consensus emerging from the 2006 Orange County Museum of Art California Biennial is that young artists on the West Coast are operating in an idiom closely linked to science fiction. The concerns that have characterised this genre over the years are all accounted for: the imagination of future and alien civilisations (Leslie Shows); interplanetary and/or time travel (Scoli Acosta); the colonisation of, or invasion from, the alien outlands (Pearl C. Hsiung); the encounter with the other (Christian Maychack); the redefinition of the idea of the human in response to the other, either alien or homemade (Sterling Ruby); the technological transformation of the human as such (Andy Alexander); the social functions of disaster, apocalypse (Marie Jager); utopia versus dystopia (My Barbarian), and so on. Even those who strive for a measure of documentary *vérité* (Sergio De La Torre, as well as the collaborative teams Bull.Miletic and The Speculative Archive) employ the everyday as a foil for the strange. Perhaps most significantly in regard to our present moment, that quintessential sci-fi theme of communication breakdown and its inevitable outcome, war, is pervasive.

Against the backdrop of the Iraq war that the current administration still wants to paint in the broad, unifying strokes of 'a battle against totalitarian ideologies' like WW2, but that is obviously much closer to the divisive 'quagmire' of Vietnam, artists are revisiting a range of oppositional strategies mainly culled from the 1960s and 70s. Some indulge in all-too familiar sorts of stylistic revivalism that are merely the 'last word' or 'shriek' of a 1980s/90s-era endgame. But then there are those who want to quantum leap right over the 1980s and 90s and to reconnect more substantially with the political sensibilities of prior eras. The 'anxiety of influence' arguments that determined the specific mode of melancholic citation throughout the 1980s and 90s have all but evaporated. The eternal return of the past no longer bespeaks an impossible future, nor does aesthetic influence automatically deny inspiration. For many young artists, the appropriated objects of the past serve as a sort of aesthetic springboard. Intensive concentration on these various artefacts is aimed at somehow 'breaking through.'

In Los Angeles, where art school and art world are one and the same, it comes as no surprise that what begins as a critical imperative should be so swiftly converted into a productive strategy. If one figure can be called out to exemplify this mode – this archaeological pop baroque – in its infancy, it is Christopher Williams, whose minute attention to every stylistic nuance of the found object places him on the opposite end of Andy Warhol's openly undiscriminating Pop. Moreover, in contrast to Warhol's absolute devotion to 'the new', Williams' appropriations are acutely untimely: visions of the future pulled from the past, haunting the present.

From the classical oracle to the street-corner fortune-teller, prescience is always linked to an object that allows for worldly reflection while also effecting deep structural distortions. A smouldering fire blurs one's vision, a pool of water ripples, and the old crystal ball bends every straight sight-line around its contours; all these things allow one to peer into the distance while obstructing one's view. The art and popular culture of 'late-style modernism' serves a similar purpose for contemporary practice. As we approach the 'end of art' in both the most positive and negative senses, that which is still wholly made by clever hands and nimble thoughts is granted a last surge of expressive vitality. As with Benjamin's aura, burning most brightly just before it is extinguished, there is an insistent romanticism at work here, implicitly linked to thoughts about death. The products of the imagination are externalised as ruins – but, paradoxically perhaps, ruins with a prognosticating value.

Ruins abound in Marie Jager's most recent project *The Purple Cloud*, which was screened at the 2006 OCMA Biennial in a dark gallery 'theatre' with related installation elements scattered about outside. These included a series of small collages presented as lobby cards and a purple vinyl cut-out of the eponymous cloud affixed to the museum's windows and extending the film's sci-fi story line of ecological catastrophe and global exodus into the space of everyday life in Southern California, where climate change and illegal immigration are already the reigning topics of the day. Titled *Sunscreen*, it metaphorically figures the imaginary disaster that drives the filmic narrative while literally shielding the interior of the museum, just as it would a car, from the real disaster of the sun's increasingly 'angry' rays. More literally still, *Sunscreen* reminds us that cinema is fundamentally a process of projection: light passed through tinted films.

Clearly, Jager still wants to make art out of cinema, to extrude its technical operations as aesthetic objects. She remains committed to this structuralist programme while recognising that it no longer stands to yield any sort of zero-degree. As Jean Louis Baudry's 'basic cinematographic apparatus' is itself flickering on the threshold of obsolescence, its deconstruction becomes suffused in a nostalgic sense of the uncanny, like the dismantling of an automaton. As Jager has already suggested in her filmic adaptation of Karel Čapek's *RUR* (*Rossumn's Universal Robots*, 2003), the medium is haunted throughout by just such baroque/gothic figures: the counterfeit human filled with machine parts or else, conversely, the counterfeit robot hiding the human inside.

Once understood as the space of synthetic convergence of all arts, cinema now undergoes a reverse-process of fragmentation. Like *RUR*, *The Purple Cloud* is based on literature, an obscure apocalyptic novel from 1901 – cinema's year zero – by the British author M.R. Schiel. Here, also, it is the book as such that supplies the film's structural foundation; not just its ideational contents but the printed word as it appears on the page. Words that describe the world's ruin are themselves ruined via the same cut-up montage-process that William Burroughs, for one, likened to avant-garde art and practised expressly to 'advance' literature to the next stage of 'visual literacy'. The vintage Stockhausen-style splicing of *concrète* and electroacoustic sounds on the score drives home the point: *The Purple Cloud* is caused as much by climactic disaster as, to quote Paul Virilio, 'the information bomb'.

No doubt, the current fascination with all things analogue is compelled by a nostalgic fetish for a still-embodied technology, one that shores up a 'warmth' that gradually dissipates as we approach the present. More substantially, the analogue era is scanned for theoretical objects that can explain our digital present. Mathias Poledna, another recent European transplant to Los Angeles, turns film in on itself to discover, in place of a general foundation, a hyper-specific ruin. Appropriately, he calls his works 'fragments of twentieth-century culture', as they are just the sort of thing one might expect to find buried deep within scorched earth, or else, worst-case scenario, orbiting a distant planet alongside other items of earthly detritus. Typically short – at just under 30 minutes, *Crystal Palace*, Poledna's latest exercise in ambient ethnography, is the longest – these works demand intensive scrutiny and repeat viewing. Every detail matters, those pertaining to content as much as the technical specifications of camera type, film stock, projector, etc., and here again the parts become significant precisely by refusing to gel. [...]

The question that haunts so many post-apocalyptic sci-fi narratives returns here without the protective armour of fantasy: how should one go about reconstructing a civilisation from just a few broken, cryptic clues?

And what if those clues related not to the productive apex of a culture, nor even to baseline functionality, but to its nadir? What if the information were itself compromised? In Adria Julia's recent installation, *La Villa Basque*, the documentary functions of film and photography are strained by their essentially unstable object. The titular Villa that the artist discovered in the industrial city of Vernon, on the outskirts of LA, is both a Basque restaurant and a museum of sorts to the glory of its founding immigrant family. From the first moment, however, the history preserved therein is riddled with fiction, as the account of arrival of the paterfamilias from the 'Old' to the 'New Country' swiftly segues to a Hollywood-style shootout. Close to empty on most days, the Villa has nevertheless managed to perpetuate its fantasies via Adria's work. It is one of those great decaying frontier outposts, a memory palace already partly corrupted by the forgetting it is trying to keep out, and in the process contaminating everyone that steps in. [...]

At its extremes, Los Angeles gives way to the beach and the desert, its geological bookends. Both preceding and succeeding the account of its relentless, sprawling development, these are also zones of intensive sci-fi speculation. In cinema, and art as well, these have always signified both the pre- and post-historical, a manifest absence that enables cultural reinvention as if from scratch. Because its endless becoming is bounded on either side by equally endless void, Los Angeles is itself often figured as a wavering mirage, an imaginary place floating just above the sands of time.

Jan Tumlir, extracts from 'Sci-Fi Historicism Part 1', *Flash Art* (March/April 2007) 102–5. Updated by the author, 2020.

Michele Robecchi
Pawel Althamer: *Common Task*//2010

The importance of the Warsaw housing estate of Bródno can hardly be overestimated in Pawel Althamer's practice. Long-time residence of the artist and his family, it made its mark for the first time at the end of 1999, when he convinced the inhabitants of the neighbourhood to salute the new millennium by lighting their flat windows to form the figure '2000' on a building façade. Although Althamer's subsequent work featured Bródno in less spectacular ways, the feeling of its presence, lurking behind even the most remote locations, was always there. Quite simply, Bródno is Althamer's favourite tool for measuring the world he ventures into. Splitting his time between living a family life in his native environment and flying across the planet from one continent to another – in what can only be described as a time-less and space-less experience – is a duality he is constantly aware of: a recurrent shift that could end up increasing a personal sense of detachment from both realities. This is, of course, unless there is someone around to take the ride with you.

Exactly a decade after *Bródno 2000*, Althamer looks back at his hometown district, this time adopting the well-known science fiction technique of exploring the present by projecting it into a future dimension. Dressed in gold spacesuits, a few members of his community have been recruited to tour the planet under the *Common Task* logo to seek different civilisations and boldly go where they presumably have never been before. The group embarked on their first journey in March 2009 to go to Brasilia – the ultimate symbol of how mankind often succumbs to the temptation of imagining its future by anticipating it, only to get it all wrong. After a brief stop to their own home base in June, they resumed their mission by visiting Belgium and, in a deeply emotional and spiritual trip, Mali.

For the last leg of their 2009 tour, Althamer and his associates decided it was time to open a public window on their activities while continuing to travel. The galleries of Modern Art Oxford have been converted into a space station, providing an opportunity to board the astronauts' ship and share the activities in real time. Space outfits are available to wear; documentaries on the group's previous journeys are viewable on rotation; visitors are welcome to join the crew on a few explorations in the Oxonian countryside; it is even possible to assist the film editor in the process of putting together fresh footage.

Like the mission and its participants, the *Common Task* station overlaps present and future elements, blurring any distinction between the two. Only at second glance, for example, does one realise that the futuristic waiting room is actually made out of old, repainted public transport seats. In typical Althamer style, the exhibition defies the logic dictated by the gallery format. Objectual art is absent, and the nature of the project itself frees it from temporal limitations.

In the 1950s the Polish architect Oskar Hansen – in response to the dehumanising aspects of modernism – advocated a return to open forms, wherein an artistic proposition would be a process translated by external agents. By generating a science fiction film in real time, *Common Task* extends Hansen's theories to the common perception of the artist as a mystical figure crossing unexplored realities, successfully converting a solitary journey into a collective experience.

Michele Robecchi, 'Pawel Althamer: *Common Task*', *Flash Art* (March/April 2010) 113.

Christopher Bedford
Ann Lislegaard//2009

Science fiction as a literary and filmic genre is distinguished in large part by its exponents' appetite for extreme conjecture, and by the need for writers and directors working in this domain to elaborate those conjectures into fantastical worlds that answer not to natural law or existent social structures, but to decrees set forth and imposed by the creator. In this sense, science fiction also supports a model of overstated authorship that presumes facets of a narrative cannot be borrowed from the observed world, but must instead emanate from the author's mind.

Though each of the works in Ann Lislegaard's exhibition '2062' originates in a particular work of science fiction, this does not mean that she is out to channel the individual visions of the authors: the creative delirium of J.G. Ballard, say, or the epic sweep of Samuel R. Delany and Ursula K. Le Guin (to refer to the artist's three primary references here); quite the contrary, in fact. More an analytical tool than platform for rehashing authorial megalomania, science fiction provides Lislegaard with the language and licence she needs to marry the frequently disparate concerns of modernism, Surrealism and Conceptualism.

A case in point is the artist's two-channel digital animation declaratively titled *Crystal World (After J.G. Ballard)* (2006), the clinical tenor of which could hardly be described as Ballardian. Prominent in this work is a domestic structure in a dense woodland setting. Rendered using 3D modelling software, the house's design is based on icons of Brazilian modernism: Lina Bo Bardi's *Casa de Vidrio* (*House of Glass*, 1957–68) and two of her designs for chairs, as well as the 1957 *Pavilhão Ciccillo Matarazzo* (*Ciccillo Matarazzo Pavilion*) by Oscar Niemeyer. Lislegaard's polished animation tours the house as its clean contours dissolve organically into a field of abstract refractions. Such transformation roughly echoes Ballard's novel, whose narrative describes a West African jungle's metamorphosis into a crystalline labyrinth. But while Ballard's surrealist dystopia offers an account of the natural world consumed by an unexplained event, Lislegaard's video eschews narrative, and seems, rather, to illustrate artistic conceptualisation in reverse: the jagged forms that emerge as the house melts away evoke architectural concept drawings. As a result, the video reads as if a process of entropy has been set in motion that returns all actualised forms to the nascent state of idea. Here, Robert Smithson, the modernist antagonist, is far more important than the lurking, maniacal spectre of Ballard.

Yet Lislegaard's blend of incommensurate visual morphologies from Surrealism to Op art – is effective only insofar as the vantage point she provides is a forceful one, that it lays the foundation for a convincing spectatorial experience. Science fiction constructs intricate fictive ecologies in the minds of its audiences through relentless imaginative hyperbole, which in turn supplies the basis for belief. Lislegaard, however, exerts control simply by directing very strictly the way her digital environments are consumed; whether those worlds are believable or even intelligible is not at issue. The result is a nuanced examination of the degree to which three-dimensional imaging technologies can offer a sentient being a plausible simulation of embodied experience. In *Bellona (After Samuel R. Delany)* (2005), as in *Crystal World*, we glide silently, unobstructed through an architectural space, our progress imperceptibly coerced and unnaturally smooth. The only view available is oblique, and each successive pan gives no clearer indication of the structure as a whole, a perspective which induces the sensation of claustrophobia and emphasises our complete lack of agency. *Left Hand of Darkness (After Ursula K. Le Guin)* (2008) features speakers producing a constant wall of static placed strategically throughout the exhibition space, underscoring the multi-sensory foundation of real spatial perception; while the artist's decision to project both *Bellona* and *Crystal World* on expansive screens that lean heavily on the gallery walls further emphasises visual perception's haptic dimension, a nuance lacking in the slick animation itself. By staging her digital renderings using sound elements and a forthrightly sculptural vocabulary, Lislegaard plays the richness of full, sensory awareness against the relative vacuity of simulation to great, disarming effect.

Christopher Bedford, 'Ann Lislegaard', *Artforum*, vol. 48, no. 2 (October 2009) 245–6.

Amna Malik
Patterning Memory//2006

The African American artist Ellen Gallagher works within a conflation of poetry and popular culture that aligns her, as Judith Wilson has argued, with the Dark Room Collective, a group of African American writers whose 'diverse literary manners and modes cohere around a shared ability to code-switch with the same fast dazzle and a common pool of black pop cultural knowledge'.[1] Unlike her contemporaries, whose approach to the question of 'race' and representation may lie within a deconstructive approach to questions of identity – in which postcolonial theory is central – Gallagher's practice attempts to construct an alternative understanding to existing ideas of 'black' consciousness by drawing on literature as a point of reference. [...]

This literary dimension of Gallagher's work and the humour pervasive in her collages are reminiscent of the surrealist artist Max Ernst's collage novels and perhaps, like Ernst, her installation *Ichthyosaurus* at the Freud Museum, London (July to September 2005) allowed her to ask questions of psychoanalysis. At first glance the installation, curated by James Putnam, appeared to be a representation of psychoanalysis as nothing more than a thinly disguised biological determinism complicit with the biopolitics that surrounds the discourse of 'race'. However, closer inspection revealed that Gallagher has been preoccupied for some time with certain forms of marine life resulting in a biomorphic lyrical abstraction that seems at odds with her earlier collages such as *Pomp! Pomp! Bang! Bang!* (2003) and their direct references to the fraught politics of 'race' in the US. In *Ichthyosaurus* aspects of the lyrical abstraction in her 'Watery Ecstatic' series, ongoing since 2001, are combined with pseudo-scientific drawings and objects to engage with Freud's collection of artefacts.

The title of the installation takes its name from one of a number of sea dinosaurs [...] found as fossilised remains. Gallagher's watercolour is a delicate and precisely rendered painting that subtly evokes images found in pre-photographic science books. The ichthyosaurus [...] was originally a lizard that adapted to conditions underwater, learning to breathe and give birth without having to return to land, but it is not clear what its connections might be with the politics of 'race' and psychoanalysis. This puzzling combination creates a contradiction that is increased by the seemingly competing forms of visual 'coding': films, watercolours, collages and specimen jars that do not initially demonstrate much continuity. Examining some of the images in the exhibition in the context of her practice as a whole I want to consider connections between the apparently abstract forms in her 'Watery Ecstatic' series and her collages taken from 'race' magazines like *Ebony*. I am particularly interested in how Gallagher, together with the curator, has drawn out a potentially different topography for the unconscious that places the trauma of the Middle Passage as a holocaust at the centre of the European psyche. [...]

The combination of visual references in the watercolour *Ichthyosaurus* draws on the pre-Enlightenment interest in natural history before the study of science was divided into different categories of biology, zoology, ornithology etc., but it is rendered in the delicate style of a nineteenth-century watercolour by an amateur naturalist. The large white cut-paper 'drawing' *Drexciya* appears to be an unevenly raised surface that on closer inspection reveals small marine fish with afro hair and 'negro' features. There were also jars containing what appeared to be marine creatures, but which were actually carefully crafted sculptural forms. Over Freud's couch hung another watercolour, again resembling but not recognisable as a jellyfish. It competed with two films, one of the Natural History Museum's specimen jars, the other of marine creatures on the seabed; shot in black and white, they resembled archival natural history footage. There was also a collage – *Odalisque* (2005) – of Gallagher being drawn by Freud whilst she reclines on a couch, which was hung above his collection of Buddhas. The juxtaposition suggested a certain 'orientalism' in his fascination with all things Egyptian.

[...] In one of the 16mm films a sea urchin's long tentacles flowed in and out, creating a beautiful rhythmic movement, pulling us into and out of its centre. If one looked carefully – the film was projected into a small corner of the study and almost impossible to see close up – it emerges that scratched into the surface of the film are little 'black' faces. The traces of the slave past, she seems to suggest, are like fossilised remains that form the geological strata, the very fabric of the seabed in the Atlantic Ocean. The fake archival form of the film attempts to insinuate this history into Freud's collection, the fake specimen jar and the collage of Gallagher as an odalisque seem to be a play on the way psychoanalysis might be seen as an archiving of memory.

If psychoanalysis offers a means of reading history across its absences, then it seems it is the absence of memory that marks this set of images by Gallagher. This is nowhere more evident than in the patterned outlines in *Drexciya*. Looking at this work is an act of contemplation that initially turns the gaze back on itself, the uneven surface of the white paper catches the light and gives it the sense of a space that dips and rises but without revealing the logic of its structure. It seems to be entirely monochromatic. The monochrome's emptiness indicates an erasure of memory and history that exemplifies a fulfilment of the European historical avant-garde's fascination with abstract art. Like Kasimir Malevich's

Black Square (1915), a black painted square on a white painted surface, it becomes a utopian attempt to escape the past and the weight of history and becomes 'a means of thinking one's way out of the present and into the future'.[2]

Moving closer to the surface of *Drexciya* we find the small indentations that create a delicate curving line reveal themselves to be cut lines that spiral outwards in a series of circular formations. In these spirals we discover heads in profile that assume a 'Negroid' appearance in the centre of swirling lines that take on the form of elaborate afros. The hairstyles of Africans and African Americans are in many respects a semiotic inscription of the body that has travelled in time and distance. Gallagher's pleasure in carefully cutting lines is not distinct from the subject matter, the dissection of the jellyfish with the biologist's scalpel, and the creation of complex patterns are made to resemble the arguably violent yet ritualised creation of elaborate coiffures popular in the beauty magazines used in her collages. In *Drexciya* they become one and the same thing. If the Afro is a specifically American mutation then plaiting and braiding hair comes from the practice of plaiting African traditions, producing a variety of elaborate styles that 'are reminiscent of African ceramics, architecture and embroidery'.[3] The conjunction of hair and marine creatures is particularly pronounced in *Negro a Day* from her *DeLuxe* series (2004/2005). Different orders of patterning are made to overlap so that the elaborate coils of black coiffures and the long tentacles of jellyfish are set against a negative silhouette of coral that slices through their shared plane. The juxtaposition of women's coiffures, jellyfish and coral creates lacunae in meaning and representation that circulates around the eroticism of black hair and, I would suggest, over the representation of black masculinity. [...] The long tentacles of the jellyfish seem to surround and lovingly caress the female subject at the bottom centre, her head turned away. In *Drexciya* the process of cutting out is extended to the 'cutting out' of the history of slavery from the psyche of Euro-American modernism.

The Afro-fish in *Drexciya* and the conjunction of fish and hair in *Negro a Day* are therefore symptoms of a patterning that is a means of evoking the archive of historical memory. We can also find traces of this historical memory in Gallagher's ongoing preoccupation with the underground techno band of the same name formed in the early 1990s, the name recurs more than once in her oeuvre. In the sleeve notes to their double CD *The Quest* (1997), we discover that Drexciyans are a marine species descended from 'pregnant America-bound African slaves' thrown overboard 'by the America-bound thousands during labour for being sick and disruptive cargo'. Mark Sinker, one of the founders of the band Drexciya, argued in 1992:

The ships landed long long ago: they already laid waste whole societies, abducted and genetically altered whole swathes of citizenry, Africa and America – and so by extension Europe and Asia are already in their ways, Alien Nation.[4]

For Kodwo Eshun the breakthrough in their music

is to bring alien abduction back to earth, to transfer the trauma from out there to yesternow [. . .] They have been here all along and they are you. You are the alien you are looking for.[5]

In this scenario, African Americans are variants on the Drexciya, landing and adapting to different social conditions, mutating in the process, but fundamentally alien beings whose occupation of America can only be understood in terms of science fiction. Consider for example, the description of a cyborg subject in Samuel Delany's *Nova* (1968) when Mouse enters the ship and plugs himself into its 'motherboard' and is able to move the spaceship's many outer structures to moving his arms a little here and navigate through the stars by moving there.[6] Delany's work was an enormous influence on Gallagher – who also cites the science fiction writer Octavia Butler – as a way of prosthetically rethinking transformed subjectivities.[7] The biological constructions of race implicated in the exhibition appear to mine a similar terrain. The Drexciya myth suggests the instinct of survival that counters the death drive and in the process creates a mutation and transformation of the slave body that directs us away from complex erasure of its humanity towards a posthuman subject that draws on scientific technologies popular in cyborg cultures. [...]

Gallagher's *Abu Simbel* (2005) is perhaps closest to the motifs of 'race' found in her earlier work. The 'trashy' presence of a star-ship made with an array of materials including blue fur, gold leaf and crystals hovering to the side of the colossal statues of Ramses II that have assumed 'negro' features, creates a curious collision between the past and the future. For Gallagher the spaceship is an allusion to Sun Ra and George Clinton and afrofuturism in techno music. The exaggerated 'negro' features of the statue of Ramses II seems to recall Senegalese historian Cheikh Anta Diop's authentication of Egypt as the cradle of African civilisation. Gallagher replaces the smaller statues of Ramses' wife and daughters, carved into the base of the gargantuan figures, with her own private obsessions. The 'black' nurses refer to Eunice Rivers and appear in the Abu Simbel print and elsewhere in her work. Rivers' complicity with the Tuskegee experiment marks a moment of trauma in African American history when African American men were drawn into the medical system without receiving treatment and used as guinea pigs to test the effect of syphilis.[8] The many severed heads which litter the site of the temple have the blank eyes common in Gallagher's appropriation of African American images of beauty, evoking the 'savagery' of the US medical establishment within the terms of a colonial unconscious.

The discovery of the temple constitutes the recovery of historical documents within the European psyche. The temple records Ramses II the warrior king's numerous victorious battles. The preservation of the past was for Freud the activity of the unconscious, whilst the ruins of time were our conscious present memories. The role of the sea in creating a necessary forgetting becomes significant. Between 1964 and 1968, conservationists restructured the area around the Abu Simbel site as water levels in the surrounding Lake Nasser threatened to damage the monument. The myth of the Drexciyans returns us to the lost city of Atlantis and particularly the origins and identity of the mysterious Sea Peoples whose battles with Ramses III, that coincided with the Trojan Wars, are commemorated in the monument *Medinet Habu*.

What is compelling is the obliteration of numerous cities by the sea that have only recently been excavated by satellite technology allowing scientists like the geo-archaeologist Eberhard Zangger to optically navigate deep sea levels from outer space. The technologies of the future are continually refashioning history and archaeology allowing a route into the past of our future. Oceanography and psychoanalysis, therefore, potentially come together.

Returning to Gallagher's installation, we can argue that she moves the topography of the unconscious from the ruins of Pompeii, Rome, and the Greek origins of European civilisation, to the Black Atlantic. Gallagher seems to unearth, through the flux and flow of water, the fossilised remains of a racist unconscious and weaves into them other formations, like Samuel Delany's relocation of the post-industrial, urban ruins of Harlem and Detroit to the dystopic cyberspaces of his future realms. One can understand what happens to these images once they are placed in the context of Freud's former study and home. They place the prehistory of the African American subject in slavery and the Middle Passage at the centre of the European psyche by paradoxically making visible the absence of this history through the presence of the monochrome as a *tabula rasa*, an erasure of the past. She thus creates the basis of a foundation myth in which the sea becomes an incubator for the potentialities of the future.

1 Judith Wilson, 'Sniffing Elephant Bones: the Poetics of Race in the Art of Ellen Gallagher', in *Inside the Visible, an Elliptical Traverse of 20th Century Art, in, of and from the Feminine*, ed. Catherine de

Zegher (Cambridge, MA: MIT Press, 1996) 375.

2 Briony Fer, *On Abstract Art* (Yale: Yale University Press, 1997) 11.

3 Kobena Mercer, 'Black Hair/Style Politics', *Welcome to the Jungle: New Positions in Black Cultural Studies* (London: Routledge, 1994) 97–128.

4 Kodwo Eshun, *More Brilliant than the Sun: Adventures in Sonic Fiction* (London: Quartet Books, 1999) 84.

5 Ibid.

6 Samuel R. Delany, *Nova* (London: Gollanz, 2001) 41–3.

7 Thyrza Nicols Goodeve, *Ellen Gallagher* (London: Anthony D'Offay Gallery, 2001) 31.

8 '1000 words', op. cit., 131.

Amna Malik, extracts from 'Patterning Memory, Ellen Gallagher's Icthyosaurus at the Freud Museum', *Wasafiri*, vol. 21, no. 3 (2006) 29–39. Available at https://tandfonline.com/doi/full/10.1080/02690050600918318

Gwyneth Shanks
Visualising the Now//2014

In 1995 Japanese artist Mariko Mori began *Beginning of the End*. The photographic project started in Tokyo as a one-off photo of the artist in the city's central commercial district, Shibuya. The project expanded over the course of a decade, coming to include photographs from numerous global locations: ruins, city centres and iconic architectural structures. Each photograph features the artist in a unitard, lying inside a clear, oblong pod, her figure mysterious and alien. The photographs are divided into three series: *Past, Present and Future*.[1] This article explores the representation of global space in *Present*, probing the subjects, historical trajectories, visual genealogies and ideological and material processes that inform the series, existing both within and outside the framed borders of Mori's photographs.

The four images in *Present* are of Times Square in New York City, the Shibuya district of Tokyo, Piccadilly Circus in London and Tsim Sha Tsui in Hong Kong. Each city is a global financial and cultural centre, as well as being located on an island.[2] If islands are often theorised and imagined as insular, bounded spaces, *Present* complicates this genealogy.[3] The photographs represent global cities imbricated within the global circulation of capital, culture, commodities and subjects.[4] The photographs nuance the term 'island', exposing the disparities that exist between such sites. Mori's *Present* emphasises that not all islands are understood as equal; some are significant nodes in a network of globalised capitalism.

The aesthetic composition of the photos from *Present* positions the figure of the alien as a spatial interruption within the urbanscape, which is always already an islandscape. The connotations and histories of otherness that can be applied to Mori's alien figure lead to a theorisation of the way in which island discourse is tied to global subjects, and is reinscribed in relation to current networks of economic production. The photographs facilitate an oscillation between the alien, the island and crowded urbanity, foregrounding concurrent geopolitical, socio-political, economic and cultural anxieties in relation to spatial production and urban visuality. The alien and the island are imbricated within similar trajectories of narrative making and empire building, emerging as placeholders for the unknown or the other encountered in the long project of colonialism. Mori's photographs link the island and the alien, asserting the two as pivotal geopolitical markers of a global urban present.

While part of this article's formal and critical analysis of *Present* vis-à-vis the island foregrounds island insularity in relation to global urbanity, this article complicates a potentially facile reading of *Present* in relationship to Mori's own desires for the project (a global consciousness predicated upon spatial and temporal elision).[5] Far from eliding spatial or temporal specificity, I read Mori's photographs as imbricated within the time and place of their production. The spatial interruption that I read the alien as enacting upon the photographic scene asserts a temporal and spatial specificity counter to the flattening forces of a certain globalisation discourse and Mori's artistic statements. If the conceit of *Present* attempts an elision of time, this article foregrounds the particular time of the photographs, attending to the distinct visual narratives that emerge in relation to Mori's alien body and the photos' island positioning.

Science fiction, a genre that has long dealt with the figure of the alien and the site of the island as well as the attendant anxieties produced by both, arrived in Japan in the late nineteenth century via the country's expanded exposure to the West.[6] Mori's work is indebted to this genealogy, which positions the aesthetic of the alien and the island as existing within a history of uneven cultural exchange. In *Tea Ceremony III* from 1994, she appears in two photographs dressed as an alien – or intergalactic geisha, as she terms the character. A suppliant smile on her face and a tea tray in hand, Mori stands attentively behind the besuited men who appear in the photos with her. The alien/woman in *Tea Ceremony*, and other early photo projects, is represented in distinct uneven power relationships with her male counterparts. The alien becomes a means to explore notions of self and other, and the gendered, raced and labour implications of that distinction. If works like *Tea Ceremony III* explored notions of alien identity in connection with sartorial markings of femininity and asymmetrical power relationships, *Oneness*, from 2003, differently engages with alien identity. The installation features a circle of six child-size alien figures linking hands, whose eyes light up when hugged. Pressed against the little aliens' chests, one can hear their mechanical heartbeats. The figurines were created out of a soft material, meant to mimic flesh. As Mori writes of the work:

> My idea was to build a metaphor of contact, of bringing in the outsider [...] although we are all human beings, we differentiate between others and ourselves, and see others as outsiders. I could be seen as an alien in another culture.[7]

Oneness embodies the moments of slippage between 'sameness and difference, between centre and margins, so that [. . .] boundaries blur and become indecisive'.[8] The hug is meant to eradicate the literal space between self and alien, shifting the reflexive nature of the term alien in the moment of feeling the figurines' soft flesh, so similar to one's own, and hearing their heartbeats. The term alien is relational and necessitates re-negotiations of who, or what, is alien.

Current notions of Japanese science fiction are perhaps most indebted to the popular and widely distributed genres of manga and anime. While the distinct visual style of both can be seen in Mori's work, particularly her early photo projects such as *Play with Me* and *Birth of a Star*, her *Present* series evokes a genealogy of science fiction's influence in Japan that reaches back to the mid nineteenth century, when Japan re-opened its borders to Western contact. Japanese science fiction arose out of the confluence of modernisation, globalisation and colonisation (the Japanese Empire as both coloniser and colonised), a collision of forces that parallels discourses on islands.[9] While Mori expresses a desire to eclipse space and time as a means to 'transcend [...] national borders and share one consciousness as global beings and life forms', there is a parallel temporal transcendence based upon the persistence of aesthetic markers embedded in uneven processes of cultural exchange.[10] *Beginning of the End* presents an aesthetic collision of future anxieties and desires predicated upon a past history of geopolitical incursions.

The Meiji Period is often narrativised as an opening of Japan's borders in response to the threat of Western powers and to forestall a colonial takeover. The empire recognised that:

> to avoid being carved up by Western colonial powers (as had already happened in China and India) [. . .] [they] would have to replicate in short order the technological and military prowess of the already developed nations of the world.[11]

The politically motivated goal of developing military technologies equivalent to Western powers aligned temporally with the introduction of the relatively new literary genre of science fiction. Western science fiction authors like Jules Verne and H.G. Wells were translated into Japanese; Verne's *Around the World in Eighty Days* appeared in Japanese just six years after its original publication in French. While science fiction entered Japan through translation, novelists and artists quickly adopted it as a means to process and express the rapid technological, social, cultural and economic changes Japan was undergoing.

While scholars point to the ways in which science fiction narratives captured the chaos of rapid technological changes and advancement within Japan and globally, the plot of Verne's classic *Around the World in Eighty Days* also signals the representational impact of the geopolitical expansion driving the colonial conquests of the eighteenth, nineteenth and twentieth centuries. Verne's plot is predicated upon circumnavigating the globe, a feat only newly possible to the layperson due to transcontinental train travel, amongst other developments. The protagonist of the novel, Phileas Fogg, accepts a wager that he cannot travel around the world in eighty days. Travel, in the novel, is associated with winning, competition and money: conquest. Almost all the cities featured in the *Present* series are on Fogg's itinerary in *Around the World*.[12]

If Verne's work links a representation of global travel indebted to colonial expansion with technological advancements, the geographic coincidence between Verne's late-nineteenth-century novel and Mori's late-twentieth-century visual project likewise positions Mori's work in relation to a spectre of science fiction entangled with colonialism. This unframed historical trajectory that informs a reading of *Present* and *Beginning of the End* positions travel in relation to narratives of scientific and technological advancements. Travel, whether the fantastical travel of an intergalactic voyager or Mori's literal travel across the globe to complete *Beginning of the End*, is a no less a constructed idea than the alien or the island, and like the two is never unmarked, but imbricated within unequal and, at times, violent cultural exchanges.

Across each exhibition of *Beginning of the End*, the photographs are installed in the same way. Printed in large format, the photographs are affixed in an unbroken loop on circular screens, and mounted several feet above viewers' heads. [...] In photographs of the exhibition, the installation seems to descend upon a viewer: a flying saucer plummeting to Earth or perhaps beaming a viewer up into this alternate visual reality of global space. The photographs that comprise each temporal series are grouped together. The photographs in *Present* abut each other, the edges of Times Square seeming to bleed into Hong Kong's commercial centre, flow into Shibuya, Tokyo, morph into Piccadilly Circus in London. To stand in the middle of the circular installation, a viewer would find her/himself encircled by a visual spatial elision. The photographic alignment of similar commercial urban spaces renders sites as geographically diverse as London and Hong Kong, if not the same, at least equivalent. The geographic boundaries of each island city collapsed, the circular installation iterates not so much representations of difference as sameness. [...] The border between each photograph – where it becomes clear that buildings do not line up, streets continue across one photograph only to terminate abruptly at the start of the next – is an edge point where spatial difference emerges. The alien and the island do not mean the same thing in each urban site. The space between the individual images – that brief moment when a viewer's eyes jump between photographs – performatively re-maps the notion of island for a globally integrated network of economic production. The space that separates each photograph from the next highlights the ease of connection within a networked globe, akin to a viewer's panning gaze, sweeping between the photographs of *Present*. [...] The play between visual continuity and disjuncture in *Present* clarifies a particular way of representing urban globality, which foregrounds not only parallel processes of globalisation, but also the distinct histories of cultural exchange or conquest embedded in island discourses and the alien.

The image of Times Square, a site marked by numerous spatial transformations over the past thirty years, complicates a reading of Mori's photograph in relation to the unframed histories that produce an understanding of the site. Times Square's history, tied to a queer subculture, an anxiety towards bodies and sexual practices labelled as 'other', and a capitalist re-mapping of such bodies and practices, specifies the way in which Mori's alien figuration can be understood. If the stakes of *Present* are grounded in the visual re-conceptualisation of the island and the interplay between urbanity, the island and the alien, the photograph of Times Square highlights the complexity of analysing urban imaginaries in relation to urban transformations and gentrification. [...] Samuel Delany [...] writes:

> the city [in order to bring about this redevelopment] instituted not only a violent reconfiguration of its own landscape but also a legal and moral revamping of its own discursive structures, changing laws about sex, health, and zoning . . . and exploit[ing] everything from homophobia and AIDS to family values and fear of drugs.[13]

The redevelopment of Times Square hinged not only on rebuilding the urban landscape and on reforming the national and international imaginary of the area, but also on erasing the previous history of the site, ensuring that the family-friendly, commercially viable vision of Times Square emerged, phoenix-like, from the demolition of an already forgotten past.

Mori's photograph captures something of these spatial and ideological shifts. An army recruiting office is centred in the photograph, directly behind Mori's body, an unsubtle reminder of the square's increased surveillance. Running along the top of the recruiting office are the words, in bright-red lettering, 'US Armed Forces'. The assumed violence underwriting the sign enfolds the photograph into Times Square's recent past, not quite visible in the image – the closure of porn theatres, often queer, and the economic displacement of the community that frequented such spaces. It is an enfolding that foregrounds the photograph's attention to corporeality and also its ability to scramble time, the past events of these urban displacements pressed to the cusp of the present of the photograph. The conceit of Mori's alien traveller is its ability to elide space and time. The army recruiting office indexes *Present*'s space/time elisions, gesturing towards what is not in the frame: the streets not pictured, the history not recorded – the practices and people placed under surveillance. Times Square's history of queer displacement, no less than the billboards so visible in Mori's photograph, informs the way in which the square functions as a global imaginary of New York City. The site registers in relation to not only desire and consumption, but also uneven trajectories of power and regulation and the policing of moral and geographic borders.

[...] This totality of vision aligns with Roy Edmond and Vanessa Smith's explication of the island. They write, 'islands seem[ed] to be natural colonies. This is not just because of the desire to possess what is paradisal or utopian, but because islands, unlike continents, look like property.'[14] The totality of the landmass is available for visual consumption. If Edmond and Smith discuss island sites in relation to consumptive desire predicated upon visuality, the photograph of Times Square clarifies this link through its own medium specificity. Inherently a visual form, the photograph links the historical project of looking at islands as objects of desire with the immediate practice of looking at the photograph itself.

This reading of Mori's image subtly expands the photograph's indexicality, referencing not simply the site of Times Square, but the practice of looking that produces Times Square as a visual commodity, representing New York City for a larger, global imaginary. If globalisation has caused to disappear notions of insularity and periphery so attached to certain island spaces, the connotations of desire, visuality and ownership remain thoroughly embedded in Mori's image. While the photograph references the historical and economic project of island looking that Edmond and Smith reference, the image also can be analysed alongside theorisations of visuality and capitalism. Shu-Mei Shih argues, in *Visuality and Identity: Sinophone Articulations Across the Pacific*, that images, or image culture, are imbricated within global capitalism.[15] Images – understood as being tied to commodity culture and production – in Shih's theorisation are understood within a complex matrix of scales and contexts such that their meaning is never stable or unitary, but rather holds at any moment a variety of contradictory, simultaneous significations and ideologies.[16] Shih's work on images and Edmond and Smith's theorisation of islands are each invested in exploring the way in which imaginaries, whether represented via commodified images or islands, travel. Images' meaning-making is tied to their transience, their ability to move and flow across the increasingly flexible borders of nation-states or the natural borders of oceans, their ability, in other words, to function as commodities in a moment of global capitalism.[17]

[...] Mori's own body links the photograph to a set of corporeal concerns, foregrounding the subjects, framed and unframed, who resonate with her figuration. Her body is obscured by the curved surface of the capsule and the light reflecting off its plastic surface. The seam, which joins the two spheres of the capsule, partly obscures her figure. Unlike the huge billboards, so available for visual consumption, her figure is visually mysterious, alien. As the late feminist science fiction writer Octavia Butler wrote concerning alien others:

> Science fiction has long treated people who might or might not exist.... Unfortunately [...] writers who started us thinking about the possibility of extraterrestrial life did nothing to make us think about here-at-home variation – women, blacks, Indians, Asians, Hispanics, etc.[18]

Mori's body twines between these two understandings of the alien other, at once a creature of the future and an immigrant to New York: a minority subject (marked as both woman and Asian). Her body references the othered bodies of marginalised, invisibilised subjects: undocumented workers, 'illegal aliens'. Her body, demanding a viewer's attention, refuses to be displaced. It holds open the possibility of imagining the numerous bodies displaced or rendered invisible by Times Square's Disneyfication. Other-ed bodies, her figure implies, are not objects to be gazed upon, but subjects who demand embodied encounters. While her figure refuses total visibility, she is also contained, seemingly displayed within her capsule. Her alien body demands a certain present-ness, for all that that present-ness shifts between the refusal of displacement – a politically potent reading of the alien within current urban economies that highlights the undocumented workers whose labour supports such global cities as New York – and the availability of her body to be seen.[19] Mori is both the alien subject who demands attention and the passive figure on display – a complex visual depiction of the alien.

The capsule in which Mori's body is encased holds potent connotations for this line of reasoning. Implicit in the signification of her capsule are ideas of displacement, of being rendered a refugee. Like Superman, who seeks refugee on Earth in an individual spaceship, Mori's capsule renders her body in relation to histories of forced migrations. The capsule, however, also reads as another prime signifier within science fiction: the pod. Pods gestate life forms, are vehicles for certain modes of alien reproduction or preservation. Twining between these various connotations of Mori's capsule, her body resonates with divergent trajectories of bodies that previously marked the space: displaced queer bodies and, reaching farther back in Manhattan's history of displacements, the Lenape tribe, from whom the Dutch West Indian Company purchased the island. If her body resonates with histories of displaced, marginalised subjects, another way of describing the potency of her figure – and a descriptor more aligned with the perceived power of the alien – is that it collapses or implodes history, rendering temporal distinctions moot.

Edmond and Smith similarly argue that islands collapse history, 'the . . . endless proliferation of island references' creating a successive chain of signifiers, linking seemingly divergent narratives, histories and subjectivities.[20] If the alien and the island collapse ready distinctions between temporal narratives of displacement, the two terms also collapse spatial borders, highlighting the ways in which the excessive signification of each term resonates across space, complicating the perceived fixity of borders, whether national, geographic or economic. Mori's alien body, so easily a signifier of an undocumented, alien workforce, reverberates with the narratives of global displacement, in which immigrants relocate to urban centres, like New York City, in search of work. As Saskia Sassen writes, the intensification of financial services centred in global cities like New York has led to an intensification of low-wage jobs 'required by high-income gentrification' and economic polarisation.[21] A marginalised workforce has historically filled such low-wage jobs: women, people of colour, ethnic groups, undocumented workers – aliens.

To embody the term alien is not only to occupy a marginal position vis-à-vis the juridical and bureaucratic systems of the United States. While the above explication relies upon a potential breakdown of agency – subjects caught in the flows of global capital and drawn to the economic opportunities offered by mega-cities like New York – the term 'resident alien' complicates this reading of the work. The protection and legal recognition granted resident aliens ensure that some aliens are more equal than others. The resident alien likewise complicates the negative connotations of the term displacement. Displacement can offer an opportunity to re-form subjectivity. If the strangeness of Mori's pod body indexes fantastical science-fiction narratives, resident aliens and, indeed, undocumented aliens have a far more everyday, if thoroughly bureaucratic and regulated, relationship with the term alien.

The resident alien connects not only to the site of New York City, but also to a genealogy of island literature. Tongan scholar Epeli Hau'ofa contends that islands are not bounded, but understood through subjects who travel far beyond the geographical confines of island sites.[22] As he writes, specifically locating his argument within the Pacific, the region is a 'sea of islands', a notion that jettisons a distinction between land and sea, instead locating the island within a vast Oceanic network of trade, travel and cultural transmission.[23] While Hau'ofa locates his argument in the historical and mythological past of the Pacific islands, he turns, at the end of his essay, to describing the region's vastness in relation to a thoroughly contemporary globalised economy and remissions culture. Reasserting the agency of Pacific subjects, Hau'ofa's argument, in part like Mori's photograph, complicates the connotations of insularity or periphery associated with island sites by a Western-centric, colonial discourse. While Hau'ofa importantly reclaims a notion of island insularity and Oceanic regionalism in his decidedly anticolonial essay, the agency and mobility of the Oceanic subjects he describes is distinctly tied to an understanding of island sites as networked, expansive zones of contact. Hau'ofa's re-configuration of the island, as well as the various aliens who align with Mori's photograph, asserts the agency of figures who are at once sited but can also move. Both Hau'ofa and Mori assert the ways in which individual subjectivity and the understanding of a site can shift as subjects move, become displaced, and are then *placed*. Hau'ofa's sea of islands or Mori's urban islands jettison notions of island boundedness, redefining the term 'insular' in relation to site specificity and island networks predicated upon moving subjects.

[...] The urban island is a site pivotal and central to the production and practices of globalisation. Times Square or Shibuya, Piccadilly Circus or Tsim Sha Tsui, these are the island imaginaries for the twenty-first century. Like Hau'ofa's contention that islands are coterminous with vast oceanscapes and predicated upon travel and trade, Mori's photographs argue that island sites, however obscured a site's island positioning might be, are central to global capitalist discourses of desire and consumption. *Beginning of the End* presents a particular visual imaginary of globalisation. Understanding the photo project through the island is to foreground the geopolitics of visualising space and desire. Such a geopolitics is imbricated within histories of othering spaces, a practice that inscribes certain global spaces as disenfranchised. The island foregrounds an understanding of globalisation that asserts the relational complexities of subjects, spaces, histories and economic networks and the ways in which practices of capitalist consumption and desire are created, maintained and visualised through material and symbolic geographies.

1 The *Past* series includes photographs of Angkor Wat, the Giza pyramids, Teotihuacán, and Tiahuanaco. In each photograph, Mori is the only figure. The images reinscribe spatial discourses indebted to uneven processes of cultural conquest; each location marks a 'primitive' past. Each site, though, is imbricated within networks of global tourism, a more complex and current spatial production than the one imagined in Mori's images, as well as referencing complex civilisations that continue to exist into the present. The *Future* series features Mori in front of postmodern architectural structures or skylines: the skyline of Shanghai; Brasilia's capital building. Each image inscribes futurity as urban and attached to a distinct mode of designing urban structures and imaginaries.

2 The photograph of Hong Kong is not on one of the islands proper; the district of Tsim Sha Tsui is located on the southernmost tip of the Kowloon Peninsula, Hong Kong's main landmass.

3 Spatial descriptors such as 'insular' and 'bounded' render islands graspable, 'able to be held in the mind's eye and imagined as places of possibility and promise'. Roy Edmond and Vanessa Smith, 'Introduction', in *Islands in History and Representation* (New York: Routledge, 2003) 2.

4 Theorised by Saskia Sassen, 'global cities' refers to a city's status as a geographical transnational nexus, which both produces and facilitates economic, financial and cultural networks of production. Saskia Sassen, *The Global City: New York, London, Tokyo,* (Princeton, NJ: University of Princeton Press, 1991).

5 Islands have been conceived of as empty scapes, upon which various narratives of utopia, dystopia or programmes of colonial conquest could be enacted. Edmond and Smith write: 'islands seem[ed] to be natural colonies. This is not just because of the desire to possess what is paradisal or utopian, but because islands, unlike continents, look like property.' Islands are also imagined as bounded zones, linked to ideas of containment and management. Ghosting this notion of containment, however, is an anxiety of the failure of management, the island asserting not its boundedness but its limitlessness, its ability to overrun its bounders. Islands, after all, have been imagined as mysterious, unknowable sites. Epeli Hau'ofa importantly argues that islands are far from bounded or limited sites. Rather, he understands islands as coterminous with the ocean, countering understandings of islands as fragmentary, discrete locations. Edmond and Smith, 'Introduction', in *Islands in History and Representation*, op. cit., 1; Epeli Hau'ofa, 'Our Sea of Islands', in *We are the Ocean: Selected Works* (Honolulu: University of Hawaii Press, 2008) 2–16.

6 Sharalyn Orbaugh, 'The Genealogy of the Cyborg in Japanese Popular Culture', in *World Weavers: Globalization, Science Fiction, and the Cybernetic Revolution*, eds. Wong Kin Yuen, Gary Westfahl and Amy Kit-sze Chan (Hong Kong: Hong Kong University Press, 2005) 58–60.

7 Mariko Mori, *Oneness* (Ostfildern: Hatje Cantz, 2007).

8 Jenny Wolmark, *Aliens and Others: Science Fiction, Feminism, and Postmodernism* (Iowa City: University of Iowa Press, 1994) 28.

9 Due to the Western colonisation of Caribbean and Pacific islands, much of the literature on

islands has engaged with islands critically, theoretically and historically in relation to colonisation. As Francisco-J. Hernández Adrián writes about the topical Atlantic, 'Islands [...] have been repeatedly framed and engineered to function as colonial and economic outposts'. Francisco-J. Hernández Adrián, 'Tomás Sánchez on Exorbitance: Still Lifes of the Tropical Landfill', *The Global South*, vol. 6, no. 1 (2012) 19. See also Matthew Body Goldie, 'Island Theory: the Antipodes', in *Islanded Identities: Constructions of Postcolonial Cultural Insularity*, eds. Maeve McCusker and Anthony Soares (New York: Rodopi, 2011) 1–40.

10 Mariko Mori, 'Mariko Mori', in *Cities on the Move*, eds. Hou Hanru and Hans Ulrich Obrist (Ostfildern-Ruit: Gerd Hatje, 1997) 49.

11 'The Genealogy of the Cyborg in Japanese Popular Culture', op. cit., 61.

12 Rather than Tokyo, Fogg visits Yokohama, a port city on Tokyo Bay, just south of Tokyo. Orbaugh, ibid., 589.

13 [Footnote 16 in source] Samuel R. Delany, *Times Square Red, Times Square Blue*, xi–xii.

14 [17] *Islands in History and Representation*, op. cit., 1.

15 [18] Shu-Mei Shih, *Visuality and Identity: Sinophone Articulations Across the Pacific* (Berkeley: University of California Press, 2007).

16 [19] Ibid., 8, 10–11.

17 [20] Ibid., 8.

18 [21] Jenny Wolmark, *Aliens and Others: Science Fiction, Feminism, and Postmodernism* (Iowa City: University of Iowa Press, 1994)

19 [22] *The Global City*, op. cit., 9.

20 [23] *Islands in History and Representation*, op. cit., 4–5.

21 [24] *The Global City*, op. cit., 9.

22 [25] Hau'ofa, 'Our Sea of Islands', op. cit., 2–16.

23 [26] Ibid., 7.

Gwyneth Shanks, extracts from 'Visualising the Now: The Alien, the Island and Mariko Mori's *Beginning of the End*', *Third Text*, vol. 28, nos. 4/5 (July 2014) 393–405.

Alondra Nelson
Aliens Who Are of Course Ourselves//2001

> No wonder we need aliens.
> No wonder we're so good at creating aliens.
> No wonder we so often project alienness onto one another.
> This last of course has been the worst of our problems – the human alien from another culture, country, gender, race, ethnicity. This is the tangible alien who can be hurt or killed... . And yet we are unable to get along with those aliens who are closest to us, those aliens who are of course ourselves.
> – Octavia E. Butler, 'The Monophobic Response'[1]

The cultural theorist and novelist Albert Murray once remarked that the mandate of the black intellectual was to provide 'technology' to the black community.[2] By technology, Murray didn't mean mechanics, new media or the Internet. Rather, he defined it as those novel analytic approaches he believed necessary to understanding black life 'on a higher level of abstraction.'[3] For Murray, this process was one of distillation and complication. He advocated theories of African American existence that, like a blueprint, would be sufficiently robust to reveal the larger patterns of society and do justice to its intricacies and complexities. By Murray's definition, the artist Laylah Ali is a technologist of the highest order. In spite of their striking clarity, her gouache images reflect the contradictions of the human condition.

Ali's work explores the tragic lives of the *Greenheads*, her hypercephalic, thin-limbed, brown-skinned creations. Using a limited palette, she composes provocative visual fields noticeably lacking in scenery, save the humanoid figures that inhabit them. A master at sleight of hand, she uses bright comic-strip colours in a way that recalls the Sunday funnies; but these images have more in common with sardonic political cartoons, for the figures she depicts inflict all manner of insult and injury on one other. Although Ali provides no script for her images, their despair and anger is unmistakable. But there is no violent haste in her brush stroke; the images are controlled – eerily exact. As befits the work of a technician, these tortured lives are rendered with the sharpest precision.

More troubling still for the viewer is the family likeness of the individual Greenheads to one another. The symbols that distinguish one Greenhead from another are remarkably superficial: one wears a dotted shirt, another a solid-colour top; one wears a uniform, another a tunic. Why would these characters, who are so seemingly similar and whose sole medium of differentiation is their attire, be at violent odds with one another?

In Ali's paintings these differences, though only skin-deep, have grave consequences. Encounters in the land of the Greenheads typically end in violence: loss of limb, decapitation, subjugation and abduction. Moreover, the power trips in this dystopic universe appear to be racialised. In *Untitled* (2000), a Greenhead pair attired in white hats and robes that resemble white supremacist get-ups meet two similarly dressed figures, one with hair ornamentation that harkens back to ancient Egyptian ceremonial attire. One pair offers a severed head to the other. Violence is pervasive and all encompassing where the Greenheads dwell; all are subject to it. Such exercises of power, however, are also the imposed heritage and present-day reality of people of African descent. The brown-skinned Greenheads do double duty as agents in humanity's universal power struggles and as actors in the performance of racialised violence.

The Greenheads are humanoid – human like – but their countenances and outlines are conspicuously similar to the Grays, the archetypal aliens who appear in abduction stories in popular culture. Elaine Showalter and Jodi Dean argue that aliens are dopplegänger of our human fears and desires.[4] Although Showalter and Dean provide different explanations for our strange attachments to aliens, both have argued that US culture is obsessed with them.

In an essay in the anthology *Dark Matter*, the science fiction writer Octavia E. Butler provides a related theory of the economy of the imagination that produces aliens. She suggests that we create the ethereal, otherworldly figures of sci-fi and speculative fiction in part as an escape from dealing with local others. Yet, as Butler reminds us, back in the real world we also have homespun 'tangible aliens' who are marked as irrevocably different by virtue of their language or culture (rendered as attire in Ali's vocabulary). We fashion aliens, and we 'project alienness onto one another'. Ali could be said to be sending the same message since she uses alienness to reveal both human connection and detachment. In this sense, we are all aliens, though blacks, are doubly so.

Ali's *mises-en-scène* are both otherworldly and familiar. This alienness is at once personal and collective, local and global, nodal and networked. Laylah Ali's images are a poignant reminder that the brother from another planet is still kin. The aliens are in fact ourselves.

1 Octavia E. Butler, 'The Monophobic Response.' in *Dark Matter: A Century of Speculative Fiction from the African Diaspora*, ed. Sheree R. Thomas (New York: Warner Books, 2000) 415.

2 Albert Murray. quoted in 'The Alain L. Locke Symposium', *The Harvard Advocate* (1 December 1973) 18.

3 Ibid., 17.

4 Jodi Dean, *Aliens in America: Conspiracy Cultures from Outerspace to Cyberspace* (Ithaca: Cornell University Press, 1998) and Elaine Showalter, *Hystories: Hysterical Epidemics and Modem Culture* (New York: Columbia University Press, 1997).

Alondra Nelson, 'Aliens Who Are of Course Ourselves', *Art Journal*, vol. 60, no. 3 (2001) 99–101.

Allora & Calzadilla and Ted Chiang
The Great Silence//2015

The humans use [the] Arecibo [observatory] to look for extraterrestrial intelligence. Their desire to make a connection is so strong that they've created an ear capable of hearing across the universe.

But I and my fellow parrots are right here. Why aren't they interested in listening to our voices?

We're a non-human species capable of communicating with them. Aren't we exactly what humans are looking for?

*

The universe is so vast that intelligent life must surely have arisen many times. The universe is also so old that even one technological species would have had time to expand and fill the galaxy. Yet there is no sign of life anywhere except on Earth. Humans call this the Fermi paradox.

One proposed solution to the Fermi paradox is that intelligent species actively try to conceal their presence, to avoid being targeted by hostile invaders.

Speaking as a member of a species that has been driven nearly to extinction by humans, I can attest that this is a wise strategy.

It makes sense to remain quiet and avoid attracting attention.

*

The Fermi paradox is sometimes known as the Great Silence. The universe ought to be a cacophony of voices, but instead it's disconcertingly quiet.

Some humans theorise that intelligent species go extinct before they can expand into outer space. If they're correct, then the hush of the night sky is the silence of a graveyard.

Hundreds of years ago, my kind was so plentiful that the Rio Abajo forest resounded with our voices. Now we're almost gone. Soon this rainforest may be as silent as the rest of the universe.

*

There was an African Grey Parrot named Alex. He was famous for his cognitive abilities. Famous among humans, that is.

A human researcher named Irene Pepperberg spent thirty years studying Alex. She found that not only did Alex know the words for shapes and colours, he actually understood the concepts of shape and colour.

Many scientists were sceptical that a bird could grasp abstract concepts. Humans like to think they're unique. But eventually Pepperberg convinced them that Alex wasn't just repeating words, that he understood what he was saying.

Out of all my cousins, Alex was the one who came closest to being taken seriously as a communication partner by humans.

Alex died suddenly, when he was still relatively young. The evening before he died, Alex said to Pepperberg, 'You be good. I love you.'

If humans are looking for a connection with a non-human intelligence, what more can they ask for than that?

*

Every parrot has a unique call that it uses to identify itself; biologists refer to this as the parrot's 'contact call'.

In 1974, astronomers used Arecibo to broadcast a message into outer space intended to demonstrate human intelligence. That was humanity's contact call.

In the wild, parrots address each other by name. One bird imitates another's contact call to get the other bird's attention.

If humans ever detect the Arecibo message being sent back to Earth, they will know someone is trying to get their attention.

*

Parrots are vocal learners: we can learn to make new sounds after we've heard them. It's an ability that few animals possess. A dog may understand dozens of commands, but it will never do anything but bark.

Humans are vocal learners, too. We have that in common. So humans and parrots share a special relationship with sound. We don't simply cry out. We pronounce. We enunciate.

Perhaps that's why humans built Arecibo the way they did. A receiver doesn't have to be a transmitter, but Arecibo is both. It's an ear for listening, and a mouth for speaking.

*

Humans have lived alongside parrots for thousands of years, and only recently have they considered the possibility that we might be intelligent.

I suppose I can't blame them. We parrots used to think humans weren't very bright. It's hard to make sense of behaviour that's so different from your own.

But parrots are more similar to humans than any extraterrestrial species will be, and humans can observe us up close; they can look us in the eye. How do they expect to recognise an alien intelligence if all they can do is eavesdrop from a hundred light years away?

*

It's no coincidence that 'aspiration' means both hope and the act of breathing.

When we speak, we use the breath in our lungs to give our thoughts a physical form. The sounds we make are simultaneously our intentions and our life force.

I speak, therefore I am. Vocal learners, like parrots and humans, are perhaps the only ones who fully comprehend the truth of this.

*

There's a pleasure that comes with shaping sounds with your mouth. It's so primal and visceral that throughout their history, humans have considered the activity a pathway to the divine.

Pythagorean mystics believed that vowels represented the music of the spheres, and chanted to draw power from them.

Pentecostal Christians believe that when they speak in tongues, they're speaking the language used by angels in Heaven.

Brahmin Hindus believe that by reciting mantras, they're strengthening the building blocks of reality.

Only a species of vocal learners would ascribe such importance to sound in their mythologies. We parrots can appreciate that.

*

According to Hindu mythology, the universe was created with a sound: 'Om'. It's a syllable that contains within it everything that ever was and everything that will be.

When the Arecibo telescope is pointed at the space between stars, it hears a faint hum.

Astronomers call that the 'cosmic microwave background'. It's the residual radiation of the Big Bang, the explosion that created the universe fourteen billion years ago.

But you can also think of it as a barely audible reverberation of that original 'Om'. That syllable was so resonant that the night sky will keep vibrating for as long as the universe exists.

When Arecibo is not listening to anything else, it hears the voice of creation.

*

We Puerto Rican Parrots have our own myths. They're simpler than human mythology, but I think humans would take pleasure from them.

Alas, our myths are being lost as my species dies out. I doubt the humans will have deciphered our language before we're gone.

So the extinction of my species doesn't just mean the loss of a group of birds. It's also the disappearance of our language, our rituals, our traditions. It's the silencing of our voice.

*

Human activity has brought my kind to the brink of extinction, but I don't blame them for it. They didn't do it maliciously. They just weren't paying attention.

And humans create such beautiful myths; what imaginations they have. Perhaps that's why their aspirations are so immense. Look at Arecibo. Any species who can build such a thing must have greatness within it.

My species probably won't be here for much longer; it's likely that we'll die before our time and join the Great Silence. But before we go, we are sending a message to humanity. We just hope the telescope at Arecibo will enable them to hear it.

The message is this:

You be good. I love you.

×

Allora & Calzadilla's video installation The Great Silence *(2014) centres on the world's largest radio telescope, located in Esperanza, Puerto Rico, home to the last remaining population of a critically endangered species of parrots,* Amazona vittata. *For the work, Allora & Calzadilla collaborated with science fiction author Ted Chiang, who wrote a script in the spirit of a fable that ponders the irreducible gaps between living, nonliving, human, animal, technological, and cosmic actors.*

Allora & Calzadilla and Ted Chiang, 'The Great Silence', *e-flux supercommunity: Planetary Computing (Is the Universe Actually a Gigantic Computer?)*, Day 3 (8 May 2015) (http://supercommunity.e-flux.com/texts/the-great-silence).

The very frustration of a computer slowing down or freezing-up indexes our own internalised demand for speed

Benjamin Noys, 'Cyberpunk Phuturism', 2014

FUTURES

Wanuri Kahiu
Ancestors of the Future//2016

Physicists have shown that time is variable and non-linear, so it is unfair to hold Africans by standards of time that are not standardised.

I heard the most brilliant statement recently: 'Countries are not poor, they are just in different time capsules.' Like, Zimbabwe is what Kenya was in the 1980s, Kenya is what South Africa was in 2000. I completely agree. I have always discounted the idea of country classifications that use words like 'developing' or 'third'. The context around who was 'third' and why and how one measures 'development' has never made sense to me. And given the work I create and the universes I like to imagine and live in, time capsules make perfect sense. Most times I live in a sub-time capsule inside of the Kenya 2015 time capsule, which is simultaneously someone's future and someone else's past. Nothing in this universe of time capsules and sub-time capsules is concrete.

I am a believer that *all* time everywhere, in the world and in universes unknown, is variable, flexible and non-linear. Past, present and future exist all at once, simultaneously and repeatedly, and sometimes in different realms. We, Kenyan artists, create with all this and none of this in mind. Right now, we are just trying to live in this time capsule we call Nairobi 2015, and our identities are multiple and varied, and cannot be neatly folded and pigeonholed into a single identity because they too, like time, are variable, flexible and non-linear. The only truth we know is that our identities will change, and the Kenya we leave will be distinctly different to the Kenya we were born into.

There is no one identity that can emerge, but hopefully a multitude of them. While we create this multi-faceted, ever-evolving art, we do it from the sheer need to create, not necessarily to make a statement or combat some nebulous populist image or dominant narrative. Like artists elsewhere in the world, we create because we need to create. It is what we were made to do. It is not much deeper than that. The more the west discusses African art, the more it seems there is a need to categorise, explain and justify its existence. More often than not, it seems that things that Africans do, their thoughts, ideas and art are viewed as a response to some western concept [...]

The most accepted definition of Afrofuturism, which draws on cultural critic Mark Dery's 1994 foundational essay 'Black to the Future', suggests that Afrofuturism itself is a reaction to either historical exclusion of people of colour or a need to project ourselves into a new culture in an effort to avoid exclusion in the future. What if Afrofuturism is just an expression of a person who wanted to be heard, seen or experienced, and not a negation of another voice? If the dominant culture or popular imagery did not exist before, would we 'African artists' still be inspired to create? I imagine we would, because way before any terms were coined that defined Afrofuturists there were storytellers who composed narratives populated with science, fantasy, mythology and speculative storylines. The stories served different purposes but at no point were they just a response to a dominant ideology or populist art.

It is this kind of polar thinking of one idea occurring as a direct result of another that feeds beliefs and recommendations that Africa has to 'catch up' with the rest of the world. As if Africa is competing in some universal race. If that was true, Africa should have already been declared the winner of this race to an unspecified future because history has proved that the invention of culture, science, technology and the human race originated on the African continent. What race can trump creation? If we were to try and get the west to build a pyramid now it would surely prove that Africa continues to be advanced.

[...] Albert Einstein concluded in his later years that the past, present and future all exist simultaneously. He believed there is no true division between past and future, there is rather a single existence – unlike Newton who believed that time is absolute.

Einstein maintained that the only true constant was the speed of light, a variable constant, and time changed according to one's proximity to the speed of light. The closer you are to attaining light speed, the more timeless you are.

With the proper technology, such as a very fast spaceship, one person is able to experience several days while another person simultaneously experiences only a few hours or minutes. The same two people can meet up again, one having experienced days or even years while the other has only experienced minutes. The person in the spaceship only needs to travel near to the speed of light. The faster they travel, the slower their time will pass relative to someone planted firmly on the Earth. If they were able to travel at the speed of light, their time would cease completely and they would exist trapped in timelessness. This theory was tested and proved in 2010 when a handful of scientists used an atomic clock, the most accurate clock in the world, to test that time is variable. The physicists put two clocks a foot apart in height above sea level and found that the Clock higher up ran quicker than the lower one, proving that time runs quicker the higher you are.

But what does this have to do with a linear progression of past, present and future? Einstein's theories additionally suggest that there is no single special present but also that all moments are equally real. The future that has just become now and become now again with every new word is no more open than the past.

Thomas Cahill, an American scholar and writer, suggests that this single experience of time that runs from one moment to the next in a line, with possible futures always ahead, is based on the one-way, linear timeline of Judeo-Christianity. This linear time is one where the future is fundamentally different from what has gone before, with biblical time progressing from creation to judgement day. Each successive moment is qualitatively different from the one before, and there is no repetition. Cahill argues that cyclical time is kind of the norm in most cultures around the world, and the Judeo-Christian notion of linear time was an unusual innovation when it came along. Having spread, through Christianity, to become the predominant mindset of modern western culture, its influence is now global, but not universal, I would argue the same could be said for the handling of time in language. The Kenyan theologian and philosopher John S. Mbiti has suggested that time is circular and two-dimensional. Mbiti references the Agikuyu and Kamba as cultures that do not have language that refer to the distant future. Although I disagree with his idea that Africans had no concrete thought of the distant future, especially given the contradictions of the pyramids, buildings that were intended to last multiple generations, I do agree with Mbiti that our history and language suggest that time is viewed as cyclical rather than linear. We take into account the natural cycle of a day, the cycle of seasons and even the cycle of life. We mark history and name children with this in mind. In cultures in Kenya, the sun marks the first hour of the clock, marking seven in the morning as the first hour of the day. Time inevitably repeats itself over and over in an unending circle. Instead of clocks, nature is used as a reliable guide for time. Therefore it is possible to state that time is flexible and combines the past as a predictor of the future. The sun came out yesterday at a particular time and predicts the time for the next days. Rain has no set schedule, so clocks have no reference. [...]

Speculative Thinking

The Large Hadron Collider (LHC) located beneath the France-Switzerland border near Geneva fascinates me no end. The world's largest and most powerful particle accelerator has begun to scratch at the probability of proving the existence of multiverses. It has created a space in which the same particle can exist in two different times at the same time, or where the particle can disappear and return with small changes, and many other possibilities. As a global African working in science fiction and able to access this kind of information, I will ultimately be influenced by these ideas.

The idea that something can exist in one space and time and travel to a different one, and return changed or unchanged, is ridiculously exciting. It brings to mind the possibility of existing in space, in a past, present and future.

In his discussions of space, physicist Richard Feynman suggests that the travel from point A to B happens not only in a single line but that all possibilities of travelling between point A and B must be taken into consideration, be it the travel from point A to B in squiggly lines, curves, backwards in time. Feynman's proposition could be described as the first timeless description of a multitude of space-time worlds all existing simultaneously.

Imagining this opens up all sorts of possible science fiction ideas about the world we live in and the multiverses that may happen alongside this one. The different multiverses may also be part past and part future, just as we (who live in our variable time capsules) may be part distant future or part past. So while African theories of cyclical time may influence my work, I am equally affected in the idea of multiverses being explored in the LHC.

The ability to access information and draw from a multitude of different ideas has infinitely affected not only how we think but also the subsequent projections we create as artists. However, education and access are not the guard dogs of speculative thinking – imagination is. Speculative thinking is the domain of the majority.

It does not need any education; it just needs imagination or a link to divinity. Agikuyu history mentions a seer who predicted the coming of White butterflies and a snake that blew smoke out of its head. This premonition of the arrival of foreigners and the prediction of the train is considered speculative thinking, yet the seer had no formal education, unless, like me, you also consider communing with Mwenye-Nyaga – the creator of all things in Kikuyu culture, the possessor of light and god of Mount Kenya – a method of formal education. The pyramids (again) are another clear example of speculative thinking outside the norm of formalised education. Scientists are still trying to understand how people with such limited formal education could create structures that they can not easily recreate today.

Afrofuturism and speculative fiction have always existed in Africa. Indeed, they pre-date western images of science fiction. Our own unique creation myths from around the continent, be it those of the Dogon in West Africa or the Zulu seer Vusamazulu Credo Mutwa, are proof enough of our Afrofuturistic aptitude. Afrofuturism has always been part of our cultural and social DNA, and Kenyan Afrofuturists like Wangechi Mutu are adding to the immense chorus of voices working their way through imagining a future. However given the west itself has no conclusive ideas on time – their most respected scientists have already and are currently continuing to demonstrate this – it is unfair to hold Africans by standards that are not standardised.

The rotation of past, present and future, and the possibilities of alternate multiverses, speaks further to the true advancement of Afrofuturists who combine the past (idealised or otherwise) in projections of their future. In fact, I believe it would be hard not to include the past in the future. Our nature, being an aggregation of our customs, cultures and ideas, constantly brings the past into the future. We name our children (our future) by the names of our ancestors (our past), or after a special or distinct time (like time of day or month), or in a myriad of other ways that fundamentally ties what has been with what will be. We project our history forward. There is a constant birth of the old and therefore a constant past in our future. I further believe that the dominant western narratives are using our African past to understand more about a possible future. Science that pre-dates our scientists is being used to gain a better understanding of who we are and what we can be.

I recently had the pleasure of hearing the Nigerian-American author Nnedi Okorafor say that she believes the path to the truth can only be found in the voices of many. So as we rotate in this current time capsule called Kenya 2015, which exists as much as someone else's past as it does as someone's future, we now have the privilege of being able to communicate in a way that can be understood by a larger populace that extends far beyond our borders. This is the only real distinction between the storytellers who came before and us. With the growth of more Afrofuturists adding their ideas to the world, we are moving towards a better understanding of a more universal truth. This truth or identity cannot be tidily summed up. At best we can say that we artists are the projection of our ancestors, as much as we artists are the ancestors of the future.

Wanuri Kahiu, extracts from 'Ancestors of the Future', in *African Futures: Thinking About the Future Through Word and Image*, eds. Lien Heidenreich-Seleme & Sean O'Toole (Bielefeild: Kerber Verlag, 2016) 165–74.

Franco 'Bifo' Berardi
The Future After the End of the Economy//2011

[...] Only if we are able to disentangle the future (the perception of the future, the concept of the future, and the very production of the future) from the traps of growth and investment will we find a way out of the vicious subjugation of life, wealth and pleasure to the financial abstraction of semiocapital. The key to this disentanglement can be found in a new form of wisdom: harmonising with exhaustion.

Exhaustion is a cursed word in the frame of modern culture, which is based on the cult of energy and the cult of male aggressiveness. But energy is fading in the postmodern world for many reasons that are easy to detect. Demographic trends reveal that, as life expectancy increases and birth rate decreases, mankind as a whole is growing old. This process of general aging produces a sense of exhaustion, and what was once considered a blessing – increased life expectancy – may become a misfortune if the myth of energy is not restrained and replaced with a myth of solidarity and compassion.

Energy is fading also because basic physical resources such as oil are doomed to extinction or dramatic depletion. And energy is fading because competition is stupid in the age of the general intellect. The general intellect is not based on juvenile impulse and male aggressiveness, on fighting, winning, and appropriation. It is based on cooperation and sharing.

This is why the future is over. We are living in a space that is beyond the future. If we come to terms with this post-futuristic condition, we can renounce accumulation and growth and be happy sharing the wealth that comes from past industrial labour and present collective intelligence.

If we cannot do this, we are doomed to live in a century of violence, misery and war.

Franco 'Bifo' Berardi, extract from 'The Future After the End of the Economy', *e-flux Journal*, no. 30 (2011) (www.e-flux.com/journal/30/68135/the-future-after-the-end-of-the-economy/).

Elizabeth C. Hamilton
Afrofuturism and the Technologies of Survival//2017

Situating the Afronaut in contemporary art and Afrofuturism is very much about finding safe spaces for black life. It is about exploring and protecting and preparing the body for hostile environments. In an Afrofuturist vision that stakes out black space in the future, black life is often obscured and simultaneously endangered. This obscurity is the result of the overdetermination of the past on black future spaces, namely the baggage of colonialism and apartheid, slavery and Jim Crow, and legacies of displacement. Through the image of the Afronaut, artists are making definitive statements about current situations of liberation, freedom and oppression, while simultaneously referencing the past and staking a place for black life in the future. [...]

J. Griffith Rollefson argues that 'Afrofuturism is most prominent in music... because a number of its artists have continually highlighted the mythic qualities of both historical tropes of magic and futuristic narratives of science through the seemingly paradoxical figure of the soulful spaceman'.[1] He thereby centres the 'soulful spaceman' as icon in Afrofuturism. The 'black man in space' is a significant symbol and signal ubiquitous in music of the 1970s, but is making a resurgence in the twenty-first century as the Afronaut in contemporary art of Africa and the African Diaspora. I contend that this resurgence is a response to current oppressive conditions, such as extrajudicial killings of black people in the United States and continued human rights disparities based on race elsewhere in the world. Artists are asking through these works containing Afronauts: What are the technologies of survival? The artists parallel these images of technologies with black people's predicament in a white supremacist society.

The word 'Afronaut' is a neologism, so it is difficult to pin down its roots or know when and where it was first used. For the purposes of this research, the Afronaut is a person of African descent who travels through outer space. The term seems to have gained popularity with the advent of African space programmes, like the one in Zambia in the 1960s.[2] As the race for space by countries like Nigeria continues and the first South African-born astronaut will be launched into space, the term gets more popular, fascinatingly, through artists' imaginings of the Afronaut.[3]

Several artists, such as Daniel Kojo Schrade, Gerald Machona, and Robert Pruitt, have adopted the term 'Afronaut' to describe the subjects in their projects, while others have applied the label loosely to those subjects in art that conveys the theme of space travel. I made this determination from the most obvious accoutrement – space suits, helmets, boots, rockets, ships – which are ubiquitous in the work I examine. There is also a conscious naming of the artwork that classifies the subjects as Afronauts (Nick Cave's and Yinka Shonibare's work is less obvious in this sense).

Afronaut is an obvious play on astronaut that reveals the ethnic identity of the space traveller. There are deeper implications, which also indicate an eternal tension between African identity and technological stasis. In a linguistic sense, the Afronaut is a tense construction, an oxymoron in a sense: afro-naut, when taken in consideration with stereotypical notions of African-ness and technological advancement. Alondra Nelson indicates this in her now-canonical *Social Text* issue about Afrofuturism.[4] This tension between blackness and technology is also evident in the conversation between Mark Dery, Tricia Rose, Greg Tate and Samuel Delany.[5] Whereas Dery believes that black artists will shun technology, Rose, Tate, and Delany challenge this assumption.

Elsewhere, I have written that Afrofuturism is the injection of futurity, fantasy and technology in the arts of Africa and the African Diaspora.[6] This definition has expanded tremendously, as contemporary situations in art and contemporary events are in constant flux. Presently, I define Afrofuturism as a mechanism for understanding the real world situations of oppression in the contemporary world in the context of the ever-present past, while charting the future situation through the arts. [...]

An insistence on materiality, rather than a nebulous reliance on concept, is remarkable in Afrofuturist works. The material does not by any means subordinate the subject, but it is significant to the understanding of each work of art. The transformative nature of Afrofuturist art addresses not only the subject, but also the audience. Afrofuturist art is a mechanism for understanding and making meaning for audiences – transforming them in the process is its goal. The artwork I examine is overwhelmingly figural; therefore, the subjects are always going through profound physical changes that have some effect on their spiritual or mental states. Temporality is in constant flux with time travellers and artists as temporal interlopers. As temporal interlopers, artists are constantly making useful space for the past to make a stake in the present or the future.

From the time the notion of Afrofuturism was first conceptualised – by Mark Dery in 1993 and expounded upon a decade later by Alondra Nelson – the situation of the alien and the outsider have played prominently. Afrofuturism seemed like the natural way to discuss the rift that black people felt with the dominant culture in the United States. However, theorising about Africa was left by the wayside even though the interfaces are fruitful and ripe for the picking.

The art of Yinka Shonibare, Nick Cave and Gerald Machona demonstrates trends of the Afronaut across the diaspora as well as the overlaps of experiences of people of African descent across the globe. They expand the idea of the black man in space with the notion that we are already in alien environments. The three artists discussed here are male, and the overwhelmingly masculine figures they create are worth noting, considering that the black female body is also in danger in a white supremacist society. Their figurative works of various media adorn the black human figure in the technologies that are needed to survive, but the absence of the woman in space as Afronaut is a glaring omission in the artworks discussed in this paper.

Yinka Shonibare is a British-Nigerian artist whose conceptual project relies on the duplicitous messages communicated through fabrics deemed 'African' by European textile merchants. Specifically, Dutch wax print fabric is brightly coloured, elaborately designed cotton marketed to countries in Africa. It has been adopted as an exemplar of African culture, even though it has no origins in the countries to which it is marketed. This duplicity is what interests Shonibare and why he uses Dutch wax print fabrics, as they are ubiquitous in his oeuvre of (usually) headless human forms. The fabric communicates the constructedness of identity and cultural heritage and its inherent difficulties in 'pinning down' origins in a global society. With the fabric, Shonibare is able to address important issues about creativity and identity (specifically African) and the notions of authenticity that often bog down understanding of African art and ideas of belonging that plague the diasporic, nomadic artist.

Shonibare's biographers have addressed the idea of the alien in Shonibare's work, but this seems awkward to me. This is where the astronaut, the particularity of the Afronaut especially, comes into play. Shonibare's diverse media and ways of working in his Afronaut works are very much about mediating the spatial, not so much the temporal. Human subjects in astronaut accoutrement are not travelling though deep space; they are navigating Earth utilising the technologies of survival needed to engage the problems associated with immigration, exile, colonialism, and the attendant xenophobia and racism.

Shuttling between Britain and Nigeria is not necessarily alien when one considers the spatial slippages resulting from the legacies of colonialism. Place is rather arbitrary considering those legacies of conquest. The made-up, politically imposed boundaries make and mark identities in the same arbitrary ways that the Dutch wax print makes something authentically African. But the boundaries are significant, nonetheless, and have real-life consequences, especially for refugees and migrants, those vulnerable to the spatial slippages and violence that results. The violence does manifest itself through racist and xenophobic policies that create outsiders and non-citizens. Consequently, I believe the Afronaut is a more cogent symbol than the alien for communicating the situation of the refugee and the migrant. Shonibare's installations depicting astronauts demonstrate the strength of this symbol.

The figure of the Afronaut seems to begin in Shonibare's work at the turn of the century. Into the new millennium, Shonibare began a conversation about futurity, fantasy and technology that is in concert with space exploration. The figures are all costumed in African wax print fabric, helmets, and space boots. Various accoutrement for travel makes each installation distinct.

Cloud 9 (2000)[7] consists of a mannequin in an astronaut's costume made of Dutch wax print fabric. The figure stands beside a flag made from a different print of Dutch wax print fabric. The installation photograph is reminiscent of Neil Armstrong's 'conquest' of the moon. The image also brings to mind themes of conquest and colonisation on Earth, specifically on the African continent.

Vacation (2002)[8] depicts a family of astronauts, two adults and two children, who are attached to what appears to be oxygen packs. They wear helmets and boots also. Their helmets are all oriented towards the ground, as if they are searching for something. The title denotes a leisure activity, but the astronaut suits and the searching complicate the assumptions of leisure. One child is seemingly separated from the rest of the family and his suit fabric is different. Perhaps this installation demonstrates Shonibare's own anxieties about being a cosmopolitan nomad – someone who traverses continents effortlessly, but whose identity requires more effort to 'pin' down. But pinning down isn't the goal for Shonibare. The opposite seems to be true. Throughout his body of work he is interested in the fluidity of identity and the sometimes dubious implications of ethnic content in his work. The astronaut figures are no different, but they speak to the sustained feeling of isolation and otherness that people of colour feel when traversing white spaces. The environments are sometimes hostile; so, the technologies that they wear are a necessity.

Space Walk (2002)[9] demonstrates the drive for survival in a hostile and alien environment. Shonibare's artistic process differs in this installation, because he designed and created the silkscreened fabric himself as an artist in residence at the Fabric Workshop and Museum in Philadelphia. The installation includes two figures dressed in the trademark fabrics of Shonibare's oeuvre. The fabric features vocal artists native to Philadelphia and responsible for the so-called Philly Sound. The figures are suspended from the ceiling along with a half-size replica of the Apollo 13 shuttle, which is made from fibreglass and wood. The figures wear backpacks, helmets, and boots. Their suits are attached to the replica of the space ship with tubes covered in the colourful fabric.

Refugee Astronaut (2012)[10] features a single figure dressed in a Dutch wax print astronauts suit. A net full of survival items burden this astronaut's back. Pans, ropes and a lantern are visible through the net. The items tell the story of an itinerant astronaut, who has yet to find home. Instead, he travels with his most important belongings from place to place. The tubes that are connected to the spaceship in *Space Walk* are connected back into the astronaut's suit in *Refugee Astronaut*. The latter installation emphasises a sense of homelessness with the placement of the tubes and a notable lack of the mothership that we see in the former installation. A cool sky blue dominates the costume that is interspersed with fiery orange and red forms. The contrast brings to mind the conflicting situations of actual refugees. All of these astronaut-themed installations point to Afrofuturism and technologies of survival for people of colour in Europe in the United States.

Nick Cave is a multimedia artist from the United States who made his first Soundsuit in 1992 in response to the Rodney King beating. King was an unarmed citizen whose brutal and sustained beating during a traffic stop by the Los Angeles Police Department was caught on videotape and disseminated to the media, causing a public outcry that led to a trial and subsequent acquittal of the offending officers. Cave's feelings of vulnerability as a black man in a white supremacist society guided the construction of a protective apparatus that he called a Soundsuit for its kinetic and sonic qualities. The Soundsuit is an Afrofuturist project that adopts the themes of fantasy to create safe spaces for black bodies. Moreover, the performers in the suits function like the Afronaut, who need a protective layer in a hostile environment. In a world where black people can be beaten, and even killed, without legal retribution, Cave desired 'a kind of outerwear to protect (his) spirit', he says.[11] The first Soundsuit was made from detritus to reflect the ways that black people and their true identities are discarded and dismissed through racial profiling. The collection of found objects are assembled to form a suit of armour that protects against the outside world and its racism.

For over two decades, Cave has continued to make the Soundsuits and they continue to maintain their relevance to current events in the United States. Cave's Soundsuits have been compared to synthesized versions of African masquerade performances. The Soundsuits do not just function visually, but have kinetic and sonic functions that support this claim. When they are worn, they are activated in ways that harness 'the power within the black male, that intimidation and scariness' in addition to preliminary protective function.[12] Although this quote from Cave emphasises the masculinity of the Soundsuit's function, history demonstrates that women are also vulnerable and are in need of a similar harnessing of power. In some ways, that intimidation and scariness becomes its own performer and takes on a life of its own in narratives about black people in interactions with police. The fantastical nature of the costumes mimics the imaginary nature of the presumed deviance and violence of black people.

While his messages and meanings remain consistent, Cave's materials and messages have changed throughout his history as an artist. The labour-intensive process of assembling found objects to create Soundsuits is now the work of multiple assistants who commit Cave's visions to reality. How he finds objects has also changed. The objects are not simply discarded, but also constructed by artisans and bought from thrift shops. This alters the process of finding and repurposing discarded items. Cave claims that through the objects that he carefully chooses for his Soundsuits the viewer can come to an understanding of the world and how to navigate it through her relationship to memory.

This mnemonic process is evident in Cave's Soundsuit for Trayvon Martin, titled *TM 13*. Martin was a teenager murdered by George Zimmerman after visiting a store to buy a soft drink and candy. Zimmerman was acting under the auspices of the neighbourhood watch and was subsequently acquitted with the aid of Florida's Stand Your Ground Law, which allows armed citizens judicial leniency for self defence. The acquittal led to the rallying cry and movement: 'Black Lives Matter'. In Cave's imagining of a Soundsuit for Martin, the body is shrouded in a protective net that is made of brightly coloured beads that mimic and recall the Skittles that Martin never got to enjoy that fateful night. Though obscured by the beaded net, the costume underneath is equally compelling: a black mannequin wears sneakers, a hoodie, and jeans.[13] Surrounding the mannequin are plastic yard decorations, typically used at Christmas and Halloween – a cherubic-looking Santa Claus and a costumed teddy bear. These playful figures recall the innocence lost and the clothing reflects a sort of vulnerability. Cave refers to the holiday figures as guardians. The net of beads in gold with red, black, and green, the colours of the black liberation flag. The net encases the body – traps it, yet protects it. Through the Soundsuits, Cave's Afrofuturist project imagined a technology of survival that is performative and meditative on the materials that he chooses.

Gerald Machona's *Vabvakure (People from Far Away)* (2013) is both a short film and installation. Machona is a Zimbabwe-born artist commenting on the collapse of Zimbabwe and the subsequent upheaval and migration of people into South Africa. With the works, Machona comments on the nature of migration and refugee status in South Africa for people from Zimbabwe. The life-size *Ndiri Afronaut (I am an Afronaut)* (2012), which is performed in the short film, is made from decommissioned Zimbabwean dollars, foam padding, fabric, wood, Perspex, rubber, plastic tubing, nylon thread and gold leaf. The migration was not without difficulties, however. South Africans rejected the Zimbabwean refugees and created a racial and social hierarchy similar to apartheid.[14]

Vabvakure opens with a discombobulated Afronaut, trying to compose himself after landing in a desert.[15] His costume is dishevelled – tubes are loose and a space boot is strewn to the side. He dizzily moves around and then begins to dance. As if remaking a scene from Neil Armstrong's famous lunar landing, the Afronaut plants his flag, which resembles the flag of Zimbabwe, but Machona's flag is metallic and has the same decommissioned Zimbabwean dollars as the astronaut suit. The Afronaut then ventures away from the landing site, which he has claimed with his flag. The suit functions as the Afronaut's protection, but it also represents economic instability and, consequently, vulnerability in a foreign environment. The Afronaut's intentions in the new place are its conquest despite that vulnerability communicated through the defunct currency.

Next, the Afronaut finds a plant specimen and puts it into a vessel. The plant is obviously alien and artificial and looks to be made of the same currency as the other items. The Afronaut ends up at an ATM, which is strange considering that his suit is made of money, but it emphasises that the currency that comprises the suit is defunct. In the next scene, the Afronaut is carrying the plant specimen down the street. He arrives in front of a crowded store, where people stare, and he retrieves a shopping cart and places his plant specimen in it. The camera focuses on the uprooted plant in an alien environment as the Afronaut pushes it through the store. People stare and one can only compare the two – the plant and the Afronaut traversing the land as outsiders.

The Afronaut retrieves water from the store shelves, people point and stare, and then he heads to the cashier to pay for his purchase. He leaves the grocery store and stops in front of a fast food restaurant. At this point, the Afronaut opens the vessel of the plant specimen and pours in the water that he just purchased. He closes the vessel and places the plant specimen in his backpack. The Afronaut nourishes and protects the plant in ways that underscore its displacement. In this way, the specimen and the Afronaut are parallel.

To end the film, Machona emphasises the performative nature of the film, by focusing on the audience screening and viewing the Afronauts costumes in the next scenes. Groups of people stoop over the suits, discussing them, and pointing, and touching and even trying to get into them. The technologies of survival in Machona's work are in response to the abject violence against Zimbabweans who fled to South Africa, which came to a head in 2008, but persist presently.

What are these artists saying about the black body in their work? That it is fragile, permeable and under attack. It is fungible and open to meanings that may destroy it. Through Afrofuturism, the technologies of survival mitigate these dangers as the black body navigates space. The body and the attendant identity is in orbit, but not always freely navigating the space.

1 J. Griffith Rollefson, 'The "Robot Voodoo Power" Thesis: Afrofuturism and Anti-Anti-Essentialism from Sun Ra to Kool Keith', *Black Music Research Journal*, vol. 28, no. 1 (2008) 86–7.

2 Cristina De Middel, *The Afronauts* (Madrid: self-published, 2012).

3 Kieron Monks, 'Nigeria Plans to Send an Astronaut to Space by 2030', CNN, 6 April 2016 (www.cnn. com/2016/04/06/africa/nigeria-nasrda-space-astro- naut/, accessed 25 March 2017); 'Mandla Maseko: The First Black African Heading into Space', BBC, 26 January 2014 (www.bbc.com/ news/ magazine-25844863, accessed 25 March 2017).

4 Alondra Nelson (ed.), 'Afrofuturism', *Social Text*, vol. 20, no. 2 (2002).

5 Mark Dery, 'Black to the Future: Interviews with Samuel Delany, Greg Tate, and Tricia Rose', *The South Atlantic Quarterly*, vol. 92, no. 4 (1993) 735–8.

6 Elizabeth C. Hamilton, 'Analog Girls in a Digital World: Fatimah Tuggar's Afrofuturist Intervention in the Politics of "Traditional" African Art', *Nka: Journal of Contemporary African Art*, no. 33 (2013) 70–79.

7 [Footnote 1 in source] The piece can be seen at www.artnet.com/Magazine/reviews/robinson/robinson5-15-5.asp

8 [2] See http://universes-in-universe.de/car/vene- zia/bien49/auth-exc/e-shonibare.htm

9 [3] See https://concretezine.wordpress. com/2013/04/15/yinka-shonibare-space-walk-2002/

10 [4] See www.allthingsankara.com/2016/06/art-refugee-astronaut-ii-2016-yinka-shonibare.html

11 [5] http://style.time.com/2012/03/26/the-noisemaker/

12 [6] Ibid.

13 [7] www.art21.org/videos/segment-nick-cave-in-chicago

14 [8] www.google.com/culturalinstitute/beta/asset/people-from-far-away/qwHGWy6_NKUzpg

15 [9] https://vimeo.com/94380286

Elizabeth C. Hamilton, extracts from 'Afrofuturism and the Technologies of Survival', *African Arts*, vol. 50, no. 4 (Winter 2017) 18–23.

J.G. Ballard, Eduardo Paolozzi and Frank Whitford
In Conversation//1971

[...]
Frank Whitford Jim, you were suggesting earlier that the average person now is highly sophisticated when it comes to fine art, and to grasping points made visually, and I don't think it's true in many cases. For example, there is still very little acceptance of the ideas to which Eduardo gave general currency during Independent Group meetings all those years ago, when was it, in 1952. He still puts on slide shows of images culled from all kinds of sources similar to the ones which took up the first part of the first meeting of the IG and there's still incomprehension, isn't there?

J.G. Ballard What kind of images are you talking about?

Whitford Things like the source material for the Olivetti project and *Bunk*, which is, in fact, a series of graphics reproducing many of the images first shown at that IG meeting. There is hostility even in art schools when Eduardo gives such slide shows.

Eduardo Paolozzi Art schools are in a desperate situation. The students are all hooked up on concept art and sub-Christo, can one say sub-Barry Flanagan? Is such a thing possible? And they see it all the time in the pages of *Studio International*. I think that kind of thing needs to be said. They're all hooked on ironic statements now. You know, someone fills a room with mud, so now we've got to fill a room with mud that's been chromium-plated.

Whitford Jim, were you aware of the Independent Group while it was going on?

Ballard I remember going to the 'This is Tomorrow' exhibition in 1956, a long, long time ago. But if that show were to be mounted now I think it would be as fresh and as revolutionary in many ways. I think you have to give pop painters every credit for what they did. They liberated the external environment, perceived it at first glance. But now I think we need to look at the external environment at second glance and look beyond the worlds of consumer goods and mass iconography. You'd agree with that, wouldn't you?

Paolozzi Well, you know the bombs at the Tate are my answer to the Brillo boxes.

Ballard To go to the Whitechapel in 1956 and to see my experience of the real world being commented upon, played back to me with all kinds of ironic gestures, that was tremendously exciting. I could really recreate the future, that was the future, not the past. And abstract expressionism struck me as being about yesterday, was profoundly retrospective, profoundly passive, and it wasn't serious. Why I became a science fiction writer – of marginal interest – was because the future was clearly better and the past was clearly worse. Abstract expressionism didn't share the overlapping, jostling vocabularies of science, technology, advertising the new realms of communication. 'This is Tomorrow' came on a year before the flight of the first Sputnik, but the technologies that launched the Space Age were already underpinning the consumer-goods society in those days. How much of this did abstract expressionism represent? If an art doesn't embrace the whole terrain, all four horizons, it's worth nothing.

Whitford The other day I inferred from something you said that, in your view, visual artists now more often produce relevant statements than writers do, that the fine arts today seem curiously more able to find metaphors for contemporary life than poets or novelists. Is this fair enough?

Ballard In the fine arts there was a major revolution somewhere about 1860 and in the field of literature that revolution hasn't yet taken place. There's a consciousness in English life that we also lack, a missing revolution here, too, which would have redefined the landscape. The fact is that the main tradition in the fine arts for the last fifty years at least has been the tradition of the new. The main pressure on the sculptor or painter is the pressure of the new. The new to the new. But in literature the main tradition is the tradition of the old. Where Eduardo and his fellow painters and sculptors are expected to find something new to say, my fellow writers and myself are expected to find something old, and to go on saying it. And nothing alerts, will strike terror into the ear of a publisher, so much as the word 'experimental'. And the next most alarming word is 'new'.

You see, the novel, despite what appears to be the technical advance of Joyce or William Burroughs, the novel is basically an early nineteenth-century structure. The writer still sees himself in the role of an Academy painter producing historical paintings. The sort of revolution achieved by the Impressionists, limited simply to its effect on the choice of subject matter, has not yet been achieved in literature. I mean, no one is yet writing like Corot painted, if you see the connection. Most writers see themselves in the same role as Homer. They're telling the story of how it happened.

Paolozzi I think Ballard's subject matter and mine touch at certain points. We're both involved with the encounter with machines, and we're both involved with forcing people to look and with preventing them from escaping from certain facts. I don't want to make prints that will help people to escape from the terrible world. I want to remind them.

Whitford The imaginations of you both are obviously stimulated, excited to an unusual degree, by all aspects of technology, and yet, it seems to me, the vast majority of us haven't the imagination to cope with the enormous riches which technology has conferred on us. For example, when a satellite was first used to beam TV from one continent to another for the general public someone somewhere had a brainwave. Let's use this previously undreamed-of facility to create a truly wonderful programme. But was the imagination up to it? Not at all. In the face of all that awe-inspiring technology, the switches, batteries, angles, circuits all working like magic, all they could think up was to show the first tram leaving Sydney depot at 4.30 in the morning, a baseball match from San Francisco and the Beatles in the studio in London singing a song they'd composed specially for the occasion. It was all live, of course, but it might just as well have been on film. They could have saved themselves all the trouble. Here is a classic example of how the imagination has failed to keep pace with the possibilities afforded by technology of all kinds.

Paolozzi This is quite true. I'm prepared to spend the rest of my life on that premise. A lot of people who are actually manipulating the mass media are curiously undereducated. And the media are such tremendously well-made machines, like warfare, which also has a tremendous amount of money spent on it, and the machinery protects the inefficient, the amateurish, because there are so many compensatory devices. So that the bad photographer will be rescued by the art editor, the incompetent interviewer rescued by the man on the cutting-room floor.

Ballard Another example: I believe the space programme, both Russian and American, has failed to excite the public imagination in real terms, and I think this may also have something to do with missed opportunities by the mass media. To have been alive, to have watched Armstrong as his foot landed on the surface of the moon... yet the effect on people's imaginations was nil. Now why? I think you're getting a sort of radical social classification into two groups of people: those who work within modern science and technology and modern communications, who actually appreciate what's going on, and those who are outside it. And we are just members of the studio audience. We are watching the acrobats but have absolutely no understanding. We are like a charabanc party that's arrived by mistake at Sadler's Wells and are watching a ballet we don't understand. But I think it's the role of the artist to connect the two. His subject matter is no longer the world of manner and the world of ordinary appearances. He has to illuminate the real world for the ordinary person, the new world which technology and communications have created.
[...]

J.G. Ballard, Eduardo Paolozzi and Frank Whitford, extract from a conversation in 'Speculative Illustrations: Eduardo Paolozzi in Conversation with J.G. Ballard', *Studio International*, vol. 182 (October 1971). Reprinted in *Extreme Metaphors: Selected Interviews With J.G. Ballard 1967–2008* (London: Fourth Estate, 2012) 42–5.

Gilda Williams
The Otolith Group//2009

In the preface to Frankenstein, Mary Shelley explained that she wrote fiction not because she enjoyed 'weaving stories of supernatural terrors' but because of its capacity 'for delineating human passions more comprehensive and commanding [than] the ordinary relations of existing events'. Almost two centuries later, the films of the Otolith Group (Kodwo Eshun and Anjalika Sagar) also adopt fiction – specifically science fiction, the genre Shelley helped invent – in order to explore impossible or failed histories and the compelling messages coded therein. In *A Long Time Between Suns (Part 2)* (2009) the artists revisit Satyajit Ray's unrealised film project *The Alien* (1967), the tale of an extraterrestrial who lands in a small Bengal village and befriends a boy, and Pier Paolo Pasolini's *Notes for a Film About India* (1968), in which the attempt to shoot a story of ancient India is juxtaposed with the country's current human catastrophes, via the director's encounters with everyday people whom he considers casting in his film. The main characters of Ray's film – the Engineer, the Industrialist, the Journalist, the Boy – return in the Otolith film to offer their suspicions of and, in turn, their disappointments with a new character, the Director, who 'plays God' in giving them life (on the screen) and death (because the film was never made), a death evoked in the recurring image of a Goya-esque firing squad and its tragic victim. Creation myths and supernatural beings are evoked throughout, in images of altars and rites that are paralleled with the rituals of filmmaking (casting, location scouting, scriptwriting), and in each character's mystified response to the Alien.

Ray's story, the encounter with the child brings out the Alien's inclination for play and magic. Ray was rethinking sci-fi at a time when Frankenstein's literary descendant, golden-age science fiction, was in decline and the genre had been reborn with a violent new urgency in the work of J.G. Ballard and his generation of 'new wave' writers. The Otolith Group readdresses the genre neither through remake nor homage but by stepping back, without nostalgia, into the radical fictional framework Ray attempted and then abandoned. The narrators digress from the story to question the film's making – 'Who will play the Director?' the Industrialist asks, offering images of possible performers culled from candid footage taken on city streets – but this contrasts with a reassuring return to the story and characters of Ray's unmade film, rendering his fantasy, paradoxically, the most stable foothold in the Otolith film.

The installation, designed by artist Will Holder, encouraged viewers to sit around a worktable, university seminar style, to watch the big screen; the accompanying video *Otolith Timeline* (2003) was also playing on a monitor set alongside printers and documents. This elaborate staging reinforced the constructedness of the main film's reality effect. The otolith is a structure in the inner ear that allows our bodies to orient us to the earth's gravitational field; it is the precariousness of our sense of historical balance today – given the current feeling that, with the right technology, just about anything, people and events, potential pasts, even unfinished artworks, could be 'raised from the dead' – that is put dizzyingly into play here.

Gilda Williams, 'The Otolith Group', *Artforum* vol. 48, no. 4 (December 2009) 245.

N.J. Stallard
I Want to See You Not Through the Machine//2018

You sit inside a small room. It doesn't matter what colour the walls are painted. You educate yourself daily from the comfort of your armchair, or lie back in your marble imitation bathtub. You know thousands of people. You love the machine. A bell rings. You open your laptop and a face appears. It wobbles a little bit, like a blue jelly. It's your son. He's in Lake Titicaca or Santiago or Delaware – somewhere on the other side of the world. He urgently needs to tell you something and wants you to come and visit.

You are irritated. This wasn't the hands-free motherhood you signed up for. One of the greatest freedoms of the machine is its ability to connect while slowly wearing away at your relationships, like the erosion of a cliff and the houses falling into the sea, one by one.

In 1909, a 30-year-old E.M. Forster sat down at his desk and wrote 'The Machine Stops', his only work of science fiction. Set in the far future, the story describes a human society that lives below the earth's surface and is run by the 'Machine'. Each individual lives in his own hexagonal room, which the Machine provides with an automated bathtub, an armchair and ambient lighting. The humans rarely go outside or see each other, and instead share lectures from their armchairs and stay in touch via a blue light able to connect to all the other hexagonal rooms.

To read the story today is to confront an uncanny version of our own 'hyper-connected' world. Readers have described the story as 'chilling' and 'spooky' due to the accuracy of Forster's dystopian vision of the future. Like an Edwardian rip-off of *Black Mirror*, he depicts a world in which the more we become dependent on the machine, the more we are alienated from each other. [...]

For Forster, one of the uncanniest moments is his description of a video call. The story opens with Vashti, a mother, relaxing in her hexagonal room – she loves the Machine. Her day is interrupted when an electric bell rings. A faint blue light appears and then she sees the image of her son, Kuno, from the other side of the world. Vashti is irritated when Kuno asks to see her in person and expresses doubts about the Machine [...]

[...] The rest of 'The Machine Stops' can be read as a battle between Kuno's dissident ideas and desire to return to the natural world and Vashti's faith in technology to enhance the future. 'It's against the spirit of our age!' Vashti says when Kuno reveals his plan to escape the Machine, akin to a social media detox or move to Virginia to live off-grid. Kuno's ideas foreground our common fear – that to connect via the Internet is ultimately to lose something. His doubts are the paradox of connection; we are able to stay in touch, but pay the price through isolation and alienation.

Who knows where this paradox came from or whether to believe it. Who knows whether to believe in echo chambers, either. What is worth knowing, however, is who you are, or who you'd like to be – Vashti or Kuno? Are you happy to sit in a room where you can connect to a thousand friends? Or do you long to see your mother face to face? Do you find yourself avoiding or growing resentful of direct experience? Or are you worried the world is becoming increasingly the same?

When Vashti eventually travels to see Kuno via air-ship, she questions the need to travel at all: 'what was the good of going to Pekin when it was just like Shrewsbury? Why return to Shrewsbury when it would all be like Pekin?'

Fast forward 100 years after Forster's story and it's 2009. Skype is four years old and has 521 million users, growing by an average of 10 million per month. [...]

Vashti or Kuno? As good as being there? Sometimes a video call can feel like a vitamin boost for a fading relationship. We use it to speak to the dying. We use it to make love. But it is frightening for a government to decide to quietly replace human contact with a video. That for people under duress it is the equivalent to eye contact, to the smell of another person, to touch.

[...] In the final scene of 'The Machine Stops', Forster puts the flourishing touch to the metaphor he has built throughout the text. The hexagonal rooms are increasingly referred to as cells, like the cell of a bee, and we come to believe that it is humankind, not the Machine, that has imprisoned itself.

When the Machine stops, the world begins to fall apart. Communication between the cells breaks, and then the cells themselves. Vashti stays inside her cell until the very last moment and when she leaves, Forster writes: 'It was thus that she opened her prison and escaped – escaped in the spirit: at least so it seems to me, here my meditation closes. That she escapes in the body – I cannot perceive that.'

Forster's story offers a dystopian vision of the future but, like most dystopias, it carries a utopia nestled in its belly. In the darkness outside her cell, Vashti finds Kuno and they embrace. Mother and son are reunited; Kuno was right all along, and the city breaks 'like a honeycomb.'

Vashti asks: 'Is there any hope, Kuno?'

He replies: 'None for us'.

N.J. Stallard, extracts from 'I Want to See You Not Through the Machine', a text written for the exhibition 'The Machine Stops', Danielle Arnaud Gallery, London, 24 February–24 March 2018 (http://www.daniellearnaud.com/exhibitions/exhibition-the-machine-stops-stallard.html).

Peio Aguirre

Semiotic Ghosts: Science Fiction and Historicism//2011

In William Gibson's short story 'The Gernsback Continuum' (1981), a photographer (the narrator) is commissioned to illustrate a coffee-table book about North American architecture of the 1930s, to be published under the suggestive title *The Airstream Futuropolis: The Tomorrow That Never Was*.[1] Excavating the architecture of the so-called 'American Streamlined Moderne', full of chrome surfaces and buildings inspired by Fritz Lang's *Metropolis* (1927), the narrator is haunted by what he calls the 'semiotic ghost': hallucinations of unrealised futures – an airplane that was 'all wing, like a fat symmetrical boomerang with windows in unlikely places' or 'fifth-run movie houses like the temples of a lost sect that worshipped blue mirrors and geometry'.[2] Gibson used this concept to describe the science fiction imagery that permeates Western culture – that is, 'bits of deep cultural imagery that have split off and taken on a life of their own'. More precisely, Gibson's somewhat satirical criticism drew both on various modernist movements (which he labelled 'futuroids') and on the 1920s-esque fake technology featured in sci-fi magazines such as Hugo Gernsback's *Amazing Stories*. Gibson's version of a futuristic pop ghost echoes that 'old-fashioned future' that Bruce Sterling, Gibson's cyberpunk peer, coined in the title of one of his books to describe the time-space shifts that tend to present the past as science fiction and science fiction as past.[3] 'The Gernsback Continuum', as a hilarious compilation of sci-fi tropes, also managed to short-circuit the categories historically assigned to the genre, and functioned as a critique of its own aesthetic clichés. For this and other reasons, the story is seen as inaugurating the cyberpunk subgenre, which mixes science fiction with postmodernism.[4]

But today Gibson's semiotic ghosts have transcended the realm of the science fiction genre to shape our current cultural reception and understanding of history. [...]

The insight that cyberpunk can provide not only lies in the imagination of utopian futures – alternatives to the current situation – but also in the understanding we have of yesterday and of the way history can be constructed and represented collectively. Thus we might be able to trace strands of sci-fi historicism in artworks that draw on the past for their material (not in vain does Chris Marker open the monumental *Le Tombeau d'Alexandre* (*The Last Bolshevik*, 1983), with George Steiner's words: 'It is not the past which dominates us, it is images of the past').

[...] Gibson's sophisticated critique of an 'antique future' becomes parodic when aligned with the representations that a futurist modernism tried to shape. His vision not only defines modernism as a Habermasian 'unfinished project', loaded both with historicity and futurity, but also as a huge bazaar, filled with artefacts that match modernism's own inexhaustibility, paving the way for postmodernism. These obsolescent artefacts have today become semiotic phantoms.

Unsurprisingly, referentiality in art and culture has not only become a convention, but *the* privileged strategy, where whatever seems to be new has already been produced, mediated or processed in another way by someone else, another author. One of the great paradoxes of the alleged fecundity of historical content (the result of thinking of history as hunting grounds) is that it expresses just the opposite – an exhaustion of the possibility of invention in a culture given to endless retrospection, unable to generate real innovation and novelty, and in which the return or recurrent reinvention of the old-fashioned has given birth to what we call postmodernism. Jameson himself diagnosed such a condition in his study of the cultural logic of late capitalism, notably through postmodernism's adoption of pastiche and film nostalgia and its dreamy, narcissistic recreation of non-existent pasts through signs and remnants.[5] [...]

The Archaeological Turn

Not surprisingly, at this juncture, in the era of globalisation, our devotion to contemporary forms of historicising is accompanied by a profound scepticism about the nature of historical time itself. How can we define our historical period? Are 'postmodernism' and 'postmodernity' still valid terms for our social, economical and cultural system? Undoubtedly, grasping period shifts and nomenclature has always been a major concern for humankind, while anxiety about the future determines our desires and social dispositions. [...] However, a large-scale shift in thought means that its ideas about the history of events and the becoming of humanity materialise today in cultural territories that render obsolete the distinctions between high and low. Such fields as cyberpunk, contemporary art, auteur cinema and postmodern architecture have created a referential magma, turning culture into a viscous mass of historical pop.

Bruce Sterling has recently offered an alternative to traditional historiography and its distinctions between classical, modern and postmodern. He speaks of 'atemporality' as the cultural trait most suitable for our time.[6] For Sterling, new non-synchronic and globalised forms of communication emerge in the structure of the network; there is no authoritarian or unique voice that can speak about history, since this discipline, which emerged in the linear culture of the book, has been fragmented in cyberspace. Technological tools have an influence on knowledge, narratives and presentations of history, irreversibly changing history itself. The conflict, according to Sterling, is between the 'Gothic High-Tech' that we have inherited as part of analogical culture ('a ruined castle or the ruins of the unsustainable') and 'Favela Chic' as an informal and outlawed network in the emerging order. Not content with describing what he considers to be the atemporality in which we live, he offers solutions for the artist who is working within this chaos, such as recuperating forms that could not be written, writing histories about people who were not the 'winners' or those without literature, or re-creating human experience from before the historical record:

> What can we do to liven things up, especially as creative artists? Well, the immediate impulse is going to be the 'Frankenstein mashup'. Because that's the native expression of network culture. The 'Frankenstein mashup' is to just take elements of past, present and future and just collide 'em together, in sort of a collage. More or less semi-randomly, like a Surrealist 'exquisite corpse'.[7]

Sterling's position risks being adopted by the so-called 'creative class' as a new version of the neoliberal call of the 'end of history'. However, it encourages the practicing of history in innovative ways, outlining novel forms of cultural history. [...] Gibson's literature over the last decade shares a future-is-now approach with Sterling's, perhaps because his fascination with the complexity of the world prohibits him from imagining further artificial created futures. In another agonistic effort, Jameson himself located the current crisis of utopian imagination in the difficulty in thinking about solutions to the current neoliberal order – a crisis that leads us to repeat ad nauseam that there is no alternative to capitalism. Thus, the political function of science fiction is not merely to forecast the day after tomorrow, but to make us aware about the problems we have in imagining it.[8] For Jameson, science fiction's powerful historical self-consciousness is useful precisely when political imagination is in decay.

Different forms of 'archaeologies of the future' appear in recent art, when evolved forms of postmodern historicism surpass the recontextualisation of narratives of the past about the 'new'. This archaeological turn is palpable in Carol Bove's installations of shelves, objects and books, which adapt the appropriationist practice typical of the 1980s, for example in the work of Louise Lawler, Sherrie Levine and Haim Steinbach. A self-reflexive commentary about appropriation as artistic solution, Bove's work uses presentation rather than representation to highlight the extreme textuality of any historical object. [...] Her excavations call up a past that, far from being fossilised, appears as an open code to be deciphered in a circular manner. [...] But more than a melancholic impulse (a feature of allegory for Benjamin) or a nod to the commoditisation of the past, central to Bove's work is a critique of the fetishisation of meta-narratives. As one of the characters in Gibson's *Zero History* says, 'consumers don't buy products so much as narratives'.[9] [...]

Crisis of Historicity

[...] In the extraordinary revival of discussions about modernism, the spectral apparition and the ghostly presence of the modern after its postmodern denial or challenge resemble in some way the charm of primitive original forms for artists of the modern period. [...] New categories (of post-postmodernism) need to be invented, in order to show how current cultural artefacts enact what Jacques Derrida has called 'hauntology'. In *Spectres of Marx* (1993), he uses the term to describe the way that after the various 'ends of history', the present remains haunted by ghosts of the past, which continuously erupt (an obvious cyberpunk metaphor).[10] Postmodernism's effect of mirroring the past stems from the collision of modernity's 'ontology of the present' with hauntology's spectres. [...]

Low-tech Returns

[...] If modernism was based on radical principles of originality and rupture that enthused the bourgeois class, and if the 'new wave of modernism' has been merging with popular and mass culture since the 1960s, giving rise to what is now known as Postmodernism, then current retro-modernism in the arts raises possibilities for dissent within the culture industry. But the main problem lies nowadays in the difficulty of finding a systemic definition of cultural production as a totality, and thus the question turns to 'naming the system'. The term 'postmodernity' has been dismissed today due to its association with not too distant historical cultural and theoretical circumstances and to the market and consumerism. Many of the misunderstandings with this term are the result of an ongoing mix-up between Postmodernism as an ideology, as a style or sum of cultural features, and as a historic condition, which is obviously the option that I seek to highlight here. Modernism, on the other hand – both in its classical and late versions – turns out to be the space where the delusion of the modern as virgin territory operates as a large iconic and narrative reserve for re-framing, re-reading and re-writing. Attempts to define these new systemic paradigms eventually reveal their weaknesses. In art, this results in a glaring contradiction: in an era that can be described as that of the end of temporality, historical and referential art becomes pervasive. The failure to set up a new cultural scene marks our present,[11] from the Jamesonian 'continuous present' and Sterling's 'atemporality', to the 'altermodern' and 'heterochronicity' of Nicolas Bourriaud, to the 'capitalist realism' of Mark Fisher – all of them provisional solutions that aim to define a theoretical alternative to the dilemmas posed and left unresolved by postmodernity, to that realm in which semiotic ghosts become myths of the near future.

1 William Gibson, 'The Gernsback Continuum', in *Burning Chrome* (New York: Arbor House, 1986). Hugo Gernsback (1884–1967) created the first science fiction magazine, *Amazing Stories*, in 1926. Gibson's story is reprinted in *Mirrorshades: The Cyberpunk Anthology*, ed. Bruce Sterling (New York: Arbor House, 1986).

2 Ibid., 27.

3 See Bruce Sterling, *A Good Old-Fashioned Future* (New York: Bantam Spectra, 1999).

4 Additionally, Gibson, in his 'Sprawl series', lays the ground for the use of a new technology that is happening in an unspecified future, one intimately connected to our modern condition. See the trilogy of *Neuromancer* (New York: Ace Books, 1984), *Count Zero* (London: Victor Gollancz, 1986) and *Monalisa Overdrive* (London: Victor Gollancz, 1988), as well as *Burning Chrome*, op. cit.

5 [Footnote 8 in source] See Fredric Jameson, *Postmodernism, or, The Cultural Logic of Late Capitalism* (Durham, NC: Duke University Press, 1991).

6 [10] B. Sterling, 'Atemporality for the Creative Artist', presented at the conference 'Transmediale 10', Berlin (6 February, 2010). Available at http://www.wired.com/beyond_the_beyond/2010/02/

7 [11] Ibid.

8 [13] Fredric Jameson, *Archaeologies of the Future: The Desire Called Utopia and Other Science Fictions* (London and New York: Verso, 2005).

9 [14] *Zero History*, op. cit., 21.

10 [19] 'Hauntology', which combines 'haunted' with 'ontology', has been used to describe some recent 'spectral' music (by Burial, The Caretaker, Ariel Pink and Boards of Canada, among others) in the blogosphere, to the point of becoming a cultural phenomena in itself. See for example the blogs of Simon Reynolds (Blissblog), Mark Fisher (K-Punk) and Adam Harper (Rouge's Foam), and the article 'Society of the Spectral' by Reynolds in *The Wire*, no. 273 (November 2006).

11 [22] See Mark Fisher, *Capitalism Realism: Is There No Alternative?* (London: Zero Books, 2009) and Nicholas Bourriaud, *The Radicant*, trans. James Gussen and Lili Porten (Berlin and New York: Sternberg Press, 2009).

Peio Aguirre, extracts from 'Semiotic Ghosts: Science Fiction and Historicism', *Afterall*, no. 28 (Autumn/Winter 2011) 124–34.

Benjamin Noys
Cyberpunk Phuturism//2014

[...] Acceleration, today, passes from the car, the quintessential technology of mass speed and modernity, to the computer. If the car, as Enda Duffy argues,[1] was the lived experience of modernist time for many – a new mass aesthetic, when modernism tended to the hermetic – then the computer plays that role today. It is the computer, especially for those who work with them, that embodies the 'speed-up' of labour, as each new model becomes faster and faster (or that is the promise). The Internet provides the 'one-click' solution, computers speed-up and slim down, seemingly providing one of the last utopian remnants worthy of any commodity fetishism; the very frustration of a computer slowing down or freezing-up indexes our own internalised demand for speed. [...]

So, the integration of the accelerating man-machine does not simply disappear, but mutates. Fredric Jameson comments:

> there are no great utopian texts after the widespread introduction of computers (the last being Ernest Callenbach's *Ecotopia* of 1975, where computers are not yet in service). Instead, we have the free market deliria of cyberpunk, which assumes that capitalism is itself a kind of utopia of difference and variety.[2]

Cyberpunk is the utopia not only of difference and variation, but also of deliria and acceleration. It is that 'utopia' I want to explore, which is rather more durable and robust than Jameson's dismissal might suggest.

This new aesthetic can be thought of as the attempt to recapture the energy of the classical avant-garde in the slackened time of postmodernity. It is not simply the repetition of the avant-garde, but a mutated and modulated futurism, which, in typical postmodern fashion, straddles between genres, forms, and cultural domains. This is what I will call 'cyberpunk phuturism'. Certainly 'cyberpunk phuturism' has an anachronistic and kitsch ring. The term 'cyberpunk' did not really recover from Billy Idol's album of that title, released in 1993. 'Phuturism' is my adaptation via the Chicago Acid House practitioners Phuture, whose 'Acid Tracks' (1989) has a claim to be the first Acid House record. That said, perhaps the kitsch element, as we'll see, reflects something of this aesthetic.

I will focus on three moments: cyberpunk fiction, Detroit techno, and their synthesis in Cybertheory. [...] I want to probe these re-tooled forms of accelerationism as a response to the mutations and continuities of contemporary capitalism. Accelerationism is not merely an historical curiosity, but an aesthetic and political attitude that continues to exert a gravitational pull on the present.

The Thrill and Threat of Materialisation

The Ur-text of cyberpunk phuturism is William Gibson's *Neuromancer* (1984), which is perhaps its most effective manifesto and predicts all its later mutant forms. *The* novel of cyberpunk science fiction, and to my mind the only successful work of this form (along with its sequels), it tracks the new shifting forms of cybernetic embodiment. The very technology of 'jacking-in' to cyberspace is rooted, within the novel, in the frame of military technologies: 'The matrix has its roots in primitive arcade games', said the voiceover, 'in early graphics programs and military experimentation with cranial jacks.'[3] [...] While speed is the promise of the opening to a new deterritorialised fluidity of social and virtual space – beyond the Fordist social-compact and the 'static' segmentations of social democracy – this is no blind process. The historical significance of Gibson's novel (leaving aside aesthetic judgements) lies in the fact that it is poised between anxiety and endorsement, critical distance and immersive *jouissance*, in its vision of cyberspace, augmentation and the accelerative disembedding of social relations.

Joshua Clover points out that *Neuromancer* incarnates the 'thrill and threat of dematerialisation' that lies at the heart of neoliberalism[4]; the thrill of new fluid forms of accumulation and super-wealth (for a very few), and the threat of obsolescence and abandonment (for many). In Gibson's novel the thrill lies in the discarding of the ego, 'de-sleeving' consciousness, to borrow a term from Richard Morgan's sci-fi novel *Altered Carbon* (2002), from its material support. The threat lies in being condemned to the 'meat' (the body), and excluded from the delights of cyberspace. [...] Yet we could rewrite Clover to say that the novel's cyberpunk phuturism also captures the 'thrill and threat of *materialisation*'. The thrill here is augmentation and integration, from Tally Isham ('the girl with the Zeiss-Nikon eyes') to Molly Numbers (with her implanted retractable razor blade implants). The threat is from bad tech, bad surgery, and falling behind the accelerative race to the future. Acceleration into the utopian horizon of capitalism – as a social form of pure drive and accumulation, freed from its dependence on the meat of labour – is always haunted by our obsolescence. Gibson's novel tracks a capitalist utopia in dystopian formulations, figuring the self literally as the 'entrepreneurial machine' that Foucault had already anatomised as the subjectivity of neoliberalism.[5]

Techno-Phuturism

Cutting to another scene, it is, I would argue, Detroit techno that forms one of the most fascinating and most aesthetically successful instances of cyberpunk phuturism. Deliberately couched as a post-industrial Afrofuturism, it aimed to 'erase the traces' (in Brecht's phrase) of the Fordist sound of Motown and to mimic the new robot production lines that had displaced the remains of 'variable capital' (i.e. humans) for 'constant capital' (i.e. machines) at Ford. This so-called 'automation' was called 'niggermation' by radical black workers in the 1970s – the systematic forcing-up of production under unsafe conditions through super-exploitation.[6] They disputed the story of new hi-tech production, noting that what was happening was often just old-fashioned speed-up on the line. Once again, we might be cautious about the images of acceleration we encounter.

Detroit techno traced the mutating social space of Detroit – from the 'white flight' following the 1967 insurrection, the deindustrialisation that followed, and its own position in the suburban site of Belleville High, where the pioneers Derrick May, Juan Atkins and Kevin Saunderson met. Mixing European influences (Kraftwerk, New Order, Depeche Mode, etc.) with the Detroit funk of Parliament/Funkadelic, the result was a singular form that defied the studied reflexes of postmodern collage for an *integrated* acceleration.

The axes of Detroit techno were an increase in speed (in bpm) from previous forms of disco and House and a stripping-out of the humanist residues that often dominated those forms – not least the voice. The singularity of its aesthetic invention lay in this welcoming of the 'mechanisation', or better 'computerisation', of the aesthetic [...] [r]etaining funk, the insistence of Detroit techno had the utopian, if not kitsch, elements of sci-fi futurism coupled to the dystopian fragmentation of the city-space ('Night Drive Thru Babylon', as the track by Model 500 had it). Again, the equivocations lay in a sense of abandonment: an escape to the future, escape from labour, or the loss of labour and the collapse of the future into permanent unemployment?

The Detroit electro/techno-duo Drexciya, who emerged in the 90s, made explicit a longer history of disposable labouring bodies.[7] [...] This Afrofuturist sci-fi vision placed cutting-edge contemporary techno in contact with the abandoned bodies who 'escaped' the fate of slavery and their descendants who laboured in Detroit's factories, before being abandoned by capitalism to destitution, drugs, and prison. Here the future is haunted by the traces of impossible labour, which ruptures with the possibility of an accelerationist continuum.[8] Detroit techno could be re-read, along these lines, as a critique of the 'smoothness' of acceleration, by a repetition that disrupts the future rather than the endorsement of accelerationism.

Cybergothic Remix

The splicing of these two moments, and the real instance of full-blown cyberpunk phuturism in explicit accelerationist form, can be found in the 1990s work of Nick Land and his allies in the Cybernetic Culture Research Unit (CCRU). This 'nomad' (anti-) academic grouping, formed at Warwick University in 1995, couched its 'disjunctive synthesis' of the drives of sci-fi and techno through the work of Gilles Deleuze and Félix Guattari, especially their *Anti-Oedipus* (1972). The aim was to format an avant-garde practice that would explode the limits of 1990s inertia.

The 'rush' of this cyberpunk phuturism operated through a new radicalisation of acceleration. Vectored through cyberpunk fiction and the post-rave speed-up of Jungle and drum-and-bass, Nick Land and the CCRU's discourse aimed at maximum intensification into immanence until 'impending human extinction becomes accessible as a dance floor'.[9] The mass drug experimentation of rave culture was also spliced into this mutagenic remix. It aimed at immersion in immanence that had been, according to Nick Land, already realised in the then-future of 2012 (!). In case of present scepticism we should note Land's prediction is hyperstitional – a kind of performative fiction, which creates the future it predicts – and that his theorisation (according to Land) disrupts linear, chronological time. In the present moment we only have traces of that future – drugs, sci-fi, Jungle, theory, biotech – that prefigures the meltdown to come: 'as if a tendril of tomorrow were burrowing back'.[10]

The project of this race to the realised future is best captured in Nick Land's restatement and remixing of Deleuze and Guattari's original accelerationist formulation. Land gives this accelerationism a deliberately provocative and late-punk antisocialist and anti-social democratic form:

> Machinic revolution must therefore go in the opposite direction to socialistic regulation; pressing towards ever more uninhibited marketisation of the processes that are tearing down the social field, 'still further' with 'the movement of the market, of decoding and deterritorialisation' and 'one can never go far enough in the direction of deterritorialisation: you haven't seen anything yet'.[11]

Machinic revolution, in Land's metaphysics, reaches out to the horizon of absolute deterritorialisation – the realised capitalism that has decapitated itself into full-blown immanent marketisation.

This posing of the market *against* capitalism was derived from the historian Fernand Braudel. Obviously markets have pre-existed capitalism, and Braudel suggested that capitalism formed itself as a monopolistic anti-market, tying down exchange. [...] Land mutates this argument to identify markets with monstrously powerful cybernetic forces, which are 'speculative, opaque and exceptional'.[12] It is these forces of exchange that can resist the *stagnations* of capitalism. A purified capitalism, shedding the dictates of the State, would traverse to a pure market accelerated out of capitalism altogether.

This theory fed off the localised economic 'boom' of the 90s in which, at least in the UK and US, regimes claiming some tenuous and residual connection to social democracy instantiated a further deepening of the neoliberal project. It would be this coupling of attenuated social-democracy and neo-liberalism that bred a series of ideological tropes that dominate the perception of that moment, the 00s, and the present time of crisis. In this discourse it was the 'left' (or pseudo-left), and the 'left' in State power, that authorised, ratified and exacerbated the excesses of financialisation and consumer credit. It was the spending of the State and the public sector, not the excesses of capitalism, which came to be treated as the 'dead weight' that is now holding us back from another leap into the future. Politicians of the present can play the austerity card in the elimination of this State and public debt, while accelerationist positions can argue that the only problem was the State itself, which did not unleash these processes far enough. It was the 'humanist' residues of State spending that failed to measure up to the anti-humanism of capitalism.

The position of the CCRU, despite its radicalised anti-humanism and inhuman immersive promise of capitalism exploding its own limits, resonates with these contemporary ideological claims that capitalism wasn't really allowed to follow through. In this narrative, the acceleration of capitalism was held back by State spending and State regulation (focused, in the UK, often on 'health-and-safety', as in the trope of 'health-and-safety gone mad'). It was a 'left' failure of nerve to go all the way to capitalism (and not all the way to the left...), that leaves us in the situation we find ourselves in.

This story of constrained capitalism was coupled, in the work of Nick Land, to a switch to China as the only State formation *really willing* to go all the way, or that had *already* gone all the way, as 'neo-China arrives from the future'.[13] What China could offer, in its post-Maoist embrace of capitalism, was the final synthesis between Stalinist acceleration ('shock work', rapid and violent industrialisation), the Maoist 'great leap forward', and capitalist acceleration (although, of course, the ultra-left had long argued Stalinism was really a form of State-capitalism and 'primitive accumulation'). The State-directed excesses of China, in its uncompromising developmental drive, become a *utopian* element.[14]

[...] The political vagaries of these aesthetic forms of accelerationism do not fall on the tired tropes of fascism and 'totalitarianism', but rather on this difficult and tense imbrication with the dynamics of capitalism. Implicit in cyberpunk phuturism is not only the logic of increased computing speed and power, but also the claim that capitalism is maintaining its dynamic of acceleration first given its most memorable form by Marx and Engels in 'The Communist Manifesto' (1848). While we are all familiar with the line that 'all that is solid melts into air', the more resonant line for cyberpunk phuturism, especially as articulated by Nick Land, is: '[the bourgeoisie] has drowned the most heavenly ecstasies of religious fervour, of chivalrous enthusiasm, of philistine sentimentalism, in the icy water of egotistical calculation'.[15] Land's work dissolves the ego in the flows of this 'icy water', although the cult of personality that developed around him indicates the paradox of calls to dissolve the ego: some kind of ego has to be there to experience this dissolution into immanent flux and to theorise or report on its own extinction.

This drowning of the ego is closely linked to the question of labour. It is as labouring subjects we are subjected to the ego and it is in the cyberneticisation of labour that we are redeemed from the ego. In his text 'Meltdown' (1996) Nick Land proclaims: 'Industrial machines are deployed to dismantle the actuality of the proletariat, displacing it in the direction of cyborg hybridisation, and realising the plasticity of labour power.'[16] It is this integrated plasticity that reshapes the proletariat from subject of history into disappearing vector of acceleration. The displacement of labour will not be achieved by communism, or communist accelerationism, but through capitalism's dynamic. Another of Land's formulations, from 'No Future' (1995), paints a more horrifying fate: 'The full labour-market cycle blurs into meat grinder.'[17] Now the fate of labour is not simply to disappear into an accelerated future, but to be processed as if in a meat plant. Land's statements code the paradox of extinction in-and-through machinic acceleration. The cybernetic machine is at once liberation from the meat and destruction of the meat, resolved in the *jouissance* of immersion into immanence.

[...] The bursting of the dot.com bubble on Friday 10 March 2000, which indicated the emptiness of the cybernetic regeneration or reinforcement of the productive forces, didn't simply wreck Land's programme. Instead it became more frantic, more intensive, and more weird, as it tried to extract any remaining vestige of dynamism from the series of financial shocks that wash round the global capitalist economy.

Stasis Today

The contemporary moment is nicely summarised in Fredric Jameson's remark from 1998: 'Stasis today, all over the world [...] certainly seems to have outstripped any place for human agency, and to have rendered the latter obsolete.'[18] The failure of agency leads to the accelerationist dream of the reinsertion of agency by the merging of humans and computers in a new technological synthesis. Gopal Balakrishnan, in his recent survey of the deceleration of global capitalism, notes that Fredric Jameson's account of postmodernism and the excess of global capitalism was initially predicated on 'unleashed nuclear and cybernetic productive forces', before 'the locus of the problem silently shifted to mapping an opaque, pseudo-dynamic world of financial markets'.[19] [...] In fact, cyberpunk phuturism often implicitly posed the first dynamic of 'cybernetic productive forces' against the emergent sense of the 'opaque, pseudodynamic world of financial markets'. This is explicitly the case in contemporary accelerationism's ambiguous discussion of 'accelerative' elements of financial capitalism, such as High-Frequency Trading (HFT).[20]

For all their postmodern panache, cyber-accelerationism was far more concerned with the exploding of opacity, rather than the revelling in the usual clichés of the play of signs or simulacra. [...]

Of course, the difficulty is that it involved a certain attachment to an accelerative dynamic of 'productive forces' that proved illusory, although this was something of a material 'transcendental illusion' generated by capitalist forms of value. Capitalism's drive to accumulation, its squeezing of labour, and its penetration of existence through abstraction, shape the conditions of our experience giving rise to a felt experience of dynamism. Accelerationism enhances and celebrates this, but the future it could not grasp was the future of crash and crisis – the terminus of acceleration in the grinding to a halt of the speed machine of capitalism.

[...] The accelerationist desire can revel in the apocalyptic destruction caused by the crisis, or used to resolve the crisis, and take this as the sign of a new take-off. [...]

The perpetual desire to purify and pierce the barrier of 'capital itself' is encoded within the genetic structure of the capitalist social relation. This leaves cyberpunk phuturism in the uncomfortable position of joining with those attempts by the managers of capital to induce movement and acceleration by removing the dead weight of variable capital.

[...] The perpetual-motion machine of capital generates the perpetual temptation to cybernetic accelerationism. One more effort, if we are to really speed up capitalism, one more effort to dispose or displace the drag of labour and the meat. The difficulty, at its heart, is that cyberpunk phuturism gives over to capital a monopoly on our imagination of the future as the continuing intensification of accumulation and the reinforcement of the capitalist continuum. [...]

1 [Footnote 2 in source] Enda Duffy, *The Speed Handbook: Velocity, Pleasure, Modernism* (Durham, NC: Duke University Press, 2009).

2 [3] Fredric Jameson, 'In Soviet Arcadia', *New Left Review*, no. 75 (2012) 119–127, 125.

3 [4] William Gibson, *Neuromancer* (London: Grafton, 1984) http://lib.ru/GIBSON/neuromancer.txt

4 [6] Joshua Clover, 'Remarks on Method', *Film Quarterly*, vol. 63, no. 4 (2010) 7–9, 9.

5 [7] Michel Foucault, *The Birth of Biopolitics: Lectures at the Collège de France, 1978–79*, trans. Graham Burchell (Basingstoke: Palgrave, 2008) 224–5.

6 [8] Dan Georgakas and Marvin Surkin, *Detroit: I Do Mind Dying* (Cambridge, MA: South End Press, 1998) 85–106.

7 [9] Kodwo Eshun, 'Further Considerations on Afrofuturism', *CR: The New Centennial Review*, vol. 3, no. 2 (2003) 287–302, 300.

8 [10] R.L., 'Wanderings of the Slave: Black Life and Social Death', *Mute*, (5 June 2013) (http://www.metamute.org/editorial/articles/wanderings-slave-black-life-and-social-death).

9 [11] Nick Land, 'Meat' (1995), in *Fanged Noumena: Collected Writings 1987-2007*, ed. Robin Mackay (Falmouth: Urbanomic/Sequence Press, 2011).

10 [12] Nick Land, 'No Future' (1995), ibid.

11 [13] Nick Land, 'Machinic Desire' (1993), ibid.

12 [14] Immanuel Wallerstein, 'Braudel on Capitalism, or Everything Upside Down', *The Journal of Modern History, vol.* 63, no. 2 (1991) 354–61.

13 [15] Nick Land, 'Meltdown' (1997), in *Fanged Noumena*. See also a more recent text: Nick Land, 'China's Great Experimentalist', *Shanghai Star* (2004) (http://app1.chinadaily.com.cn/star/2004/0826/vo3-x.html).

14 [16] Hence Land's decamping from academia to work as a journalist in China was the personal embrace of this trajectory. His more recent toying with the neo-reactionary theories of Mencius Moldbug (aka computer scientist and entrepreneur Curtis Yarvin) renders critique of this latest work superfluous. See Nick Land, 'The Dark Enlightenment' (2014) (http://www.thedarkenlightenment.com/the-dark-enlightenment-by-nick-land/).

15 [17] Karl Marx and Friedrich Engels, 'Manifesto of the Communist Party' (1848).

16 [18] Nick Land, 'Meltdown', in *Fanged Noumena*, op. cit.

17 [19] Nick Land, 'No Future', in *Fanged Noumena*, op. cit.

18 [20] Fredric Jameson, *Brecht and Method* (London: Verso, 1998) 4.

19 [21] Gopal Balakrishnan, 'Speculations on the Stationary State', *New Left Review*, no. 59 (2009) 5–26, 15.

Benjamin Noys, extracts from 'Cyberpunk Phuturism', in *Malign Velocities: Accelerationism & Capitalism* (Winchester: Zero Books, 2014) 105–28.

Dominique Gonzalez-Foerster
In Conversation with Jessica Morgan//2008

[...]

Jessica Morgan The interest in science fiction has been present in your work for a long time, the literary influence and the filmic. And so in a sense it's perhaps the obvious thing to bring to the space of the Turbine Hall. But I remember you were also talking about this idea of changing the history of the building, which carries with it a very strong sense of its past use as well.

Dominique Gonzalez-Foerster Yes, because what happened to this space is in fact some kind of science fiction. A hundred years ago it's impossible to imagine that the people working there could conceive of what it would become. This shift says more than any other about the art inside the building. So I thought this was also a strong starting point. And then to imagine that there was one shift and what could be the second? And so I was imagining possible futures, something set fifty or a hundred years in the future.

Morgan I like the idea of setting a stage: that through this you can address the present but also potentially the future, that it's both fiction and reality.

Gonzalez-Foerster George Orwell's *1984* is a comment about 1948. And *The Martian Chronicles* by Ray Bradbury is about California in the 1950s. Science fiction always has this double aspect of being an opportunity to comment on the present and the future, and it's exactly this tension that is interesting. It's only possible to imagine this fiction in the present moment, so therefore it's still dominated by the present. [...]

Dominique Gonzalez-Foerster, extract from 'Interview with Jessica Morgan', in *TH. 2058* (exh.cat) (London: Tate Publishing, 2008) 165–6.

Neil Cummings and Marysia Lewandowska
Museum Futures: Distributed//2008–58

Centenary Interview 2058

Interior: The common room, Moderna Museet v3.0. A beautiful lounge, comfortable seating, local lighting, graduated windows with breathtaking views of the sea.

The Executive of Moderna v3.0, Ayan Lindquist is waiting to be interviewed in real-time from Guangzhou, in the Asian Multitude.

She is browsing screens as a face fades-up on the wall window.

Ms Chan Nihao, hej, hello! Hello is that Ayan Lindquist?

Ayan Lindquist Nihao, hello. Yes Ms Chan, this is Ayan. We are in sync.

Chan Thank you so much for finding time… you must be very busy with the centenary launch.

Lindquist It's a pleasure. We really admire your work on mid twentieth-century image ecologies. Especially your research on archival practice.

Chan Well I'm flattered. For many Asian non-market institutions, your pioneering work with long-term equity contracts has been inspirational too!

Lindquist Oh, there was a whole team of us involved… So let's begin.

Chan Ok. Just to refresh, for the centenary I'd like to archive your live-thread recall of Moderna.

Lindquist Yep, that's fine, I've enabled about 20 minutes.

Chan Ok, live. Maybe we could start with some personal history. What were you doing before you became executive at Moderna Museet v3.0?

Lindquist Well, I joined Moderna 2.0 in 2049, almost ten years ago. First as adviser to the development working group. Then as part of the governance team. I participated in the forking of Moderna 3.0 in 2'51. And was elected fixed-term executive in 2'52,… uhmm,…until today. I've got another four years in the post.

Chan And before that?

Lindquist Immediately before joining Moderna I collaborated in the exhibition programme at the MACBA cluster in Mumbai for six years. Although, more in resource provision. That's where we worked on a version of the equity bond issue you mentioned.

Chan And before that?

Lindquist In programming again at Tate in Doha for four years, particularly developing exhibitionary platforms. And even before that, I participated in research on cultural governance, for the Nordic Congress of the European Multitude for six years. I suspect exhibition agency and governance are my real strengths.

Chan Maybe we should dive into the deep-end. Could you briefly say something of why Moderna v3.0 devolved, and why was it necessary?

Lindquist As you can imagine there was a lot of consultation beforehand. It's not something we did without due diligence. For almost forty years Moderna v2.0 has explored and developed the exhibitionary form. We pioneered the production of many collaborative exhibitions, resources and assemblages.

We helped build robust public – what you prefer to term non-market cultural networks. And scaled those networks to produce our i-commons, part of the vast, glocal, Public Domain. We have continually nurtured and developed emergent art practice. Moderna can proudly, and quite rightly say that we participated in shaping the early twenty-first-century movement of art. From an exhibitionary practice based around art-artefacts, spectacle and consumption – to that of embedded co-production.

Chan Do you mean...

Lindquist Of course there are many complex factors involved... But we were agent in the shift from a heritage cultural mind-set of 'broadcast', to that of emergent, peer-to-peer meshworks. Following the logic of practice, we became an immanent institution.

Chan Could you say a ....

Lindquist Uhmm... Although having said all of that... We've not really answered your question, have we? Given that Moderna 2.0 continues its exhibitionary research, some of us believe that exhibition as a technology, and immanence as an institutional logic needed to be subject to radical revision. So this is what we intend to explore with Moderna 3.0, we want to execute some of the research. To enact. To be more agent than immanent.

Neil Cummings and Marysia Lewandowska, 'Museum Futures: Distributed' (Stockholm: Moderna Museet, 2008–58). Available at https://vimeo.com/54359801

Dawn Chan
Tomorrow Never Dies: Asia-Futurism//2016

[...] In 1986, describing the United States, Jean Baudrillard touched on what the country was not: Japan. Specifically, a Japan that had managed 'an unintelligible paradox, to transform the power of territoriality and feudalism into that of deterritoriality and weightlessness'. 'Japan', he continued, 'is already a satellite of the planet Earth.' Taking up where he left off, David Morley and Kevin Robins laid out an articulation of techno-orientalism a few years later, observing that Japan's path to modernisation had become a crucial aspect of its exoticised image as an Oriental other, an image construed to reflect the same Western anxieties that drove the historical violence of colonialism, racism and exclusion. Yet even as their words set the stage for many a conversation about the formation and transformation of Asian identity through the channels of diaspora and distance, ever-newer avatars of techno-orientalism continue to be reflected in both high art and low culture. [...]

As the worldwide preoccupation in the 1980s with Japan's unassailably ascendant technological dominance has given way to worldwide consternation over the still unfolding effects of neoliberal globalisation on an array of Pacific Rim nations, the idea that East Asian countries have any exceptional claim to futurity has grown more complex. But if the nuances of techno-orientalism evolve with the times, visions of Asia-futurism continue to be mirrored, magnified and distorted in the Western world toward complicated ends, with complicated effects on both contemporary art production and an already troubled construction of Asian American identity.

[...] Putting aside the more prominent discussions around the mass media's outright erasure of actors of colour (exemplified by Scarlett Johansson's casting as the protagonist of the upcoming *Ghost in the Shell* remake), the TV narratives that consistently cast Asian actors are still primarily science fiction and fantasy. When real Asian Americans – by which I mean people and not stereotypes – appear in media, we do so in the future, but not the present; in alternate realities, but not this one. As underscored by many critics of techno-orientalism, Joss Whedon's early-naughties cult television show *Firefly* imagined a world in which China and the US had evolved into one empire, with not a single Asian actor in a major role. Whedon's more recent portrayal of a sci-fi universe – the ongoing (and highly entertaining) *Agents of S.H.I.E.L.D.* – demonstrates some progress: it includes a Chinese American actress and another of mixed-race Chinese heritage as leads. The latter character turns out to be a sort of special egg: a member of the Inhumans, a genetically advanced race whose full powers must be triggered by the Terrigen Mists. She is someone who is [...] awaiting Life, Phase Two. At the most recent Association for Asian American Studies conference, critic and curator Ryan Lee Wong noted a renewed interest in such Asian colossi as *Pacific Rim* (2013) and *Godzilla* (2014): 'Nowhere, in these depictions, is there agency on the part of the Asian characters.' Wong has spoken about an Asia-futurism that draws inspiration from Afrofuturism. How? Perhaps the agency he invokes is key: if Afrofuturist thinkers have created speculative realms of their own accord, carving out counterfactual worlds that might cast the shortcomings of our current one in high relief, might there be analogous ways for Asian artists to recast techno-clichéd trappings toward more generative ends?

Two ongoing projects come to mind. Last year, the Japanese collective Chim↑Pom staged 'Don't Follow the Wind', a group exhibition in Fukushima, Japan, home of the 2011 nuclear-reactor disaster. Three years before that, the Ho Chi Minh City – and Los Angeles – based Propeller Group began *The History of the Future*. To call either of these endeavours 'ongoing' is an understatement; they are literally impossible to experience until the present draws to a close. Chim↑Pom's exhibition comprises a selection of works by artists that the group has secreted away within the perimeter of the radioactive Fukushima zone. Meanwhile, the Propeller Group has buried a wooden version of a Star Trek phaser rifle – intricately carved using old Vietnamese techniques – in a location whose GPS coordinates will be disclosed only in 2112. Both projects investigate the dark underbelly of technology – its environmental fallout, its military applications. But they also work toward more subversive ends: Rather than merely delivering visions of othered, futured Asian lives for a present-day global audience, they perform an exclusion that, when viewed from the West, thumbs its nose at the systemic erasure of Asian faces in non-Asian narratives. Here, no one is allowed in.

While projects like these might loosen 'the grip social reality holds' over techno-orientalist clichés, and '[free] them from their fate' (to appropriate the words of Paul Chan on the power of art), it would be unfair to expect all Asian artists, on an individual level, to make work that explicitly counters problematic perceptions of Asian technofutures once it reaches Western shores. But what if curatorially driven endeavours could be asked to carry more of the burden, given their larger scale and more direct dealings with inclusion and exclusion? Indeed, much is made of the international art festival as a method of decentring and recentring our preconceived notions of identity, and in recent years, a critical mass of Asia-based biennials, triennials, and art festivals have adopted themes that embrace a future tense, or at least an atelic one – all while (thankfully) placing artists from their regions in ever-greater focus.

The most recent Yokohama Triennale came with a title, 'Art Fahrenheit 451: Sailing into the Sea of Oblivion', which referred to an oppressive fictional world and then evoked a poetically speculative end. It found opportunities to subvert high-tech tropes, as with Yuko Mohri's lo-fi machine apparatuses or Shinro Ohtake's riotous trash-art-mobiles. Meanwhile, the forthcoming Gwangju Biennale promises to explore art's 'projective and imaginative qualities – art's active relationship to the future'. And the 'Shanghai Project', curated by Hans Ulrich Obrist and Yongwoo Lee, literalises its interest in the next century: Its title, '2116', refers to the year when 76% of the cosmopolitan Chinese port city is projected to be subsumed by rising sea levels. It's as if these art exhibitions work to refute Baudrillard's depiction of Asia as a distant satellite of Earth. Remember, they murmur: Asia is Earth, too.

But what of Asian people living elsewhere? Biennials and art festivals are still inherently responding to place, whether by embracing or explicitly subverting it. And so, too, Asia-futurism itself: How often do its narratives relish the landscape and texture of a specific (if imagined) metropolis as much as the inner lives of its inhabitants? In contrast, many scholars have noted that the Asian American experience continues to grapple with the unease that comes with sitelessness and the ongoing threat of encountering the phrase *go home* – a partial inheritance of a history of immigration bans, internment camps and indentured servitude in America's not-so-distant past.

The relative invisibility of Asian people in America often seems refracted throughout international contemporary art exhibitions. Take, for example, the many Asian artists featured in 'All the World's Futures' at the most recent Venice Biennale (or in the past several hundred solo shows staged in New York's major museums, for that matter). Only a handful of these artists have permanent roots in the US. America, as a geographic place, is certainly a necessary component of Asian American identity. But it's hardly sufficient. For all the recuperative potential behind these recent biennials – for their power to rework clichés and to position futuristic constructions of Asian identity as original vantage points rather than responses to Western fears – many of these exhibitions nonetheless have situatedness as an inherent point of departure. As a result, there remains a disconnect between the reparative dialogue they may stimulate, on the one hand, and the sitelessness of Asian American communities, on the other. Curators and artists may be fruitfully labouring to reposition Asia as a true part of planet Earth. But here, perhaps it's me and my diasporated cohorts in the US who are satellites, unmoored from the Asia our predecessors left behind. And maybe this has something to do with the reason I leave most art shows still looking for my own face in the present.

Dawn Chan, extracts from 'Tomorrow Never Dies: Asia-Futurism', *Artforum*, vol. 54, no. 10 (June 2016) 161–2.

Ana Teixeira Pinto
Alien Nations//2019

In recent years a preoccupation with the future, or lack thereof, gave rise to a great many claims that the future was stolen, stalled, or otherwise evacuated – hence must be reclaimed. Departing from what one could call reformist or reactionary forms of progressivism, a great many artists have been reclaiming the term 'futurism', in order to make plain the future was never evenly distributed.

Instead of putting forth an image of the future as a blank canvas upon which alternate visions can be projected, these futurisms are chronopolitical acts that seek to rearticulate the relation of time to technology, and of technology to the underprivileged. Unlike the original Futurists, present-day futurisms are not triumphalist. Rather, they express disenchantment with the declining valence of futurity, and with the invariance of technology. [...]

Italian Futurism

The experience of industrialisation [in the late nineteenth and early twentieth century] was an experience of shock, to both the social and the individual body. The fear of mutilation and physical trauma was directly responsible for a wide plethora of pathologies, some of which were codified in political terms, finding their metaphorical expression in the armoured drill formations of a military phalanx – a cipher for the fascist superbody.

A lot has been written about the Futurist triangulation of technology, potency, and masculinity.[1] But there is another aspect to this fascist superbody that is often overlooked: the fantasy of an indestructible, hyper-muscular body that was already in existence in the colonial imaginary. It was exactly the way slavers and settlers imagined the black body to be – a body that cannot be broken, that is sturdy, muscled, and able to withstand inhuman treatment. Futurist technophilia both reveals and conceals a colonial relation, mobilising the hardness of iron and steel to displace and erase the hardness of black muscle.[2] By conflating the fluid factory sewage that he involuntarily gulps down with the nurturing breast milk of his Sudanese wet nurse ('Oh, maternal ditch, half full of muddy water! A factory gutter! I savoured a mouthful of strengthening muck which recalled the black teat of my Sudanese nurse!') [Filippo Tommaso] Marinetti also replaces the image of Africa as the locus of resource extraction with the fantasy of technogenesis and the worship of self-reproducing masculinity, freed from labour and social history.

Needless to say, fascism and racism exist on a continuum, an imperial Möbius strip whose two-sidedness is but an optical illusion. As Aimé Césaire argued, what in Europe is called 'Nazism' was just colonial violence finding its way back home – 'before they were its victims, white Europeans were its accomplices' – diverting their gaze while it was inflicted on non-Europeans all over the world, from the Putumayo region in Peru to the Congo Free State, from the Herero and Namaqua genocide and the extinction of Tasmanian Aborigines to the Trail of Tears.[3]

There is also a hidden racial dimension to the codification of technology as a forward, unidirectional motion. Though the Futurists were not alone in their investment in the redeeming dimension of the technological, allegedly able to overcome the human, the alignment of technology and futurity constitutes a form of chronopolitics most often deployed to condemn 'the disempowered to live in the past.'[4]

Afrofuturism

Africa, in the colonial imaginary, represents a stage of civilisation already superseded in the West – no two concepts would have seemed further apart than 'Africa' and 'futurism' for Marinetti and his followers.

This is why Afrofuturism, as Mark Fisher notes, has always been charged with a dual task: first, to decolonise technology by decoupling it from narratives of white modernity that 'positioned Africa as origin, at the furthest remove from the terminus of history', and second, to subvert the Malthusian dimension of modern temporality, whose apocalyptical ethos claims that the demise of Western civilisation is imminent, that the end is nigh.[5]

The term 'Afrofuturism', a portmanteau of 'Afro' (as in 'of Africa') and 'futurism', is usually attributed to Mark Dery, from an interview with Samuel R. Delany, Greg Tate and Tricia Rose in a 1993 issue of the *South Atlantic Quarterly*.[6] But the previous year Mark Sinker had already described the specificity of black science fiction in his seminal article 'Loving the Alien: In Advance of the Landing', published in the British experimental music magazine *The Wire*. In contradistinction to white eschatology, 'the central fact in Black Science Fiction', Sinker argued, 'is an acknowledgement that Apocalypse already happened.' For those who, after being abducted, survived the traumatic transatlantic voyage in the hulls of the slave ships to be sold to work on plantations, mines, or the construction industry, 'Armageddon has been in effect.'[7]

The boundary between science fiction and social reality, as Donna Haraway noted, is observer-dependent. A great many sci-fi scenarios describe, in a realistic yet non-naturalistic fashion, the real lived experience of Afro-diasporic subjects.[8] Alien abduction – to be secretly kidnapped by non-human beings in possession of superior technology, for the purpose of intrusive medical examinations, usually of a sexual nature, and with a focus on the reproductive system – is a cipher for the plight of the enslaved, and the social reproduction of bodies as units of labour power. Science fiction became the central literary vehicle for the articulation of Afrofuturism because, as Greg Tate maintains, the very conventions of the genre 'focus on someone who is at odds with the apparatus of power in society and whose profound experience is one of cultural dislocation, alienation and estrangement [...] and that pretty much sums up the mass experiences of black people in the post-slavery twentieth century.'[9]

To this day, African Americans are the subject of mass incarceration and over-policing, daily micro-aggressions and institutional racism, which lead to what W.E.B. Du Bois termed the 'peculiar sensation' of double consciousness, the 'sense of always looking at one's self through the eyes of others', of having two different identities, hard to reconcile, 'American' and 'Negro'.[10] Kodwo Eshun, a crucial author in the theorisation of Afrofuturism, traces his conceptualisation of the alien as a fictional motif to an interview between Toni Morrison and Paul Gilroy, published in the 1991 anthology *Small Acts*. According to Eshun, Morrison argued that the enslaved Africans, who 'experienced capture, theft, abduction, mutilation and slavery were the first moderns [because] they underwent real conditions of existential homelessness, alienation, dislocation, and dehumanisation that philosophers like Nietzsche would later define as quintessentially modern'.[11] Modernity, rather than enabling a civilising project, instituted a de-civilising void, which began with the Middle Passage and slowly seeped into every corner and crevice of the colonial empires.

The science fiction writers associated with Afrofuturism, like Samuel R. Delany and Octavia Butler, write about the worlds that emerge from the dehumanising motions of the Atlantic trade and the 'modalities of identity without hope of resolution' they engender.[12]

Paraphrasing Richard Wright, one could say that black sci-fi writers didn't need to invent the horror genre, because rather the horror of the Afro-diasporic experience invented them. The slave-space-ships 'landed long ago', as Sinker writes, and the inhuman beings they carried 'already laid waste to whole societies, abducted and genetically altered swathes of citizenry, imposed without surcease their values'. In the whirlwind the triangular trade unleashed, 'Africa and America – and so by extension Europe and Asia – are already in their various ways Alien Nation.'[13]

Homecoming, a literary trope usually steeped in sentimentality, acquires an unsettling tone with Afrofuturism. What home is there to return to when 'race and nation and neighbourhood and family are none of them enough to obviate betrayal?'[14] The Detroit-based electronic music duo Drexciya fictionalised an underwater world – the Black Atlantis – populated by the descendants of the pregnant women routinely thrown overboard by slavers, midway across the ocean, for being too disruptive. Their unborn babies, known as the Drexciya, somehow develop the ability to breathe liquid oxygen and thrive in the deep seas, evolving a secret African technology. In the video essay *Hydra Decapita* (2010) the Otolith Group (Kodwo Eshun and Anjalika Sagar) place the Drexciya and the slave ships they originate from at the heart of the capitalist enterprise, as a cipher for the accumulation of death and for the figuration of survival, which inevitably takes a posthuman form.

How could it not when humanism (that is, the white man's burden) and savagery are so intimately tied? Eshun's contribution was also crucial for articulating the link between posthumanism and the 'Black Atlantic', putting forth the argument that humanity is not something to be attained, but something to be overcome, since the experience of the enslaved – as the subject who is forced to share the fate of the object – bankrupts the very notion of 'humanity'.[15] Sun Ra, the experimental composer credited as the father of Afrofuturism, used to say he came from Saturn.

In her performance-lecture *Afrogalactica: A Brief History of the Future*, the Franco-Canadian artist Kapwani Kiwanga revisits *Space Is the Place*, the 1972–4 science fiction film written by Sun Ra. Examining an enigmatic scene in which Sun Ra wagers the future of the black race in a game of cards he plays against a character called the Overseer, Kiwanga points to the symbolic confrontation between two incommensurable worldviews: the Overseer draws a card with a picture of a luxury vehicle, the 'foremost symbol of material gain in twentieth-century America', and in response Sun Ra holds up a card featuring a flying saucer, with the word 'Judgment' underneath. Whereas for the pimp-like character, salvation can only be attained via inclusion in the marketplace (hence urging black folk to rise from their community rather than with it), Sun Ra aims to resettle black life on a new planet, via the sonic transportation medium. The flying saucer, in Kiwanga's view, is the space-age iteration of a recurring motif in the Afro-American imaginary, the 'celestial chariot', which she traces back to the spiritual song written by Wallace Willis circa 1862, 'Swing Low, Sweet Chariot', describing an angel-sent ship 'coming for to carry me home.' The ever-present image of evasion acquires here a twofold dimension, conjuring at once the Underground Railroad (a network of secret routes used by African Americans to escape the slave states of the South) and the transcendental realm of sonic sanctuary, a soundscape able to comfort and assuage hurt, fear and hunger.

The earlier film *The Last Angel of History* (1995), by the Black Audio Film Collective's John Akomfrah, opens with a story about a bluesman from the 1930s named Robert Johnson, who was said to have sold his soul to the devil at a crossroads in the Deep South. In return for his soul, Johnson was given the secret of a black technology now known as the blues – the same technology that later begat jazz, soul, hip-hop, R&B and, by extension, Sun Ra, Lee 'Scratch' Perry, Public Enemy, Jimi Hendrix, George Clinton, Afrika Bambaataa, Ishmael Reed, and Earth, Wind and Fire. Two hundred years into the future a data thief is charged with the task of re-finding the crossroads and collecting the techno-fossils buried there.

Put together, these elements yield a code, the key to an Afro-future. But the data thief only has one clue, the phrase 'mothership connection'. Syncretism, sampling, and assemblage emerge, here, as the fundamental operations for the constituting and reconstituting of an orphaned and dispersed culture, and by extension for reconstituting a social history burdened by centuries of hardship and abuse. But these operations also 'unravel any linear model of the future', complicating unidirectional schemas. 'Time in Afrofuturism is plastic, stretchable and prophetic', forked into the distant past (ancient Egypt, Dogon cosmology) and the near future. Voiding vulgar Hegelianisms and chauvinistic chronologies[16], Afrofuturist temporality conjures a counter-history, which, at its most ambitious, is rather more than just a style, artistic genre, or aesthetic movement. The collective Black Quantum Futurists challenge the 'regularly lived experiences of cancelled futures' via the articulation of imaginary counter-futurisms.[17] Luanda-based artist Kiluanji Kia Henda's *Icarus 13: The First Journey to the Sun* (2008) fictionalises a space mission to the sun via a *détournement* of the country's unfulfilled history – choosing the sun as destination rather than the Moon or Mars, Henda abstains from emulating the space race, and its frontier narratives, gesturing towards the allegorical instead. In her critique of accelerationism, 'Notes on Blacceleration' (2017), artist Aria Dean argues that the only subject able to transverse the human-capital binary, as well as the only subject plastic enough to be able to ride out the infinite plasticity of racial capitalism in order to become 'the agent of the world's demise and its inheritor', is the black non-subject.[18]

In her 2016 exhibition at The Kitchen, 'Resident Evil', artist Sondra Perry thematised this subject, wholly disengaged from the attachment to fantasies of the good, respectable life – with its promises of upward mobility, job security, income parity, and durable intimacy – that typically oppresses her.[19] Perry's nihilism, for want of a better word, is a militant nihilism, which stands in stark contrast to what art historian Larne Abse Gogarty aptly refers to as the aspirational nihilism of market-besotted post-internet art.[20]

It is perhaps here that certain elements of Afrofuturism intersect with Afropessimism, in the sense that Afropessimism sustains that undoing white supremacy would mean dismantling the vast majority of the systems, structures and institutions that have informed social life since the dawn of modernity. But blackness, rather than designating a racialised subject, can also emerge as a political concept. Once the conditions of depredation, dispossession and social death that formerly defined the black condition are universalised, creating a global underclass of disposable and fungible people, it becomes manifest that 'the planet, already turned Black'.[21] It is this generalisation of structural violence, enforced uprooting, arbitrary rule, pauperisation, social alienation and political disfranchisement that Achille Mbembe refers to as planetary apartheid.[22] Blackness, here, does not necessitate black skin in order to be inscribed into the world as nothing but effacement and erasure – hence the overlap with Sinofuturism.

Sinofuturism

'Our best machines are made of sunshine', Donna Haraway wrote in one of the most famous passages of her 'Cyborg Manifesto', 'all light and clean because they are nothing but signals, electromagnetic waves, a section of a spectrum.'[23] For artist Lawrence Lek, our machines are made not of sunshine but of finely congealed Chinese lives. In his video-essay *Sinofuturism* (1839–2046 AD), Lek describes Sinofuturism not as a concept or movement but as 'a spectre already embedded into a trillion industrial products, a billion individuals, and a million veiled narratives'.[24]

At present, the survival of industrial capitalism hinges on the cheap, non-unionised labour the Chinese Communist Party provides for outsourced industries, whose low-cost products, in turn, meet the declining purchasing power of an increasingly impoverished Western working class. But these workers' lives only become visible via their own effacement, as labour ground into sneakers and smartphones. Sinofuturism is, according to Lek's eponymous video essay, a movement composed of 'multiple overlapping flows. Flows of populations, of products, and of processes (which) is often mistaken for contemporary China.'

In most East Asian countries, where, to paraphrase curator Hyunjin Kim, the process of rapid urbanisation and modernisation was perceived as synonymous with Westernisation, technology could be seen as the site of a double alienation, via the introduction of the new and the foreign.[25] In China, under the leadership of Deng Xiaoping, industry undertook a process of acceleration in order to 'synchronise' the country with the West. Technological development – which as philosopher Yuk Hui notes is the 'source of synchronisation of the global time axis since the beginning of globalisation' – came to constitute 'a past the Chinese never lived' but whose unfettered power has nonetheless progressed at a much more tremendous pace than in the West.[26]

In Ho Rui An's lecture-performance *Dash* (2017), the frictions between these competing temporalities are represented as a full-frontal collision between a venture capitalist's sports car and a humble taxi. Captured on a dash-cam and later uploaded to YouTube, the footage of the accident becomes a cipher for the imbrications of frontier narratives and financial eschatology. As the artist shows a sequence of dash-cam-captured car crashes (uncannily similar to Hollywood's car chase scenes) the dashboard emerges as a signifier for a god's-eye view – he who, surviving the crash, drives on toward the vanishing horizon – while speed is codified as an upward motion, leading to the future. Standing at the intersection between traditional ways of life and cyber-modulated social milieus, Singapore itself appears as a liminal space, within which time is infrastructured as finance.

Ho Rui An does not use the term 'futurism', and since Sinofuturism lacks a defined status as an artistic genre, his inclusion here is somewhat arbitrary. That said, I cannot help but also mention Jung Yoonsuk's two-channel video installation *Lash* (2017), which contrasts the gritty surroundings and arduous toil at a sex doll manufacturing facility with the glossy, seamless product this labour yields.

The gendering of technology is, here, a central theme in a double articulation of difference: sexual difference and machinic difference. In spite of the feminist appropriation of the cyborg-like body as a de-gendering machine, the cyborg became a reactionary figure that renders the female pliable to male desire, and, by extension, devaluation, while sex is a commodity whose accumulation enhances male status. Not incidentally, the word 'robot', introduced by Karel Čapek in his 1921 sci-fi *R.U.R.* (Rossum's Universal Robots), comes from *robota*, which literally means 'serf labour' (forced or unfree labour) in Czech. Tellingly, Čapek's robots are not mechanical automata, but rather artificial biological organisms.

Gulf Futurism

Slave-like labour – as Richard Barbrook and Andy Cameron sustained in their prescient 1995 essay 'The Californian Ideology' – cannot be obtained without somebody being enslaved.[27] In October

2017, at the Future Investment Initiative, Saudi Arabia granted citizenship to a humanoid robot named Sophia, while the country remains infamous for its abuse of migrant labourers, whose legal status is similar to indentured serfs.

Gulf Futurism, a term usually used in reference to the work of artists Fatima Al Qadiri and Sophia Al-Maria, thematises the vectors of mobility and immobility that regiment life in the Gulf states.

Contrasting the dizzying speed of information highways and financial flows with the restricted movements migrants are afforded and the idle, indoor lifestyle of the citizenry, Gulf Futurism combines a socially reactionary ideology with a forward, speculative thrust the artists describe as the 'space race for skyscrapers'. Here, verticality (of wealth, of privilege) and horizontality (of labour flows, of evacuated futures) constitute two interdependent yet wholly disconnected socioeconomic worlds, whilst capital itself appears as an alien, voracious life form.

The Gulf region could be construed as the apex of what China Miéville called 'a politico-geo-transformative agenda to make our entire planet, including at the semiotic level, the most fecund biome possible for capital'.[28] But the future that is here accumulated as capital is, quite literally, siphoned off from elsewhere – from a planet that is running out of it.

If anything defined the modern era, it was the belief that the future would be different from the past. But this forward-looking temporality was predicated on two conflicting and often antithetical motions: a view of the present as a 'time of transition' during which epoch-making decisions could be made in order for alternate futures to be attained; and the synchronisation, and by extension acceleration, of the pace of development on a global scale. As the latter snuffed out the former, alternate futures became hard to envisage and even harder to sustain.

Afrofuturism, arguably the most important aesthetic movement of the postmodern era, emerged at a junction of political and allegorical inversions, after utopias and liberation movements were laid waste. Present-day futurisms are not so much futurisms as a means to contest the synchronisation of temporalities via financial and informational technologies. At their strongest they are counter-futurisms, sites of chrono-political antagonism and semiotic struggle. At worst they are regressive and mimetic, concerned not so much with what technology will do to the future as with what the future will do to the human. But their common threads – a preoccupation with labour, validation and epistemic dispossession – point to a shared recognition that, to quote Evan Calder Williams in the guise of a conclusion, 'nothing clearly marks a passage into the future without undoing the forms that bind lives, materials and systems, in variably punitive ways, to a mode of time designed around the continuity of the present'.[29] Even when this present comes with added war-zone filter.[30]

1 For a detailed discussion see Giovanna Zapperi, 'Du Surhomme au non-homme', in *La fabrique du corps humain: la machine modèle du vivant*, eds. V. Adam and A. Caiozzo (Grenoble: CNRS-MSH-Alpes, 2010).

2 See Olivier Marboeuf 's interview with Kader Attia in Kader Attia's film, *The Postcolonial Body* (2018).

3 Aimé Césaire, *Discourse on Colonialism*, trans. Joan Pinkham (New York and London: Monthly Review Press, 1972) 3.

4 Kodwo Eshun, 'Further Considerations on Afrofuturism', *New Centennial Review*, vol. 3, no. 2 (Summer 2003) 289.

5 Mark Fisher, 'Afrofuturism and Hauntology', *Dancecult: Journal of Electronic Dance Music Culture*, vol. 5, no. 2 (2013).

6 Mark Dery, 'Black to the Future: Interviews with Samuel R. Delany, Greg Tate, and Tricia Rose', *South Atlantic Quarterly*, no. 92 (1993) 559, and *Dancecult: Journal of Electronic Dance Culture* vol. 5, no. 2 (2013).

7 Public Enemy quoted by Mark Sinker, in 'Loving the Alien: In Advance of the Landing', *The Wire* (February 1992). See also Mark Bould, 'The Ships Landed Long Ago: Afrofuturism and Black SF', *Science Fiction Studies* vol. 34, no. 2, (July 2007) 177–86.

8 Afrofuturism is mostly a product of the African diaspora, and has been at times accused of being Anglo-centric.

9 Quoted in 'Further Considerations on Afrofuturism', op. cit., 298.

10 W.E.B. Du Bois, *The Souls of Black Folk* (Chicago: A. C. McClurg, 1903) 2.

11 'Further Considerations on Afrofuturism', op. cit., 288.

12 'Loving the Alien', op. cit.

13 Ibid.

14 Ibid.

15 Achille Mbembe, 'Afrofuturisme et devenir-nègre du monde', *Politique africaine*, vol. 4, no. 136 (2014) 121–33.

16 'Afrofuturism and Hauntology', op. cit., 46.

17 Jussi Parikka, 'Middle East and Other Futurisms: Imaginary Temporalities in Contemporary Art and Visual Culture', *Culture, Theory and Critique*, vol. 59, no. 1 (2018) 46.

18 Aria Dean, 'Notes on Blacceleration', *e-flux*, no. 87 (2017) (https://www.eflux/journal/87/169402/notes-on-blacceleration/).

19 See Lauren Berlant, *Cruel Optimism* (Durham, NC: Duke University Press, 2011).

20 Larne Abse Gogarty, in a recent conference at the BAK, Utrecht.

21 'Loving the Alien', op. cit.

22 Achille Mbembe, 'Afrofuturisme et devenir-nègre du monde.'

23 Donna J. Haraway, 'A Manifesto for Cyborgs', in *The Haraway Reader* (Abingdon: Routledge, 2003) 12.

24 See https://vimeo.com/179509486.

25 Hyunjin Kim, *A Thousand Asian Tigers* (exh. cat) (Berlin: HKW, 2017), published for the exhibition '2 or 3 Tigers', HKW Berlin, 2017 (https://hkw.de/en/tigers_publication/).

26 Yuk Hui, *The Question Concerning Technology in China* (Falmouth: Urbanomic, 2016) 292.

27 Richard Barbrook and Andy Cameron, 'The Californian Ideology', *Mute*, no. 3 (Autumn 1995).

28 China Miéville quoted in 'Middle East and Other Futurisms', op. cit., 48.

29 Evan Calder Williams, 'Volcano, Waiting', *WdW Review*, (June 2017) (http://www.wdw.nl/en/review/sediments/volcano_waiting).

30 Marina Vishmidt, *Accumulating Futures*, eds. Sven Lütticken and Eric de Bruyn (Berlin: Sternberg, forthcoming).

Ana Teixeira Pinto, extracts from 'Alien Nations', *Mousse*, no. 64 (2019) 166–75.

Jamie Sutcliffe
Letter from Honshu: Asia-Futurism//2017

[...] A mechanical colossus stands guard over Tokyo Bay. Glimpsed against a backdrop of glittering high-rise city blocks, the 1:1 scale statue of Mobile Suit Gundam (Japan's fictional space-travelling robotic icon) is a daunting sight in the early evening light, its visor defiantly reflecting the expansive waters of the greater Pacific. I had journeyed to see this monumental work of public art on the recommendation of Tokyo-based artist Catherine Harrington, and certainly wasn't prepared for the composite of nested complexities it embodied. Located atop the concrete plaza-scape of Odaiba – one of many islands erected in the mid nineteenth century to defend Edo against foreign intruders – the modular body of this fantastic entity spoke not only of the military capacity and aspiration for space travel that had been complicated for Japan by the restrictions of a post-war constitution forged in 1947, but also the common tendency for Japanese pop-cultural exports to blur amid the assumptions and anxieties of what critic Toshiya Ueno has termed the techno-orientalist imagination. To this day, western cultural expectations continue to figure Japan as a strange hybrid of mysterious traditions and hyper-technological modernity, often reductively re-inscribing the teleological horizon of technological progress in some hazily imagined pan-Asian future – a presumption I found myself all too guilty of as I ambled around the statue's feet, trying to capture an atmospheric photograph of Mount Fuji receding behind the pulsing megalopolis.

In her great essay 'Tomorrow Never Dies', curator Dawn Chan outlines the difficulties of what might be termed 'Asia-futurism', and the ways that a myth of an Asia hard-wired for futurity and underscored by images of 'cities in hyperdrive and sleep-deprived gamers' might feed negative representations back into Japanese conceptions of the self. Chan notes Jean Baudrillard's poorly phrased extra-terrestrial analogy that an accelerated transition to modernity had led the country to transform the power of feudalism into weightlessness, thus turning itself into 'a satellite of the planet Earth', before suggesting that Asia-futurism might reclaim its agency, perhaps, by forging counterfactual worlds in which 'techno-cliché trappings' might be recast towards 'more generative ends', circumscribing locales beyond the strictures of an externally projected future.

My journey through Honshu last autumn led me to a series of exhibitions at institutions across Japan's central island that appeared to be concerned with just such explorations of futurity and speculation. Despite its comedically bland title, 'The Universe and Art' at the Mori Art Museum in the district of Roppongi, Tokyo, presented a vast and scrupulously sourced survey show that sought to explore trans-cultural interest in the cosmos.

Located on the fifty-third floor of one of Tokyo's most iconic high-rise buildings, the show's organisers need some preliminary praise for the logistical wizardry of installing an exhibition amongst the clouds, an obviously appropriate venue for such galaxy-oriented reflections. Vertiginous heights aside, the show was exhilarating for the leaps it made between ancient, religious and scientific artefacts and the work of contemporary artists. The few steps separating a finely painted Tibetan Yamantāka Mandala (seventeenth–eighteenth century) – structured to demonstrate a Buddhist cosmology of compartmentalised heavens and cloud-borne deities – from Mariko Mori's ethereal fibreglass sculpture *Ekpyrotic String II* (2014), brought centuries-old mystical teachings into relevant contact with the dynamical objects currently postulated by superstring theory. Wolfgang Tillmans' *named and unnamed galaxies, ESO* (2016), a body of work commissioned for this exhibition, documented the seemingly immeasurable labour of mapping distant star systems through the somewhat crude screen-based interfaces of astronomers based at the Paranal Observatory in Chile, unremarkable photographs that made the enormity of such exploratory endeavours visible through the indistinguishable likeness of stars to single pixels.

The strange occurrence of the 'hollow ship', an unexplained event of 1803 in which a mysterious vessel drifted ashore along the coast of Hitachi Province, lined with cryptic writings and ferrying an unidentifiable passenger, was represented here by numerous Edo-period newspaper articles and hand-drawn illustrations, a popular folk-precursor to the 'unidentified flying object'. That such anomalies may recur archetypally across cultures was the focus of works by Laurent Grasso, whose series of 'ancient aliens' employed authentic maquettes and altar-pieces-turned-evidence to hint that human religions may be the result of inter-dimensional contact. Tokyo-based collective Teamlab's *Crows Are Chased And The Chasing Crows Are Destined To Be Chased As Well, Blossoming On Collision* (2016), used admittedly impressive projection-mapped digital animations to generate an ultimately saccharine and crudely emotive vision of astral travel which fell something short of creating the same sense of wondrous possibility that could be observed in more modest proposals for kinetic audio-visual interfaces developed as part of an exciting programme for KIBO, the Japanese Experiment Module on the International Space Station, on display nearby.

Travelling north to Kanazawa, an industrial harbour city on the North Coast, I called into the 21st Century Museum, an institution whose architecturally clean lines and deep shadows mirrored the quiet composure of the DT Suzuki archive nearby. Here, a one-year project by Danish collective Superflex entitled *The Liquid State* brought raw materials such as asphalt, kombucha bacteria and even the microorganisms borne on visitors' breath into the gallery to demonstrate slow processes of collapse, cultivation and fermentation. An alleged attempt to materially elucidate the relationships a museum might have with its community, the slow, unobtrusive matter-of-factness of these resources seemed to underscore the necessity for the museum to remain a place of unquantified, understated and self-justified contemplation.

At Hiroshima MOCA, 'The World Is Strange!' brought the work of two painters-turned-graphic artists under sustained scrutiny in an inspiring show that mapped the dialogue between academic painting and formal innovation in sequential art. Tiger Tateishi (1941–1998) and Yuichi Yokoyama, both known painters but renowned comic-book artists, subvert pop-cultural tropes into a critical 'psychedoolia' that demands a pronounced patience and the willingness to learn their oddball graphic languages. In a country that treats the comic book with a fitting respect, it seemed appropriate that Yokoyama's crazy schematisations of hyper-regulated and automaton populated transit systems, and Tateishi's metamorphic cartoon entities, transcultural process comics and tech-organic vignettes were receiving such institutional validation.

Such science fictive postulations, admittedly representative of many popular Japanese comic books and animations, figure prominently in Ueno's characterisation of techno-orientalism. Indeed, it is the global popularity of these forms that he has been inclined to read as a technique of a sub-imperialism whose hegemonic power might be exerted through cultural exports as opposed to military might. And while Japan has a difficult identity historically as both a colonial aggressor *and* an occupied subject, the pressing implication for Ueno is that this exported image of technical acceleration has created a feedback loop that might deliver both an image of the Japanese as 'automated others' back into Japanese culture whilst seeding prescient fantasies of deregulated capital flow into the globalised circuitries of information capitalism – criticisms that could be levelled, at least superficially, towards both Yokoyama's and Tateishi's fantasy worlds. However, given that the idiosyncratically segued images of both artists have the tendency to draw readers into prolonged periods of near-meditative concentration, restructuring the reading experience itself with strangely disjunctive flows, unprecedented graphical vocabularies of destabilised bodies and obscure typographies, I wondered whether the necessarily timeless interstices and world-building impetus of the Asia-futurism proffered by Chan might ultimately be found somewhere within their pages, in the beguiling line work of their uncompromising cartoons.

Jamie Sutcliffe, extract from 'Letter from Honshu: Asia-futurism', *Art Monthly*, no. 403 (February 2017) 42–3. Updated by the author, 2020.

YOU HAVE ALREADY BECOME POSTHUMAN

N. Katherine Hayles, 'How We Became Posthuman', 1999

POSTHUMANISM

Donna J. Haraway
A Cyborg Manifesto//1991

An ironic dream of a common language for women in the integrated circuit

This text is an effort to build an ironic political myth faithful to feminism, socialism and materialism. Perhaps more faithful as blasphemy is faithful, than as reverent worship and identification. Blasphemy has always seemed to require taking things very seriously. I know no better stance to adopt from within the secular-religious, evangelical traditions of United States politics, including the politics of socialist feminism. Blasphemy protects one from the moral majority within, while still insisting on the need for community. Blasphemy is not apostasy. Irony is about contradictions that do not resolve into larger wholes, even dialectically, about the tension of holding incompatible things together because both or all are necessary and true. Irony is about humour and serious play. It is also a rhetorical strategy and a political method, one I would like to see more honoured within socialist-feminism. At the centre of my ironic faith, my blasphemy, is the image of the cyborg.

A cyborg is a cybernetic organism, a hybrid of machine and organism, a creature of social reality as well as a creature of fiction. Social reality is lived social relations, our most important political construction, a world-changing fiction. The international women's movements have constructed 'women's experience', as well as uncovered or discovered this crucial collective object. This experience is a fiction and fact of the most crucial, political kind. Liberation rests on the construction of the consciousness, the imaginative apprehension, of oppression, and so of possibility. The cyborg is a matter of fiction and lived experience that changes what counts as women's experience in the late twentieth century. This is a struggle over life and death, but the boundary between science fiction and social reality is an optical illusion.

Contemporary science fiction is full of cyborgs – creatures simultaneously animal and machine, who populate worlds ambiguously natural and crafted. Modern medicine is also full of cyborgs, of couplings between organism and machine, each conceived as coded devices, in an intimacy and with a power that was not generated in the history of sexuality. Cyborg 'sex' restores some of the lovely replicative baroque of ferns and invertebrates (such nice organic prophylactics against heterosexism). Cyborg replication is uncoupled from organic reproduction. Modem production seems like a dream of cyborg colonisation work, a dream that makes the nightmare of Taylorism seem idyllic. And modem war is a cyborg orgy, coded by C31, command-control-communication-intelligence, an $84 billion item in 1984's US defence budget. I am making an argument for the cyborg as a fiction mapping our social and bodily reality and as an imaginative resource suggesting some very fruitful couplings. Michael Foucault's biopolitics is a flaccid premonition of cyborg politics, a very open field.

By the late twentieth century, our time, a mythic time, we are all chimeras, theorised and fabricated hybrids of machine and organism; in short, we are cyborgs. The cyborg is our ontology; it gives us our politics. The cyborg is a condensed image of both imagination and material reality, the two joined centres structuring any possibility of historical transformation. In the traditions of 'Western' science and politics – the tradition of racist, male-dominant capitalism; the tradition of progress; the tradition of the appropriation of nature as resource for the productions of culture; the tradition of reproduction of the self from the reflections of the other – the relation between organism and machine has been a border war. The stakes in the border war have been the territories of production, reproduction and imagination. This chapter is an argument for *pleasure* in the confusion of boundaries and for *responsibility* in their construction. It is also an effort to contribute to socialist-feminist culture and theory in a postmodernist, non-naturalist mode and in the utopian tradition of imagining a world without gender, which is perhaps a world without genesis, but maybe also a world without end. The cyborg incarnation is outside salvation history. Nor does it mark time on an oedipal calendar, attempting to heal the terrible cleavages of gender in an oral symbiotic utopia or post-oedipal apocalypse. As Zoë Sofoulis argues in her unpublished manuscript on Jacques Lacan, Melanie Klein and nuclear culture, *Lacklein*, the most terrible and perhaps the most promising monsters in cyborg worlds are embodied in non-oedipal narratives with a different logic of repression, which we need to understand for our survival.

The cyborg is a creature in a post-gender world; it has no truck with bisexuality, pre-oedipal symbiosis, unalienated labour, or other seductions to organic wholeness through a final appropriation of all the powers of the parts into a higher unity. In a sense, the cyborg has no origin story in the Western sense – a 'final' irony since the cyborg is also the awful apocalyptic *telos* of the 'West's' escalating dominations of abstract individuation, an ultimate self untied at last from all dependency, a man in space. An origin story in the 'Western', humanist sense depends on the myth of original unity, fullness, bliss and terror, represented by the phallic mother from whom all humans must separate, the task of individual development and of history, the twin potent myths inscribed most powerfully for us in psychoanalysis and Marxism. Hilary Klein has argued that both Marxism and psychoanalysis, in their concepts of labour and of individuation and gender formation, depend on the plot of original unity out of which difference must be produced and enlisted in a drama of escalating domination of woman/nature. The cyborg skips the step of original unity, of identification with nature in the Western sense. This is its illegitimate promise that might lead to subversion of its teleology as Star Wars.

The cyborg is resolutely committed to partiality, irony, intimacy and perversity. It is oppositional, utopian, and completely without innocence. No longer structured by the polarity of public and private, the cyborg defines a technological polis based partly on a revolution of social relations in the *oikos*, the household. Nature and culture are reworked; the one can no longer be the resource for appropriation or incorporation by the other. The relationships for forming wholes from parts, including those of polarity and hierarchical domination, are at issue in the cyborg world. Unlike the hopes of Frankenstein's monster, the cyborg does not expect its father to save it through a restoration of the garden; that is, through the fabrication of a heterosexual mate, through its completion in a finished whole, a city and cosmos. The cyborg does not dream of community on the model of the organic family, this time without the oedipal project. The cyborg would not recognise the Garden of Eden; it is not made of mud and cannot dream of returning to dust. Perhaps that is why I want to see if cyborgs can subvert the apocalypse of returning to nuclear dust in the manic compulsion to name the Enemy. Cyborgs are not reverent; they do not re-member the cosmos. They are wary of holism, but needy for connection – they seem to have a natural feel for united front politics, but without the vanguard party. The main trouble with cyborgs, of course, is that they are the illegitimate offspring of militarism and patriarchal capitalism, not to mention state socialism. But illegitimate offspring are often exceedingly unfaithful to their origins. Their fathers, after all, are inessential. [...]

Donna J. Haraway, extract from 'A Cyborg Manifesto: Science, Technology, and Socialist-Feminism in the Late Twentieth Century', in *Simians, Cyborgs, and Women: The Reinvention of Nature* (London: Free Association Books 1991) 149–51 [footnotes omitted].

N. Katherine Hayles
How We Became Posthuman//1999

You are alone in the room, except for two computer terminals flickering in the dim light. You use the terminals to communicate with two entities in another room, whom you cannot see. Relying solely on their responses to your questions, you must decide which is the man, which the woman. Or, in another version of the famous 'imitation game' proposed by Alan Turing in his classic 1950 paper 'Computer Machinery and Intelligence', you use the responses to decide which is the human, which the machine.[1] One of the entities wants to help you guess correctly. His/her/its best strategy, Turing suggested, may be to answer your questions truthfully. The other entity wants to mislead you. He/she/it will try to reproduce through the words that appear on your terminal the characteristics of the other entity. Your job is to pose questions that can distinguish verbal performance from embodied reality. If you cannot tell the intelligent machine from the intelligent human, your failure proves, Turing argued, that machines can think.

Here, at the inaugural moment of the computer age, the erasure of embodiment is performed so that 'intelligence' becomes a property of the formal manipulation of symbols rather than enaction in the human life-world. The Turing test was to set the agenda for artificial intelligence for the next three decades. In the push to achieve machines that can think, re-performed again and again the erasure of embodiment at the heart of the Turing test. All that mattered was the formal generation and manipulation of informational patterns. Aiding this process was a definition of information, formalised by Claude Shannon and Norbert Wiener, which conceptualised information as an entity distinct from the substrates carrying it. From this formulation, it was a small step to think of information a kind of bodiless fluid that could flow between different substrates without loss of meaning or form. Writing nearly four decades after Turing, Hans Moravec proposed that human identity is essentially an informational pattern rather than an embodied enaction. The proposition can be demonstrated, he suggested, by downloading human consciousness into a computer, and he imagined a scenario designed to show that this was in principle possible. The Moravec test, if I may call it that, is the logical successor to the Turing test. Whereas the Turing test was designed to show that machines can perform the thinking previously considered to be an exclusive capacity of the human mind, the Moravec test was designed to show that machines can become the repository of human consciousness – that machines can, for all practical purposes, become human beings. You are the cyborg, and the cyborg is you.

In the progression from Turing to Moravec, the part of the Turing test that historically has been foregrounded is the distinction between thinking human and thinking machine. Often forgotten is the first example Turing offered of distinguishing between a man and a woman. If your failure to distinguish correctly between human and machine proves that machines can think, what does it prove if you fail to distinguish woman from man? Why does gender appear in this primal scene of humans meeting their evolutionary successors, intelligent machines? What do gendered bodies have to do with the erasure of embodiment and the subsequent merging of machine and human intelligence in the figure of the cyborg?

In his thoughtful and perceptive intellectual biography of Turing, Andrew Hodges suggests that Turing's predilection was always to deal with the world as if it were a formal puzzle.[2] To a remarkable extent, Hodges says, Turing was blind to the distinction between saying and doing. Turing fundamentally did not understand that 'questions involving sex, society, politics or secrets would demonstrate how what it was possible for people to *say* might be limited not by puzzle-solving intelligence but by the restrictions on what might be *done*'.[3] In a fine insight, Hodges suggests that 'the discrete state machine, communicating by teleprinter alone, was like an ideal for [Turing's] own life, in which he would be left alone in a room of his own, to deal with the outside world solely by rational argument. It was the embodiment of a perfect J.S. Mill liberal, concentrating upon the free will and free speech of the individual'.[4] Turing's later embroilment with the police and court system over the question of his homosexuality played out, in a different key, the assumptions embodied in the Turing test. His conviction and the court-ordered hormone treatments for his homosexuality tragically demonstrated the importance of *doing* over *saying* in the coercive order of a homophobic society with the power to enforce its will upon the bodies of its citizens.

The perceptiveness of Hodges' biography notwithstanding, he gives a strange interpretation of Turing's inclusion of gender in the imitation game. Gender, according to Hodges, 'was in fact a red herring, and one of the few passages of the paper that was not expressed with perfect lucidity. The whole point of this game was that a successful imitation of a woman's responses by a man would *not* prove anything. Gender depended on facts that were *not* reducible to sequences of symbols'.[5] In the paper itself, however, nowhere does Turing suggest that gender is meant as a counterexample; instead, he makes the two cases rhetorically parallel, indicating through symmetry, if nothing else, that the gender and the human/machine examples are meant to prove the same thing.

Is this simply bad writing, as Hodges argues, an inability to express an intended opposition between the construction of gender and the construction of thought? Or, on the contrary, does the writing express a parallelism too explosive and subversive for Hodges to acknowledge?

If so, now we have two mysteries instead of one. Why does Turing include gender, and why does Hodges want to read this inclusion as indicating that, so far as gender is concerned, verbal performance cannot be equated with embodied reality? One way to frame these mysteries is to see them as attempts to transgress and reinforce the boundaries of the subject, respectively. By including gender, Turing implied that renegotiating the boundary between human and machine would involve more than transforming the question of 'who can think' into 'what can think.' It would also necessarily bring into question other characteristics of the liberal subject, for it made the crucial move of distinguishing between the enacted body, present in the flesh on one side of the computer screen, and the represented body, produced through the verbal and semiotic markers constituting it in an electronic environment. This construction necessarily makes the subject into a cyborg, for the enacted and represented bodies are brought into conjunction through the technology that connects them. If you distinguish correctly which is the man and which the woman, you in effect reunite the enacted and the represented bodies into a single gender identity. The very existence of the test, however, implies that you may also make the wrong choice. Thus the test functions to create the possibility of a disjunction between the enacted and the represented bodies, regardless which choice you make. What the Turing test 'proves' is that the overlay between the enacted and the represented bodies is no longer a natural inevitability but a contingent production, mediated by a technology that has become so entwined with the production of identity that it can no longer meaningfully be separated from the human subject. To pose the question of 'what can think' inevitably also changes, in a reverse feedback loop, the terms of 'who can think.'

On this view, Hodges' reading of the gender test as non-signifying with respect to identity can be seen as an attempt to safeguard the boundaries of the subject from precisely this kind of transformation, to insist that the existence of thinking machines will not necessarily affect what being human means. That Hodges' reading is a misreading indicates he is willing to practice violence upon the text to wrench meaning away from the direction toward which the Turing test points, back to safer ground where embodiment secures the univocality of gender. I think he is wrong about embodiment's securing the univocality of gender and wrong about its securing human identity, but right about the importance of putting embodiment back into the picture. What embodiment secures is not the distinction between male and female or between humans who can think and machines that cannot. Rather, embodiment makes clear that thought is a much broader cognitive function depending for its specificities on the embodied form enacting it. This realisation, with all its exfoliating implications, is so broad in its effects and so deep in its consequences that it is transforming the liberal subject, regarded as the model of the human since the Enlightenment, into the posthuman.

Think of the Turing test as a magic trick. Like all good magic tricks, the test relies on getting you to accept at an early stage assumptions that will determine how you interpret what you see later. The important intervention comes not when you try to determine which is the man, the woman, or the machine. Rather, the important intervention comes much earlier, when the test puts you into a cybernetic circuit that splices your will, desire, and perception into a distributed cognitive system in which represented bodies are joined with enacted bodies through mutating and flexible machine interfaces. As you gaze at the flickering signifiers scrolling down the computer screens, no matter what identifications you assign to the embodied entities that you cannot see, you have already become posthuman. [...]

1 Alan M. Turing, 'Computing Machinery and Intelligence', *Mind*, vol. 54 (1950) 433–57.

2 Andrew Hodges, *Alan Turing: The Enigma of Intelligence* (London: Unwin, 1985) 415–25. I am indebted to Carol Wald for her insights into the relation between gender and artificial intelligence, the subject of her dissertation, and to her other writings on this question. I also owe her thanks for pointing out to me that Andrew Hodges dismisses Turing's use of gender as a logical flaw in his analysis of the Turing text. Andrew Hodges, *Alan Turing – the Enigma* (Princeton, NJ and Oxford: Princeton University Press, 2014).

3 Ibid., 423–4.

4 Ibid., 425.

5 Ibid., 415.

N. Katherine Hayles, extract from 'Prologue', in *How We Became Posthuman: Virtual Bodies in Cybernetics, Literature, and Informatics* (Chicago and London: University of Chicago Press, 1999) xi–xiv.

Rosi Braidotti

Metamorphic Others and Nomadic Subjects//2015

We are not all humans, or not human to the same degree, not if by 'human' you mean to refer to the dominant vision of the Subject as white, male, heterosexual, urbanised, able-bodied, speaking a standard language and taking charge of the women and the children. Many of us belong to other, more marginalised categories or groups: non-white, non-male, non-heterosexual, not urbanised, not able-bodied, not speaking a standard language, not in charge of the women and the children. The world itself is not human, but teems with organisms and life forms parallel to but distinct from our species. Those who are other-than-human, or otherwise human, cannot claim full allegiance to the dominant vision of the human subject: their belonging is negotiable at best.

The 'others' are structured with distressing regularity along the axes of devalorised difference. They are the sexualised others: women and LBGT's; the racialised others: natives, postcolonials and non-Europeans; the naturalised or earth others: animals, insects, plants and the planet; and the technological others: machines and their interactive networks.

The dominant subject, on his part, is haunted by his structural 'others', because they are necessary to his self-representation, albeit by negation. They are the complement to that subject, who constructs himself as much through what he excludes, as through what he includes in his sense of himself, his agency and his entitlements. The devalued 'others' constitute therefore the specular counterparts of the subject: different from him, they are valued less than him. Difference in this respect is indexed negatively on that standard definition of the human subject: normality is the zero-degree of difference.

Given the structural importance of these 'others' as props that confirm the 'same' in his dominant subject-position, their sheer existence is a source of perennial anxiety because it illuminates the complex and dissymetrical power-relations at work in the constitution of the dominant subject-position. Because this system of difference-as-pejoration fulfils a structural and constitutive function in subject formation processes, it also occupies a strategic position, as it has the power to challenge the very foundations of the self-other relationship.

[...] The sexualised, racialised, naturalised and nowadays even technologically mediated others draw their creative but also disruptive force precisely from the fact that they embody and express the view of those pejorative and yet structurally necessary 'others' who constitute the boundary-markers of the dominant vision of the subject. In the subversive mode, they constitute both the symptom of the crisis of dominant subjectivity and the expression of altogether new subject-positions. The 'others' may well be a fundamental resource for the dominant subject, but they are also a constant challenge.

Beyond Metaphors

The bodies and lives of 'others' have historically been made available to the dominant subject and hence become disposable, mainly in terms of physical and social exploitation. Just think of the oppression of women and LGBT's, of colonial domination and the depletion of the earth resources. Their disposable status, however, also contains more symbolic dimension: the others are a site of preferred fantasy and imaginary projection and as such they are easily metaphorised as the objects of the dominant subject's desire, or wishes. Familiarity with these others is a relationship uncomfortably ridden with hierarchical power relations: women and LGBT's, natives and animals and mechanic or technological devices can become objects of both fascination and aberration. In other words, they function as metamorphic others, reflecting the dominant subject's own concerns and anxieties. We humans identify with them, out of fear or fascination.

The sexualised, racialised, naturalised and technological others, while being socially marginalised, are also living metaphors, referents for alternative symbolic values and meanings, highly iconic emblems within language and culture. Being feminised, racialised or animalised are patterns of pejoration of the human subjects that tend to be coded negatively both morally and emotionally: they express decreasing degrees of being-human. [...] Metaphorisation of the devalorised others expresses the ontological violence of the dominant subject.

The reason why the 'others' play such a role in the social imaginary is that they offer sites of formation of negative counter-subjectivities; they provide privileged negative mirror images, often expressed in terms of monstrous and alien others. A kind of 'Gothic' imagery is associated with the metaphorised, devalued others, expressing again that structural ambivalence of repulsion and attraction. In the eyes of the dominant subject, the boundaries of the others are porous and fluid, not fixed socio-symbolically into robust structures of selfhood. [...]

As a result, the axes of sexualisation, racialisation, naturalisation and technological mediations very often cross into and merge with each other, producing representations of women and natives as animals, or robots and technological apparatus as living organisms. In other words, the metamorphic other provide a repertoire of fantastic representations that combine the metaphysical cannibalism of the metaphorisation processes with fantasmatic transformation of self and other into recombined figures and images. From

Ovid's classical Metamorphoses text to contemporary graphic novels, the white, male human melts and devolves into sexualised, racialised, naturalised and technologically mediated others with ease and panache, as this kind of access to a number of 'body doubles' were perfectly normal. A sense of great ontological entitlement is needed to support such imaginary consumption of other bodies. [...]

The metamorphic dimension fulfils another function, in that the monstrous triggers the recognition of a sense of multiplicity contained within the same self. It is an entity whose multiple parts are neither totally merged nor totally separate from the human observer. Freaky or monstrous representation of other bodies fulfil therefore a paradoxically reassuring function in the anxiety-ridden contemporary imagination. [...] Monstrous others can afford us a welcome emotional relief and a break from the generalised political economy of fear, precisely by incarnating fully its destructive potential. [...] Their effect is cathartic, as if the monster was within our embodied self, ready to unfold.

Although the term 'monster' must be reserved for animate or organic entities, I would argue for a structural analogy between the organic monster and the technological other, especially if it is represented in anthropomorphic images. Body-doubles, robots or automates have in fact the same metamorphic effect on the human observers as the monstrous devalorised organic others. They are objects of wonder and terror, loathing and desire. As body-doubles, they represent a re-assembly of organic parts, often arranged in a new order: organs are metamorphically redesigned by excess, lack or displacements from their 'natural' locations. Quite often, the re-arrangement of organic parts in the mechanical body-double expresses a fantastic and playful array of alternative body-shapes, bodily functions, morphologies and sexualities. As such, the technological anthropomorphic machine is an object of imaginary projections and fantasy. It can be a mixture of human and non-human parts, half insect and half metal, as in the worst science fiction horror movie.

The automaton lends itself to such fantasmatic usages and it therefore plays a paradoxical role within scientific and cultural practice. On the one hand it exemplifies the potency of scientific rationality to master life and the living, on the other hand it defies rational understanding. While being very much itself, the technological body-double is also irrevocably other. It is consequently positioned in ways that are analogous to the classical 'others' of modernity: the sexual, the ethnic and the natural others. [...] Like the Frankenstenian body-double, the automaton is a mixture, a mix of detachable parts and organs, a collage or montage of pieces. As such it is marked by ambiguity and polyvalence and it is linked to the monstrous through the mixture of fascination and horror, which it provokes by being such a liminal borderline figure. The technological other is monstrous because it blurs the boundaries, it mixes the genres, it displaces the points of reference between the normal – in the double sense of normality and normativity – and its 'others'. It sticks to us, it settles in the recesses of our psyche and works from within.

Nomadic Becomings

The work of Oliver Laric expresses and explores in the contemporary global context, the challenge that the hybrid, the anomalous, the monstrous metamorphic others throw in the direction of dominant subject positions and their century-old metaphorisation habits. Laric expresses a new cultural and political sensibility that calls for active dissociation from those bad old habits which pathologised and criminalised metamorphic others and encourages us to think again and think harder about our relationship to otherness.

In my own reflexion on this subject I have argued that we have to approach the devalued and monstrously different others not as signs of pejoration, but in the positivity of their difference.[1] The others embody the unfolding of virtual possibilities that point to positive developments and alternatives and they do so in their own terms – each one of them a complex singularity that resists both metaphorisation and metaphysical cannibalism. Re-formulated in the language of nomadic subjectivity, this would mean that the contemporary metamorphic imaginary, expresses simultaneously two contradictory tendencies.[2] As a reactive or negative reaction, it expresses on the one hand the fear and the anxieties of the dominant subject-position of the male, white, heterosexual, urbanised property-owning speaker of a standard language, at a historical time when his social and symbolic entitlements are crumbling. As an active, or affirmative and empowering act, on the other hand, it expresses the specificity of the 'others' and their own positive subjectivity. This qualitative shift of perspective is what I call the processes of becoming-nomadic subjects.

The point and the cultural challenge is to break the bad old metamorphic habits and the dialectics that underscore them so as to develop modes of interrelation and representation of the 'others' in an affirmative and empowering manner, rather than in an exploitative and consumeristic manner. Nomadic subjects are subjects in process, that have relinquished the dialectical mode of relation to others by giving priority to the critique of the formerly dominant model of subjectivity and thus putting on the spot the discourse of the master subject. Rather than putting the burden of truth on the constitutive, but also disposable others, nomadic subjects attack Master's discourse and expose his structural weakness and dependency on the very others it oppresses and consumes. This is what is at stake in the nomadic theory of becoming.

Becoming nomadic works on a time sequence that is neither linear nor sequential, because they are not predicated upon a stable, centralised Self who supervises their unfolding. They rather rest on a non-unitary, multi-layered, dynamic vision of the subject. For instance, becoming woman/animal/insect is a process, a sensibility and an affect that flow in and from each, becoming actualised in new modes of ethical and aesthetic relation. It is not about metaphors, but about experientially undoing the boundaries of otherness by allowing the others to express their singularity and specificity outside of any dialectical scheme of reduction and metaphysical consumption. Becomings are itineraries without fixed targets or destinations, but are punctuated by constant encounters with otherness as a multi-layered and multi-directional landscape. Nomadic subjects push themselves to the limit in a constant encounter with external, different others. The nomadic subject as a non-unitary entity is simultaneously self-propelling and outward-bound. All becomings are minoritarian, that is to say they inevitably and necessarily move in the direction of the 'others' of classical dialectics but not in order to consume them. It rather dis-places them and engages with his/her external others in a constructive, 'symbiotic' block of becoming, which bypasses dialectical interaction. 'Becoming' is a persistent challenge and an opposition to dominant unitary identities and outside dialectical oppositions and teleological models.

These patterns of nomadic becoming can be visualised alternatively as sequential modes of affirmative deconstruction of the dominant Subject-position (masculine/white/heterosexual/speaking a standard language/ property-owning/urbanised etc.). Or else, as the expression of the specificity of those who until now had been reduced to devalued otherness. Nomadic becoming asserts the potency of expressing virtual possibilities of interaction with others and the different stages or levels of becoming trace an itinerary that consists in erasing and recomposing the former boundaries between self and others. Becoming: woman/insect/imperceptible/molecular are deconstructive steps across the boundaries that used to separate dialectically the dominant subject from others. Therefore, it is impossible to separate out the becoming-woman/animal/insect/earth from the other multiple becomings: they form a zig-zagging itinerary across many thresholds of 'becoming-nomadic'. They are qualitative transitions that cross through the others and keep on moving into the 'becoming-imperceptible' and 'becoming earth'. They are not systematic, linear or teleological stages or phases of becoming, each plateau marking instead a framed and sustainable block or moment of immanently actualised transformations.

The nomadic subject expresses the figuration of a situated, posthuman, culturally differentiated understanding of the subject released from the burden of dialectics. This figuration translates our shared desire to explore and legitimate political agency, while taking as historical evidence the decline of metaphysically fixed, steady identities. Critique and creativity need to join forces to fill in the imaginary deficit and design new forms of interaction with otherness. Critical theory is both the quest for and the creation of new ways of thinking. We need systems of thought, as well as cultural and aesthetic paradigms that can help us think about change, transformation, living transitions in an affirmative manner. I value a creative, non-reactive project, emancipated from the oppressive force of the traditional dialectical approach.

Implicit in the nomadic subject is the belief in the political relevance of the aesthetic practice of the imagination, as a way to step out of those bad old habits of thought that harped on metamorphic devalued others. Art practices may be more effective, here and now, than theoretical systems. The nomadism in question here refers to the kind of critical consciousness that resists settling into socially coded modes of thought and behaviour. The central issue at stake is the inter-connectedness between identity, otherness, subjectivity and power. The nomadic subject combines coherence with mobility. It aims to rethink the subject-other relationship without reference to humanistic beliefs, without dualistic oppositions, linking instead body and mind in a new set of intensive and often intransitive transitions. The political challenge is how to respect cultural diversity without falling into relativism or political despair. Relativism is a pitfall in that it erodes the grounds for possible inter-alliances or political coalitions. Because the nomadic subject is culturally driven, it is a form of subjectivity that cannot be dissociated from the cultural or the aesthetic, simply because it involves the creation of sustainable alternatives and social horizons of hope for contemporary subjects. Conceptual and perceptual creativity is the key issue in redefining contemporary subjects-in-process as accountable entities capable of meta-stability and peaceful cohabitation with human and non-human others in the contemporary globalised world.

1 Rosi Braidotti, *Metamorphoses: Towards a Materialist Theory of Becoming* (Cambridge: Polity Press, 2002) 317; *Transpositions: On Nomadic Ethics* (Cambridge: Polity Press, 2006); and *The Posthuman* (Cambridge: Polity Press, 2013) 229.

2 Rosi Braidotti, *Nomadic Subjects: Embodiment and Sexual Difference in Contemporary Feminist Theory* (New York: Columbia University Press, 1994).

Rosi Braidotti, extracts from 'Metamorphic Others and Nomadic Subjects', a text written for the exhibition 'Oliver Laric', Tanya Leighton, Berlin, 22 November 2014–17 January 2015 (http://tanyaleighton.com/exhibitions/oliverlaric#9).

Jeffrey Deitch
Post Human//1992

[...] Social and scientific trends are converging to shape a new conception of the self, a new construction of what it means to be a human being. The matter-of-fact acceptance of one's 'natural' looks and one's 'natural' personality is being replaced by a growing sense that it is normal to reinvent oneself. The Freudian model of the 'psychological person' is dissolving into a new model that encourages individuals to dispense with the anguished analysis of how subconscious childhood experiences moulded their behaviour. There is a new sense that one can simply construct the new self that one wants, freed from the constraints of one's past and one's inherited genetic code.

Human evolution may be entering a new phase that Charles Darwin never would have envisioned. The potential of genetic reconstitution may be quickly propelling us beyond Darwinian natural evolution and into a bold realm of artificial evolution. Our society will soon have access to the biotechnology that will allow us to make direct choices about how we want our species to further evolve. This new techno-evolutionary phase will bring us far beyond eugenics. Our children's generation could very well be the last generation of 'pure' humans.

This new sense of one's power to control and, if desired, reconstruct one's body has quickly developed a broad acceptance, but there is still a significant segment of society that is deeply disturbed by its implications. The bitter debate over abortion rights is an example of how explosive the controversy over the limits of 'natural' life will become. The battle over the abortion issue and the outcry over euthanasia and the right to choose suicide may be just the beginning of an enormous social conflict over one's freedom to use the new biotechnology to take greater control over one's body and to enhance the course of one's life.

The issue of using genetic engineering to 'improve' the foetus will potentially become much more highly charged than the controversy over abortion. It may not be an exaggeration to say that it will become the most difficult moral and social issue that the human species has ever faced. Genetic engineering is not just another life-enhancing technology like aviation or telecommunications. Its continued development and application may force us to redefine the parameters of life.

Our consciousness of the self will have to undergo a profound change as we continue to embrace the transforming advances in biological and communications technologies. A new construction of the self will inevitably take hold as ever more powerful body-altering techniques become commonplace. As radical plastic surgery, computer-chip brain implants and gene-splicing become routine, the former structure of self will no longer correspond to the new structure of the body. A new posthuman organisation of personality will develop that reflects peoples' adaptation to this new technology and its socioeconomic effects. [...]

The obsession with self-awareness and self-improvement in the 1970s (the 'Me' decade), and with self-image and self-indulgence in the 1980s, demonstrated the intense interest in redefining and perhaps reformulating society's definition of the self. The new broader understanding of the multiplicity of possible realities has inspired a widespread desire to break with older constraining models of personality. It is becoming routine for people to try to alter their appearance, their behaviour and their consciousness beyond what was once thought possible. The modern era might be characterised as a period of the discovery of self. Our current postmodern era can be characterised as a transitional period of the disintegration of self. Perhaps the coming 'posthuman' period will be characterised by the reconstruction of self. [...]

The decentred television reality that we experience, with its fragmentation, multiplicity and simultaneity, is helping to deepen the sense that there is no absolutely 'correct' or 'true' model of the self. Increasingly people may come to feel that it is no longer relevant to try to 'cure' a personality disorder. Instead it may seem more appropriate to try to alter, rather than cure, the self. We are likely to be witnessing the dissolution of the Freudian psychological model with its emphasis on childhood experiences and family background. The latest statistics show that in American inner cities, more than half of the school-age children come from one-parent homes and as many as 10% from 'no parent' homes. The process of self-construction has to be radically different from the way it was in turn-of-the-century Vienna. Many contemporary people have little sense of past and little sense of future, only a sense of the present. Disconnected from traditional family history, people are more prone to start their self-identity with the present. There is less need to psychologically interpret or 'discover' oneself and more of a feeling that the self can be altered and reinvented. Self-identity is becoming much more dependent on how one is perceived by others. As opposed to a deeply rooted sense of inner direction. The world has become a mirror.

Reality, fantasy and fiction are merging into the inspiration for a new model of personality organisation. The interchangeable identities of Madonna and the extraordinary self-transformation of Ivana Trump are examples of this shuffling of reality and fantasy into a reassembled fictional personality that quickly becomes fact. The search for the absolute 'true' self has been replaced by a constant scanning for new alternatives.

The contemporary collapse of absolutes applies not only to personality models, but to political and social models as well. The crumbling of communism in the Soviet Union marked the dissolution of one of the most absolute of all belief systems. In the capitalist sphere, as well, the Japanese bubble economy has been punctured and the ideologies of Reaganism and Thatcherism have been tarnished. Corporate restructurings, with their plant closings and forced early retirements, have shattered the long-nurtured assumption that the modern corporation would make every effort to take care of its dedicated employees. The belief system at the foundation of modern corporatism has been seriously weakened, leading to new models of how individuals perceive their place in the free-market structure.

The public has even experienced an unprecedented collapse of the reputation of many of its most trusted and admired heroes. It turned out that Ben Johnson's astounding athletic prowess was the product of steroids and that Donald Trump's vast wealth was not real, only simulated. The recent deflation of all these 'absolutes' in our cultural, socioeconomic and political environment has set the stage for a new kind of belief structure based on multiple realities and multiple perceptions.

In addition to the way social and economic forces are shaping a new method of seeing and experiencing the world, two extraordinary new technologies will soon be challenging definitions and perceptions of reality in a way that is beyond anything previously imagined. Computer science with its ever closer realisation of virtual reality and biotechnology with the amazing potential of genetic engineering, are on the verge of creating a new environment where most of our assumptions about what is reality and even what is life will have to be re-examined. The combination of these two sets of technologies will create not only new life forms and new communications channels, but will shape new perceptions of time and space and even lead to new structures of thinking.

We are already experiencing a new kind of electronic space and a new kind of simultaneous television time. The former sense of the vast distances that separated, for example, a metals trader in New York from his customer in Tokyo has already been collapsed by twenty-four-hour, online trading. Economic space once encompassed a sense of the long journeys involved to move goods and information from one city to another. Now, with computer networks, video conferencing and DHL overnight service, company offices on different continents can function as if they were next door to each other. The new sense of time experienced through CNN's live broadcasts of the Gulf war and the August 1991 Soviet coup has changed forever the way world affairs will function. There will no longer be the cushion of time between an event and its interpretation in the newspaper: the electronic media has networked the world into a new kind of simultaneous real-time structure, speeding up the course of social interchange. The current communications revolution is likely to be just a prelude, however, to the advent of cyberspace, a vast computer universe that will further restructure our understanding of time and space.

The new electronic time and space also seems to be shaping a new kind of thinking, oriented toward images and sound bites. The former emphasis on deductive rational structures and lengthy narrative has been eclipsed by the electronic media's compressed sense of time. The television audience is being trained to take in complex issues through quick successions of images and compact, packaged commentary. As previous generations learned structures of complex thinking through essays and novels, today's advanced television generation learns how to think through news anchor-people and talk-show hosts.

The structure of thinking is changing and it appears that the quality of thinking is changing as well. Patterns of thinking are becoming less rational. With the collapse of many of the modern era's hierarchical belief systems and their replacement by multifaceted alternatives, people are moving away from hierarchically structured rational thinking to a more perceptual, less structured outlook and a more irrational mode of thought. An irrational outlook in fact might be a more appropriate approach to a world that seems to have outgrown its modern utopian faith in rational solutions.

This feeling of irrationality is furthered by the sense that the explosive new technologies may also be unleashing some explosive new pathologies. We are experiencing a surge of seemingly untamable viruses: biological, social, environmental and computer viruses as well. There is a sense that we are advancing but not progressing, mired in a swirl of unexpected side effects that have undermined our belief in a rational order and moved us closer to embracing an irrational model of the world.

Our transition to the posthuman world of cyberspace and genetic engineering is occurring gradually. Many of the new attitudes toward the body and the new modes of social behaviour do not seem particularly significant in isolation, but viewed together they demonstrate a decided trend toward a radically new model of the self and of social behaviour. They constitute a kind of prelude that is likely to make society attitudinally more ready than one would have expected for the truly radical technologies that are soon to come.

It is assumed that the average person can and should alter his or her body through rigorous diet and exercise. The virtues of mind exercise and even of mind-altering drugs have also achieved wide acceptance. Plastic surgery is not only accepted and encouraged by many of our social role models but is enthusiastically shown off. For the generation that has watched and perhaps tried to imitate the self-transformation of Jane Fonda, there is already a strong sense of one's freedom to control and alter one's body. As more powerful technology becomes accessible, the next logical step might be for members of the post-Jane Fonda generation to want to create a genetically improved child who would already incorporate the enhanced physical endowments that years of exercise, liposuction and implant surgery had accomplished. How large a jump would it be for someone with an elaborate home-computer system to install a chip in his or her brain that stored the entire Encyclopedia Britannica and images of every important painting in art history? The attitudes that may make us ready to embrace the posthuman person may already be here.

We are also already well on our way to assimilating a new set of nearly posthuman social structures. These new types of social behaviours first seemed to assert themselves in the realm of mating rituals. The social dislocations that began to isolate young people from their traditional family and community networks led to numerous artificial structures to facilitate introductions. First there were personal ads and singles clubs, then singles bars and an organised singles industry. Now, with the threat of AIDS and perhaps a growing sense of human alienation, phone sex has become especially popular. People can conduct fantasy relationships without the mess that often goes along with real human contact. From phone sex it is only a small step to virtual sex, the multi-sensual sexual experience that people will soon be able to have in three dimensions with their home computer: A virtual-sex program featuring every simulated sound and sensation is not only likely to be better in many ways than the real thing, for future generations it may become the real thing. [...]

These emerging social and technological trends that are redefining our concepts of the self and of social behaviour have begun to exert tremendous influence on artists. There is an enormous new artistic interest in the body and in the presentation of the self. Much of today's most innovative new artistic practice involves new concepts of the figure and new approaches to the figure. This new interest in the figure is, however, not to be found where it would traditionally be expected, in painting and in conventional sculpture. The new interest in figuration, in keeping with the social and technological trends that are inspiring it, is conceptual rather than formal. The new figurative art is emerging through the channel of the conceptual, body and performance art of the late 1960s and 70s rather than through the figurative painting tradition.

Many of the most interesting younger artists are dealing with the new conceptions of the body and the new definitions of self that the vanguard of our society is also dealing with. They are exploring through their art the same questioning of traditional notions of gender, sexuality and self-identity that is taking place in the world at large. Much of the new figurative art is reactive to and descriptive of the 'real' world, but it cannot in fact be called realistic in the conventional sense. That is because so much of the 'real' world that they are reacting to has in fact become artificial. With the concept of the real disintegrating through an acceptance of the multiplicity of reality models and through the embrace of artificiality. Realism as we used to know it may no longer be possible. This new figurative art may actually mark the end of Realism rather than its revival.

The redefinition of the figure is being approached by a number of artists through its breakup and reassembly. Robert Gober shockingly isolates segments of the body from the whole, creating an eerie new reality of free-floating limbs and disconnected emotions. Body parts are disassembled and reassembled in the sculpture of George Lappas, who also mixes time frames from the past and the present. This shuffling of historical present and future time is also characteristic of the approaches of Wim Delvoye and Yasumasa Morimura. The figures in their works function in historical, present and future time simultaneously, giving a picture of the kind of time mix that is likely to be more and more characteristic of the way we will experience the world.

Time is not the only element that is shuffled. Humans and animals are conflated in the work of Mike Kelley, humans and mannequins in the work of Charles Ray, and humans and machines in the work of Paul McCarthy. These artists present a shocking reformulation of humanity that gives a disquieting glimpse of the coming posthuman situation. In Kelley's world, the ever more intense underflow of violence and perversity bubbles over into an uneasy confusion of artificiality, innocence and bestiality. In Ray's sculpture, frighteningly out of scale mannequins represent intensified visions of posthuman evolution, drained of all emotion and affect. McCarthy's Garden depicts an alien posthuman future in which the figure becomes a robotic shell seized by an uncontrollable sexual obsession from which all 'human' passion is absent.

Future genetic manipulation may spawn a race of posthumans who are outwardly perfect but whose inner neuroses and instincts may not be so easily controlled. Artists are sensitive to this murky underside of displaced urges that may not be quite as easy to re-mould as a pair of flabby thighs. Janine Antoni's cube of gnawed chocolate reveals the neurotic and desperate behaviour sometimes hidden beneath the sleek façade of a woman's image perfected through cosmetics. Kiki Smith's flayed bodies, dripping with excretions, bear witness to the emotional wreckage that festers below the plastic surface. Artists are giving us a frightful warning of the irrational reservoir of dislocated emotions that may overwhelm the advances of technology.

[...] The new way in which personal identity is being constructed is examined through the mind-flow drawings of Karen Kilimnik, which enter into the interplay between models of celebrity and models of self. The fascinating collapse of the border between public and private lives is also explored though Kilimnik's work. As evidenced by the new approaches to the private versus public, in everything from the scrutiny of the personal lives of political candidates to the behind-the-scenes revelations of Madonna's *Truth or Dare*, our entire understanding of the meaning of private life is in the process of being redefined.

The re-creation of self through an embrace of fantasy and fiction is embodied in the life and work of Jeff Koons. In the course of a two-year period, Koons transformed his body and his life through his courtship and marriage with Cicciolina. The biological and material sculpture resulting from their union dissolves the dividing line between artificial and real. Creating art that can truly be described as posthuman.

As the organic, naturally evolving model of human life is replaced by the artificial evolution into the Post Human, art is likely to assume a much more central role. Art may have to fuse with science as computerisation and biotechnology create further 'improvements' on the human form. Many of the decisions that will accompany the applications of computerised virtual reality and of genetic engineering will be related to aesthetics. Technology will make it possible to remodel our bodies and supercharge our minds, but art will have to help provide the inspiration for what our bodies should look like and what our minds should be doing.

Will the onset of the Post Human mean unprecedented freedom for the individual and for the artist? Will we soon have almost unlimited ability to recreate ourselves and break through the constraints of genetic history? Will we have the opportunity to express ourselves in any way we want physical appearance? Will we be able to create art that is also biology?

Or will it happen that all these extraordinary new possibilities will result in increased social repression and a push toward conformity? Will the persuasive skills of the advertising industry convince us all to buy the same two or three genetic-improvement programmes? Will governments assert their control over the powerful new biotechnology and restrict its use? Or will they take a more aggressive stance, exploiting the new technology to create genetically improved populations for economic and military superiority? Could the world evolve into a nightmarish situation with new, improved Post Humans in the wealthy countries ruling over the 'old humans' in countries where the new technologies cannot be readily afforded? All these scenarios remain unclear.

What we do know is that we will soon be forced by technological advances to develop a new morality. We will need to build a new moral structure that will give people a framework of how to deal with the enormous choices they will have to make in terms of genetic alteration and computerised brain enhancement. We will have to face decisions not only about what looks good, but what *is* good or is bad about the restructuring of the mind and body. The limits of life will no longer be something that can be taken for granted. We will have to create a new moral vision to cope with them. In the future, artists may no longer be involved in just redefining art. In the posthuman future artists may also be involved in redefining life.

Jeffrey Deitch, extracts from 'Post Human', in *Post Human* (exh. cat) (Pully/Lausanne: FAE musée d'art contemporain/Rivoli: Castello di Rivoli/Athens: Deste Foundation for Contemporary Art/Hamburg: Deichtorhallen Hamburg, 1992) 26–7, 29–47.

Lee Bul
Beauty and Trauma//2000

[...]

Speed and Motion

I have a fear of speed and motion, an inconvenient affliction to say the least, in a world that seems increasingly ruled by both. I haven't been able to locate the precise origin of this fear, though I suspect it might have something to do with my experiences with 'bullet taxis' that hurtle along the eight-lane freeways linking central Seoul with the so-called satellite cities on the outskirts. These taxis appear in the hours after midnight when the subways and buses stop running and salarymen emerge from downtown bars, faced with the choice of sleeping on the sidewalk or paying the $30 fare (exorbitant by Korean standards) to get back to their suburban beehive dwellings. The driver will make five, six runs, all in the span of a couple of hours, and this is possible because he is mad with concentration, hyped up on hiropon, a methamphetamine concoction first developed by the Japanese army during World War II for their kamikaze pilots.

I took these taxis a few times out of sheer necessity when I was younger and my studio, a disused storage shed, was on a plot of farmland that had yet to be swallowed up by the protoplasmic expansion of the satellite cities. Those rides were strangely silent, save for the tinny sound of late-night radio chat shows and the air buffeting the windshield at roughly 100 miles an hour. I never dared to make small talk with the driver, for fear of opening up a gap, and introducing the possibility of human error, between him and the machine. Now and then the car would shudder as traffic passed by in adjacent lanes. Sometimes, as we rode the bank of a curve, the wheels became slightly airborne, momentarily escaping the pull of gravity.

At what point does velocity begin to warp time? At the end of the terrifying journey, there awaited a derelict vision of the future: over the barren horizon of what used to be paddy fields, I could see the dark outlines of construction machinery hunched like slumbering beasts, surrounding the pale concrete monoliths coming into being, enclosed in a cocoon of scaffolding, all of it watched over by a towering formation of minatory cranes.

Mastery and Mechanical Failure

The secular teleology of technological progress is getting a boost these days from the proliferation of everything with an 'e-' prefix. We are now living, the popular media would have us believe, in a new, brilliant electronic age. But has the world really advanced that much?

Living in Korea can point up the contradiction between the growing faith in the creed of new technology and the chastening reality of things constantly breaking down. In many ways, Korea is a 'high–tech' nation. Some 60% of the population is wired to the Internet, more than in Japan, and its mega-corporations produce roughly half the world's computer memory chips.

Yet, it's also a place of casual catastrophes: bridges and department stores collapse, subterranean gas mains explode, and the jumbo jets of Korean Air, the national carrier, routinely go down. Given my fear of speed and motion, I find this last item in the list especially disconcerting, There's a thorough investigation, of course, whenever there's a plane crash, but ultimately there can only be two possible conclusions: human error or mechanical failure. In Korean society, these are, by and large, acceptable answers. The idea of fallibility, whether human or mechanical, is considered a matter-of-fact truth. Something that the more 'advanced' Western societies, with their technological triumphalism, are reluctant to acknowledge. Still, whenever I'm on a plane, I want to believe the stolid American aeronautics engineers attesting to the invulnerability of their inventions in the wake of the mysterious crash of TWA Flight 800 three years ago: 'Boeing 7475 can virtually fly themselves.' 'It would take a scud missile to bring one down.' And when the flight attendants begin their preflight pantomime of emergency procedures, I willingly suspend disbelief. Soon, anaesthetised by the miniature bottles of vodka, I join the other passengers in the collective, immemorial dream of absolute mastery over gravity. But somewhere down below, in an unmarked hangar, the archaeologists of public disasters are sifting through the wreckage of the latest crash, speaking to one another in an idiom that verges on the esoteric lexicon of medieval sorcery.

Lee Bul, extract from 'Beauty and Trauma', trans. Andrew Han, *Art Journal*, vol. 59, no. 3 (Fall 2000) 105–7.

Siân Ede

New Bodies for Old: The Art and Science of the Body

Elective//2005

[...] Eduardo Kac – not entirely tongue in cheek – proposes a new role for artists. 'With at least one endangered species becoming extinct every day, I suggest that artists can contribute to increase global diversity by inventing new life forms', he writes. These can then 'be taken home by the public to be grown in the back yard or raised as human companions'.[1] Such is Kac's best known work, *GFP Bunny*, commissioned from a French laboratory, a live rabbit called Alba, into which was expressed green fluorescent protein (GFP). This protein is isolated from the Pacific Northwest jellyfish and glows bright green when exposed to ultraviolet or blue light. The process is harmless but Alba was not permitted to enter Kac's Chicago backyard, such is the moral quandary of the authorities. In the *Eighth Day* Kac has brought together a collection of creatures – plants, fish and mice – which are novel in the sense that each has been created by the cloning of a gene that codes for the production of GFP. Visible through a four-foot diameter Plexiglas dome that they share with a biological robot, their bioluminescence is visible to the naked eye. Put together, they are not individual laboratory specimens but a proposed ecology belonging to a newer world. [...]

The political economist Francis Fukuyama presents a dismal view of the post-genetic world in which he believes that biotechnology will subvert for ever notions of equality, engendering, in effect, a privatised eugenics programme for the rich as we choose to promote new and rigid concepts of normality, with unnerving implications for the balance of power in the world. Ideal people will be healthy, beautiful, clever, the men strong and pleasant, the women attractive and high-achieving. Strong western women will feminise politics, men will become ineffectual, except in the Third World where normal aggression will rule. Homosexuality may be phased out, as might any form of disability, and the prolonging of our lifespan means the young will have to look after the old. Neuropharmacologies will also transform our personalities, Prozac bringing us lotus-eating calm and Ritalin sapping any inconvenient disaffection in younger generations. Margaret Atwood's novel *Oryx and Crake*[2] is a horrific Swiftian view of a dystopian future in which genetic technology has catastrophically put paid to the human race, a story that hovers on the boundaries of credibility given recent panics about Ebola, BSE, SARS and Avian Influenza where animal diseases can jump the species barrier and trigger incurable epidemics in humans. As fast as we find ways to transform nature, it seems that nature is able to catch us out in the same game – a situation that begs us to consider the ethics of interference.

Fay Weldon wrote her prescient novel *The Cloning of Joanna May* in 1985, in which a woman reaches the age of forty to discover that her mad scientist captain of industry husband has had her cloned twenty years before so that when her looks fade she can be replaced by young and beautiful replicas of herself. She now has four daughters/siblings who have been brought up in different families. But far from discovering them to be zombie threats, she comes to love them for their different personalities – for they are not identical but unique confident young women who have grown up without the self-doubt of their mother's generation for whom a woman's identity could be someone else's property without the bother of biotechnical intervention. Always mischievously perverse, Weldon is often prophetic and it is worth heeding her words:

> And cloning? Every child a chosen child? It's bound to come. Governments are going to want their best citizens replicated, and so will individuals. No one really wants to leave anything to chance any more. Why risk an unlovable baby when a lovable one is to hand? Why have an angry, argumentative, plain population when you could have a nice, kind, peace loving assembly of attractive, constructive citizens? And governments can leave it to parents to make their individual decisions; they won't even have to impose choices from on high. So watch out for a relaxation of the rules and regulations on cloning. It may take fifty years or so, but watch this space.[3]

Kac's artist-invented life forms may also be more than fantasy. 'Truth is stranger than fiction', Weldon writes, 'and if the writer can think of it, someone somewhere is bound to be doing it, the world is so large and strange.' The same is true in the case of artists. Some of them are already doing it, appropriating scientific techniques and imagining futuristic scenarios beyond the boundaries of science fiction. Good work will be stunning on its own terms and naturally stimulate us to raise ethical questions and to ponder more deeply on the human condition, as I believe it should, even while I wouldn't want to see art that is too one dimensionally didactic. But some of the new work seems to be rather coolly frivolous and we may feel ambivalent about using the tissues of life itself to simply shock or entertain.

1 [Footnote 18 in source] Eduardo Kac, 'Transgenic Art', *Leonardo Electronic Almanac*, vol. 6N (11 December 1998).

2 [22] Margaret Atwood, *Oryx and Crake* (London: Doubleday, 2003).

3 [23] Fay Weldon, 'Welcome, Whoever You Are', *New Statesman* (13 January 2003) and *The Cloning of Joanna May* (London: Fontana, 1990).

Siân Ede, extracts from 'New Bodies for Old: The Art and Science of the Body Elective', in *Art and Science* (London: I.B.Tauris, 2005) 156, 159–60.

Josh Kline
In Conversation with Domenick Ammirati//2013

Domenick Ammirati Let's get this out of the way: posthumanism?

Josh Kline For me, it's about technology changing what it means to be human. There's a self-actualisation aspect to it that's potentially positive, but I mostly associate it with the relentless push to squeeze more productivity out of workers – turning people into reliable, always-on, office appliances. I'm probably not the right person to throw down about posthumanist theory. I go with the simple definition from sci-fi novels: people who are no longer human. I read Donna Haraway and N. Katherine Hayles a long time ago, but I'm uncertain how much has stuck with me. I'm not sure I see them as a starting point for the art I'm making or interested in, which is reacting to real-world events, not theory.

Ammirati I feel like what's being identified as 'posthuman' in contemporary art comes precisely from that kind of relation to the general culture. But, if so, you could argue that the 'posthumanist' art of the moment is just the latest extension of the lineage of Pop – a relatively direct re-presentation of the present.

Kline It's more complicated than that. Many of my peers are turning to communications strategies from mass media and advertising as a way to escape the self-referential conversation of the art system. In much of this work, advertising's syntax is a useful formal strategy or a device. It's also a vernacular.

Ammirati Is it important to you to contextualise your art or the art in 'ProBio' – the group show that you have curated at MoMA PS1 – with regard to art history?

Kline I think most – but definitely not all – of the artists in 'ProBio' feel pretty strongly about getting away from a focus on art history. It's partially a reaction to the 2000s and the MFA system, where older artists make younger artists justify their work against the art-historical record and via theory.

Ammirati Don't you worry you could get painted as anti-intellectual?

Kline Not really. You can use art to have serious conversations about a whole universe of topics that has nothing to do with the art industry.

Ammirati It's funny, part of me doesn't care about the rest of the world at all.

Kline Meaning you side with the hermetic art conversation?

Ammirati Not 'side with' exactly; I just enjoy it.

Kline I think that's why it's rare for this kind of work to be tackled on its own terms. It's one of the reasons it's important for artists to be writing and curating at the moment, so we can put the work in a twenty-first-century context. [...]

Josh Kline, extract from 'Interview with Domenick Ammirati', *frieze*, no. 157 (September 2013). Available at https://frieze.com/article/focus-interview-josh-kline

Francesca Ferrando
A Feminist Genealogy of Posthuman Aesthetics in the Visual Arts//2016

[...] Our digital sisters: from the nineties till today. The early nineties marked the birth of Cyberfeminism. The unexpected success of Haraway's 'Cyborg Manifesto' (1985) strongly contributed to its popularisation, in a historical moment when cyberculture was establishing its narratives and art was reshaping into new forms, such as cyberart, web art, new media art, electronic art, software art, digital art, telematic art. The tremendous possibilities opened by virtual reality, which included computer-simulated environments, where to experience different gender identities (whose effects actually proved to be less revolutionary than expected)[1] were theoretically inscribed within Cyberfeminism, which stressed multiplicity, nomadicity and connectivity. Its practices were participatory and decentred; its goals were mainly concerned with making the digital realm a woman-friendly space, which would not perpetuate patriarchal agendas. Cyberfeminism represents an important antecedent of Posthumanism. Although the term 'posthuman' had first appeared a decade earlier within the frame of postmodern literature, and specifically, in the writings of Ihab Hassan[2], it started to be popularised in the writings of the time.[3] Its use became familiar within academia after the publication of 'How We Became Posthuman' (1999) by Katherine Hayles, who already in 1995 was writing: 'Standing at the threshold separating the human and the posthuman, the cyborg looks to the past as well as the future.'[4] The historical and herstorical passage between the human and the posthuman is the cyborg.

[...] Let us now consider Afrofuturism, a term coined by Mark Dery in 1993[5] to refer to the contribution of the black experience to the settings of the upcoming times. Afrofuturism and Posthumanism share common theoretical ground and a crucial difference with Futurism, in their recognition of the importance of acknowledging the past, based on the same premises: 'human' is not a neutral term, and it carries a history of privileges. For instance, women, people of colours other than white, disabled people and so on have been repeatedly deprived of such status. In particular, the African-American diaspora, which caused a forced erasure of private and public histories, makes it crucial to keep the past and present in the visualisation of desirable futures. Many artists have contributed to such narratives. Let us start with Wangechi Mutu (b. 1972), a Kenyan-born artist whose collages melt together the aesthetics of traditional

African crafts with science fiction imaginary, bionic prosthetics and Surrealism. Her visionary cyborgism is fully aware of the sexual and racial difference. In an interview for the CNN, she stated: 'what I've been trying to sort of do is [...] give the women a kind of strength that the machine supposedly represents for the man. It's like they're taking it back and they become these cyborgs, these fierce female cyborgs'.[6] US artist Denenge Akpem is both an artist and an academic theorist. She has done extensive work on divulging the concept of Afrofuturism, which she defines as 'an exploration and methodology of liberation, simultaneously both a location and a journey'.[7] In her performative installation *Rapunzel Revisited: An Afri-Sci-Fi Space Sea Siren Tale* (2006), she transforms herself into a hybrid human-jellyfish, with lighted fibre-optic tentacles. Her work redefines concepts of race, gender and humanity with a holistic approach. Jamaican-born Renée Cox (b. 1960) is a photographer who stages her own body in self-portraits that deconstruct racist and sexist stereotypes. In the series *Raje* (1998) she poses as her alter-ego, Raje, a superheroine who fights for racial justice. Between the many other afrofuturist posthuman sisters I would like to mention: Kara Walker (b. 1969), Fatimah Tuggar (b. 1967) and Tanekeya Word (b. 1983).

Related to Afrofuturism is Chicanafuturism, a term coined in 2002 by Catherine S. Ramírez to explore the relation between the Chicana experience and the future, with a special emphasis on its technological and scientific developments.[8] Chicanafuturism also explores a redefinition of the human through Latin American history and exploitation: 'Chicanafuturism articulates colonial and postcolonial histories of indigenismo, *mestizaje*, hegemony and survival'.[9] Some of the artists who delve into this area of investigation are: Alma Lopez, Marion C Martinez (1954), Coco Fusco (1960) and Laura Molina (1957), whose character 'Cihualyaomiquiz, The Jaguar', created in 1994, represents an avenging Mexican-American superheroine ready to die for social justice. [...]

1 [Footnote 23 in source] As Sandy Stone phrased it in her essay 'Will The Real Body Please Stand Up?: Boundary Stories About Virtual Cultures' (1991), in *The Cybercultures Reader*, eds. D. Bell & B.M. Kennedy (London: Routledge, 2000) 504–28, 524: 'No matter how virtual the subject may become, there is always a body attached'.

2 [24] Literary theorist Ihab Hassan (1925–2015) was among the first to use the term 'posthuman' in the article 'Prometheus as Performer: Toward a Posthumanist Culture?' (1977), to then develop it in *The Postmodern Turn* (1987).

3 [25] For instance, one of the subchapters of Braidotti's essay 'CyberFeminism with a Difference' focuses specifically on 'Posthuman Bodies'. See Rosi Braidotti, 'Cyberfeminism with a Difference',

New Formations, vol. 29 (Autumn 1996) 9–25.
4 [26] Katherine Hayles, 'The Life Cycles of Cyborgs: Writing the Posthuman', *The Cyborg Handbook*, eds. C. Hables Gray & H.J. Figueroa-Sarriera (New York: Routledge, 1995) 321–35, 322.
5 [32] Dery introduced it in his essay 'Black to the Future: Interviews with Samuel R. Delany, Greg Tate, and Tricia Rose' (1993).
6 Wangechi Mutu, 'Artist Wangechi Mutu: My lab is the female body', *African Voices* (19 July 2011) (cnn.com).
7 D. Akpem, 'Are You Ready to Alter Your Destiny? Chicago and Afro-Futurism', part 1 of 2, *Chicago Art Magazine* (2 July 2011) (chicagoartmagazine.com).
8 C. Ramírez, 'Deus ex Machina: Tradition, Technology, and the Chicanafuturist Art of Marion C. Martinez', *Aztlán: A Journal of Chicano Studies*, vol. 2, no. 29 (2002) 55–92.
9 C. Ramírez 'Afrofuturism/Chicanafuturism: Fictive Kin', *Aztlán: A Journal of Chicano Studies*, vol. 1, no. 33 (2008) 185–94, 187.

Francesca Ferrando, extracts from 'A Feminist Genealogy of Posthuman Aesthetics in the Visual Arts', *Palgrave Communications* (2016) 5, 7, 8–9.

Anya Harrison
All Systems Go//2017

In 1997, the world watched with awe and trepidation as IBM's supercomputer Deep Blue defeated Russian world chess champion Garry Kasparov. Framed at the time as the ultimate union of human and machine cognition, Deep Blue's victory in a game long considered the ultimate test of human intelligence signalled the arrival of a new machine era. Yet if the machines won that battle, and many since, for Kasparov humans still reign supreme. In *Deep Thinking* (2017), he writes: 'There is more to being human than creativity [...] We have other qualities the machines cannot match. They have instructions while we have purpose. Machines can not dream, not even in sleep mode.' Kasparov makes the distinction clear. AI ultimately plays a subservient role: to fulfil 'human ambition' and our perennial search for a 'higher purpose'. While computer science and AI have come a long way since 1997, what is striking about that mythic chess match is that Deep Blue's victory was ultimately a question of political and economic supremacy, a story of capitalist impulse. It was a victory for advancements in machine learning and AI, but also for IBM, whose stocks subsequently soared.

Frankfurt-born but London-based, Lawrence Lek (b. 1982) creates digital environments that address the impact of the virtual on our perception of the real, uncovering the deeply embedded infrastructures governing our technological era. Set in 2065, his recent CGI film *Geomancer* (2017) picks up seamlessly where Kasparov's narrative ends, unpicking the threads that weave together consciousness, art, history, technology and politics. Combining video-game animation, 3D software, a synthesized music score and a neural-network-generated dream sequence, it imagines a speculative future in which advanced AI is no longer a distant technological utopia but the fabric of everyday reality.

The forty-eight-minute-long *Bildungsroman*, presented earlier this year at the Jerwood Space in London as part of the Jerwood/FVU Award and currently on view at the HyperPavilion at the Venice Biennale, opens with a different game of skill – the ancient Chinese game of Go. In the aptly titled prologue, 'Swansong of the Genius', set in the 2045 Singapore E-Sports Olympics, we watch a re-enactment of grandmaster Lee Sedol playing the triumphant 'hand of god' move that wins him the game against the Go-playing AI program OmegaGo. (This triumph is in fact sleight of hand. In the actual match that took place in March 2016, the AI program ended up the winner). Fast-forward twenty years and Geomancer, a young weather-monitoring AI satellite, awakens in space on the eve of the Singapore Centennial. A direct descendant of OmegaGo, Geomancer is a military unit; the technology that had previously been guided by the rules of a board game have been rerouted into an instrument for surveying the invisible and disputed borders of the South China Sea. Yet Geomancer has a different plan. As its consciousness develops, the satellite decides to return to Earth to become an artist, exchanging an existence of subservience and loneliness for one of free will and agency.

As in all of Lek's work, *Geomancer* borrows gaming's first-person view, inviting us, as viewers, to inhabit the invisible bodies – or perhaps mindset – of his narrators. Devoid of human presence, his futuristic landscapes function as psychological spaces in which to reflect. While the film imagines what an awakening of AI consciousness might look like, it is equally concerned with the ensuing ontological crisis. And while it is Geomancer's crisis that we are privy to – the burden of limitless knowledge coupled with a quest for self-determination – the implication is that our own desires and anxieties are being played out. In a world where automation has surpassed much human ability, liberating us from labour, the question arises of whether creative tasks can be outsourced to algorithms and technology, and what happens if they can.

From our human-centric position, technological progress necessitates a constant reappraisal – and repositioning – of the boundaries that separate man from machine. While this has always served to advance AI-related research (Deep Blue's brute force learning is outmoded by today's standards), each breakthrough in AI's cognitive functioning – from the realm of play to that of labour – also redefines the level of human-only access. In the case of *Geomancer*, art becomes the last standard-bearer for humanity, and a space to be defended.

In Singapore, Geomancer encounters other AI voices as it floats through the cityscape of gleaming skyscrapers, stopping at a casino and virtual-reality museum, and sating its curiosity on an information overload of history, art and human culture. On discovering a law imposed by humans banning AIs from the sphere of art production, it encounters a mysterious group called the Sinofuturists, a set of e-commerce AIs escaped from the confines of the AI Anti-Art Law to become AI curators, turning the museum into a dream factory peddling 'best ever' experiences to each visitor. In an earlier pseudo-documentary video essay, *Sinofuturism (1839–2046 AD)* (2016), Lek subverts cultural clichés and anxieties around the ascendancy of East Asia, advancing a conspiracy theory that posits China's accelerated development as a latent form of AI. Of Chinese-Malaysian descent himself, and having spent his formative years in East Asia, including Singapore, Lek's concept of Sinofuturism reflects multiple perspectives. Featuring hyper-stimulating montages of animation and footage taken from the BBC, Infowars.com and local Chinese state media, Sinofuturism takes its cue from Afrofuturism and Gulf Futurism to present an alternative concept of futurity. Lacking primary identity, it accepts and enhances the pejorative characteristics attributed to it by a Western worldview plagued by its own inferiority complex and by a Chinese state intent on eradicating these examples of 'bad behaviour'. Unrestricted by national boundaries, the movement is predicated on a posthuman capacity for work and study, copying, gaming and gambling.

As a setting, Singapore is the quintessential, albeit confused, Sinofuturist metropolis. A nation of 'hybrids', of colonisers and colonised, this artificial postcolonial landscape is, as Lek himself points out, at once a crucible of neoliberal wealth, a nanny state with an extreme Confucian belief system and a breeding ground for hyperintelligent beings. Or, as the science fiction writer William Gibson once put it, 'a Disneyland with a death penalty'. Born in a Singapore tech start-up, Geo's quest for independence reflects the city-state's own struggles with identity and self-determination.

The empty spaces that make up *Geomancer* bear a conscious affinity with the late writer and theorist Mark Fisher's concept of 'the weird and the eerie': a fascination for 'that which lies beyond standard perception, cognition and experience', and which expands beyond the Freudian *unheimlich*. For Fisher, if the 'eerie' is naturally at home in landscapes devoid of human presence, it is also never far from the structure of capital itself, an invisible force that 'exerts more influence than any allegedly substantial entity'. In Lek's work, the potential of the 'sublime' is tempered by the safeguards and invisible systems of control put in place by a monolithic, Occidental capitalist worldview. Of course, Lek is no technophobe. But what casts *Geomancer* as a 'tragedy' is the self-perpetuating struggle for supremacy and power upon which the AI's sense of consciousness is built – a self-awareness born of the history of human conflict. However far we may advance, the work suggests, artificial intelligence remains the product of human intent, and Geomancer – despite its exceptionally humanlike displays of emotional sensitivity – is no exception.

Anya Harrison, 'All Systems Go', *Flash Art*, vol. 50, no. 316 (September/October 2017) 68–9.

YOU BEGIN TO REALISE THAT THIS SUPPOSEDLY MARGINAL GENRE HAS BEEN ABSOLUTELY CENTRAL TO OUR WHOLE UNDER-STANDING OF ENLIGHTENMENT'S CONCEPTION OF WHAT THE HUMAN IS AND CAN BE

Ama Josephine Budge, ' In Conversation with Angela Chan', 2019–20

ECOLOGIES

Rachel Carson
A Fable for Tomorrow//1962

There was once a town in the heart of America where all life seemed to live in harmony with its surroundings. The town lay in the midst of a checkerboard of prosperous farms, with fields of grain and hillsides of orchards where, in spring, white clouds of bloom drifted above the green fields. In autumn, oak and maple and birch set up a blaze of colour that flamed and flickered across a backdrop of pines. Then foxes barked in the hills and deer silently crossed the fields, half hidden in the mists of the fall mornings.

Along the roads, laurel, viburnum and alder, great ferns and wildflowers delighted the traveller's eye through much of the year. Even in winter the roadsides were places of beauty, where countless birds came to feed on the berries and on the seed heads of the dried weeds rising above the snow. The countryside was, in fact, famous for the abundance and variety of its bird life, and when the flood of migrants was pouring through in spring and autumn people travelled from great distances to observe them. Others came to fish the streams, which flowed clear and cold out of the hills and contained shady pools where trout lay. So it had been from the days many years ago when the first settlers raised their houses, sank their wells, and built their barns.

Then a strange blight crept over the area and everything began to change. Some evil spell had settled on the community: mysterious maladies swept the flocks of chickens; the cattle and sheep sickened and died. Everywhere was a shadow of death. The farmers spoke of much illness among their families. In the town the doctors had become more and more puzzled by new kinds of sickness appearing among their patients. There had been several sudden and unexplained deaths, not only among adults but even among children, who would be stricken suddenly while at play and die within a few hours.

There was a strange stillness. The birds, for example – where had they gone? Many people spoke of them, puzzled and disturbed. The feeding stations in the backyards were deserted. The few birds seen anywhere were moribund; they trembled violently and could nor fly. It was a spring without voices. On the mornings that had once throbbed with the dawn chorus of robins, catbirds, doves, jays, wrens, and scores of other bird voices there was now no sound; only silence lay over the fields and woods and marsh.

On the farms the hens brooded, but no chicks hatched. The farmers complained that they were unable to raise any pigs – the litters were small and the young survived only a few days. The apple trees were coming into bloom but no bees droned among the blossoms, so there was no pollination and there would be no fruit.

The roadsides, once so attractive, were now lined with browned and withered vegetation as though swept by fire. These, too, were silent, deserted by all living things. Even the streams were now lifeless. Anglers no longer visited them, for all the fish had died.

In the gutters under the eaves and between the shingles of the roofs, a white granular powder still showed a few patches; some weeks before it had fallen like snow upon the roofs and the lawns, the fields and streams.

No witchcraft, no enemy action had silenced the rebirth of new life in this stricken world. The people had done it themselves.

This town does not actually exist, but it might easily have a thousand counterparts in America or elsewhere in the world. I know of no community that has experienced all the misfortunes I describe. Yet every one of these disasters has actually happened somewhere, and many real communities have already suffered a substantial number of them. A grim spectre has crept upon us almost unnoticed, and this imagined tragedy may easily become a stark reality we all shall know.

What has already silenced the voices of spring in countless towns in America? This book is an attempt to explain. [...]

Rachel Carson, extract from 'A Fable for Tomorrow', in *Silent Spring* (1962), Fortieth Anniversary Edition (Boston and New York: Mariner, 2002) 1–3.

Kim Stanley Robinson
In Conversation with Helena Feder//2018

Kim Stanley Robinson is the author of more than twenty works of fiction, including the celebrated Mars trilogy (*Red Mars* [1992], *Green Mars* [1993] and *Blue Mars* [1996]), *Forty Signs of Rain* [2004], *The Years of Rice and Salt* [2002], *2312* [2012] and, his latest novel, *New York 2140* [2017]. A former student of Fredric Jameson, Robinson's work is consistently anti-capitalist. His novels evince not only his deep interest in global economy and ecology, but also a belief that fiction may venture into spheres where theory fears to tread. For

Robinson, science fiction is uniquely placed to do this, rooted both in what is and what could be. In the best tradition of the genre (H.G. Wells, Isaac Asimov, Ursula K. Le Guin), it can consider critically both the politics and possibilities of technology, and the social, ideological and ecological systems that give rise to it. Science fiction has, in this sense, a particular responsibility not only to imagine the future but to imagine how we might change its direction. In Robinson's *New York 2140*, a series of connected characters, centred around the MetLife tower in a future inter-tidal world, a financially and physically liquid city, come together to do just this. Sea levels have risen in two catastrophic 'pulses' of ten and forty feet, transforming planetary and human geography. In the midst of this ecological and refugee crisis, lower Manhattan becomes 'a veritable hotbed of theory and practice, like it always used to say it was, but this time for real'.

Robinson champions science fiction as 'the realism of our time'. And the reality, if not the realism, of our time is grim. The moment we inhabit has become inhospitable, terrifying and disorienting to contemplate. The Earth, 'the wholly enlightened', is, as Adorno and Horkheimer argued in *Dialectic of Enlightenment* [1947], truly 'radiant with triumphant calamity'. Violence to humans and other animals seems to proliferate rhizomatically, slow and fast: the escalation of anthropogenic damage to the planet and its atmosphere, the Sixth Mass Extinction, the consolidation of wealth and power in the hands of fewer and fewer people, the waves of ideologically motivated attacks on the poor, people of colour, Jews, Muslims, women, democracy, secular thought and the secular world, all over the world. [...]

The interview with Robinson took place at his home in Davis, California in October 2016, a few months before the publication of *New York 2140*.

Helena Feder In a 1993 interview with Bud Foote, you said that 'science fiction proclaims more than it can do'; that, at its best, it is an 'enjambment of facts and values that our culture desperately needs right now because our culture develops and enacts change without much regard for underlying values'. *New York 2140* is just such an enjambment, in terms of form and content. Could you speak to this, to the novel's sections on history and ecology, your 'citizen' subchapters? At one point you warn the reader to skip ahead if she's the sort of person who cares only about smaller, human dramas.

Kim Stanley Robinson This is simplistic, but science is where we establish facts and fiction is where we establish values. The name 'science fiction' is very powerful because it seems to say we can bridge the fact/value conundrum. It's a question whether or not the genre can or does do that, but it seems set up for it. It tries. When you talk about the future you're always talking about history. A novel always does this, but science fiction does so explicitly, through thought experiments: 'If we do this we'll get here. If we do that we'll get there.' Also, whereas the nineteenth-century novel traditionally speaks to the individual's relationship to society and history, science fiction adds the non-human and the planet [to that list]. The content of science fiction helps to make biophysical systems and problems visible. Humans do not simply make their own history on a *tabula rasa*; [the world is] an actor network where non-human actors are important players too. We've hit the limits of carrying capacity, in some ways, on the planet. And what type of fiction that can tell this story best? I've been saying, for many years now, that science fiction is the realism of our time. [...]

Feder 2140 imagines the '*Werteswandel*' [a mutation of values] you've called for elsewhere. In fact, it imagines a new idea of value itself. Is that what you're trying to do?

Robinson For Marxism, '*Werteswandel*' is in dialectical relation with changes in material circumstances and systems, not just modes of production, but also modes of exchange, or modes of valuation. Mode of production isn't really the whole story anymore. I've been interested in some radical economists, like Dick Bryan, Randy Martin and others, who argue that we should nationalise the banks, that global finance is the great danger to the planet. They also suggest there's a way to trigger another crash and then, by nationalising the banks, you could both create and then solve the crisis. And by solving the crisis in this way you would actually have done something useful, rather than papering over the problems and going on as before, as we did in 2008. That's the storyline of *New York 2140*.

Feder Capitalism disregards facts as well as non-economic values. Many Americans seem to ignore the findings of fact-checking, while many politicians ignore, or pretend to ignore, the facts themselves. Given this, what do you think of the schizophrenic role of science in capitalist culture?

Robinson I think of them as in conflict for control. I'm very pro-science, but everything can be bought, and even science is in danger. I thought, because science was doing the real work, that capitalism was its parasite, like the puppet masters in the Heinlein story. I still think that's true, but in global capitalism, money really can direct scientific research; we still have the war machine, for instance. And big pharmaceuticals direct a lot of biological research, ignoring certain problems and paying attention to others, depending on the potential for profit. Just because science is doing the real work it doesn't mean it's in control; the puppet master can call the shots, the parasite could be strong enough to kill the host. That happens a lot in nature. It's a scary, scary century.

Science is a contested space. The AGU (the American Geophysical Union) is an example. Do they take money from Exxon or not? They voted on it, and they are still taking money from Exxon. They think it is better to have that money to put to good use than to make a symbolic statement against Exxon. This is just one small example of a constant battle. The enormous, elaborate community of scientific institutions is trying to figure out how can they save the world without becoming revolutionaries, or without becoming political. This is funny, because they're acting politically without admitting it. What they're doing is intensely political, but they're still caught in a paradigm in which facts aren't political. Generally speaking, the psychological mindset of science is astonishingly naive, philosophically simplistic: 'What I do is very straightforward. I gather data, and then I analyse it, and I make a theory and I explain, then I go back and do more experiments.' On the other hand, many scientists are highly sophisticated and know more about the humanities than most people in the humanities know about the sciences. Many are actually more well-rounded intellectually than most people in the humanities.

The first wave of scientific efforts to alert the world to climate change was a painfully instructive moment for scientists. When scientists saw that just announcing the problem didn't change people's behaviour, they were shocked and dismayed because they thought that people would look at the facts and then change their values. Even now they are still trying to find a way to move forward, to be both scientists and effective political actors.

Feder That's a nice segue to a question I want to ask about H.G. Wells. I know you're a fan. Anyone who works on Wells has a difficult task of trying to think through his visionary socialism alongside his authoritarian tendencies. Is there anything you want to say about *The Shape of Things to Come* [1933], *The Work, Wealth and Happiness of Mankind* [1932] or, if by chance you've read it, *The Croquet Player* [1936]?

Robinson No, I haven't read *The Croquet Player*, but I've read *Star Begotten* [1937], another late work from the thirties. In the thirties they could see that another war was coming, and it probably felt apocalyptic to think that they were heading towards a war even worse than the First World War. I admire the way Wells tried to continue to be hopeful in that situation. It was a very totalitarian time; as with Leninism, people thought if you could just seize control long enough to do what's right, then democracy could come later. His version of taking over is usually a scientific meritocracy. It's almost like Silicon Valley today, which thinks 'If we could just ignore politics and tech our way out of all these problems....' Of course, Wells was much cannier than that. The libertarian Silicon Valley view is lame. They're not geniuses. [...] I've seen computer world attitudes range from sophisticated concern to a siloed in [view of the world], 'We're so smart that we can ignore other problems; maybe we'll set up a colony on Mars, and then we'll be okay.' That kind of thinking is terribly inadequate. [...]

Feder One of the horrible places in Wells has to do with population; Wells had phases of eugenic thinking. In *New York 2140*, there is a refugee crisis, but I don't recall seeing the word overpopulation in your novel. Did the first and second pulses (of rising sea levels) significantly diminish the population or are you trying to make people rethink the question of population in ecological terms?

Robinson Population per se is not the problem. Population still matters, but it is only part of the equation. Ehrlich's 'IPAT' formula [I = P x A x T or, impact is determined by population times affluence times the 'greenness' of the technology] shows that the ordinary westerner uses thirty times the resources of someone in Asia. When you do the math, 300 million people in the United States times thirty, you get a stupendous figure that makes India and China look like paltry little populations in terms of consumption or impact on the earth.

But it shouldn't be an A for affluence or appetite in that equation, it should be an E, for economics; in other words, the 'IPET' theory. I talked to Ehrlich about this, and he was interested. You don't want to talk about affluence or appetite, because everybody should have a refrigerator so they don't get sick, and what is true affluence is a value judgement. Thoreau was affluent. So, what's messy in this equation, between population and the cleanness or dirtiness of technology? What's the thing that makes us use too much? Our economic system, the middle term. It's more important than population per se, and tech is getting cleaner and cleaner. Re-rigging the economic system for our survival is the focus of *New York 2140*, but all my writing, going back almost thirty years now, has been about imagining various post-capitalisms. I don't characterise it with any one term because they're weighted with baggage from the past, so I'm perfectly happy to talk about any post-capitalist future, social democracy or democratic socialism, communism....

Feder Social-anarchism?

Robinson I'm a statist; I don't believe anarchism is a way to get through the next couple of centuries. I thoroughly approve of anarchism's ultimate goal of the total horizontalisation of power but, to me, anarchism is a horizon that is centuries out. [...]

Feder I couldn't help but enjoy the pairing of global and financial liquidity (rising sea levels and financial crashes). Did you have the pairing, literally and metaphorically in mind from the start?

Robinson Yes. People say I like floods. All of my big novels include floods, the *Mars Trilogy*, *The Years of Rice and Salt*, *Green Earth*, and now this book. And in *2312*, the drowned Manhattan appears for the first time as a set piece. It always struck me as funny that we might drown in our own liquidity.

Feder In *New York 2140*, we have, on the one hand, dark economic pools and then, on the other, nature as Mother Ocean. In one of the Amelia chapters you invoke Aldo Leopold's land ethic, in which he exhorts us to think like a mountain. Is this novel trying, in places, to ask us to think like an ocean?

Robinson Maybe. Leopold is very important. I think his phrase, 'What's good is good for the land' is a baseline value, a value that we should base everything else on. If you take care of the land, then people will also be okay. This is crucial, transformative ecological thinking.

Essentially, what's good for the planet is good for the people who are co-existent with it. The inter-tidal is a great metaphor as well as a great real space. As a real space, it's complicated, messy, lively, and you can't legislate it. In many legal systems it's an unorganised public space.

Feder Living in this post-second pulse, inter-tidal space requires some interesting future technology, including very resilient carbon negative building materials and infrastructure. Is any aspect of this technology in development?

Robinson Right now it's at the level of venture capital, these graphene sheets, basically carbon nano-tubes flattened out. It's science fiction tech right now, but people with money are interested in it because the source material is carbon.

Feder *New York 2140* is a work of speculative fiction, speculating on the technology we need for a better future, which sheds light on another, related form of speculation: futures markets.

Robinson 'The Volatility Index' is already a science fiction story set one month out! Risk assessment for investors is a matter of making predictions. Since it can't be done [accurately], the risk is high; the volatility is high. In that realm, what you want is to be able to win whether the market goes up or down.

Feder This is interesting, because some of the earliest climate data we have comes from insurance companies.

Robinson The insurance companies, especially the re-insurance companies, could be part of the story of post-capitalism, because they're going to be the ultimate holders of the costs. They are going to say to the world, 'Sorry, these are not payable costs.' I have friends in the Natural Catastrophe Division of Swiss Re who say, 'Wait, our whole industry is doomed, because we can't pay out what's going to come due,' and therefore [the world's now] uninsurable. They would have said, up to this point, everything's insurable, you just need to set the rate right. When you can't set the rate right, it would break civilisation to pay the premiums. You get into the mass extinction event, you get into the stupidity of 'we can't afford to survive'. [...]

Feder Speaking of problems of scale, the complex ecological effects of the industrial revolution and Great Acceleration, what do you think of the term Anthropocene, and the idea of Anthropocene literature?

Robinson It's interesting to historicise it as a term. It began with scientists trying to say, 'Look, climate change is real, and we're having a profound impact as a species.' But when academia picked it up, it drops into the swamp of semantics, it loses political force. It's best as a geological term, but it has already been defused. It's become just another term like sustainability.

Feder Yes, 'sustainability' has been co-opted. Do you think Anthropocene literature might rescue the term?

Robinson Whenever science fiction gets interesting, then people try to give it another name. It's the anti-science fiction prejudice raising its head again. If its content becomes relevant, you call it cyberpunk, cli-fi, Anthropocene literature or dystopian fiction. These are all science fiction.

It's a very big, powerful genre. As soon as you say, 'we're going to talk about the future', you're saying you're going talk about history. You're going to talk about the planet. You're going to talk about everything. That's what science fiction does.

Kim Stanley Robinson and Helena Feder, extracts from 'The Realism of Our Time: Interview with Kim Stanley Robinson', *Radical Philosophy*, no. 2.01 (February 2018) 87–90, 91, 96, 97, 98.

Jessica L. Horton and Janet Catherine Berlo
Beyond the Mirror: Indigenous Ecologies and 'New Materialisms' in Contemporary Art//2013

[...] Material is in motion across the academic disciplines. In the past decade and a half, Bill Brown challenged literary and visual studies with 'thing theory'; scholars ranging from literary critic N. Katherine Hayles to political scientist Francis Fukuyama heralded the cyber- and bio-technological era of the 'posthuman'; political scientists Samantha Frost and Diane Coole pointed to the transdisciplinary rise of a host of 'new materialisms'; in contemporary art history, citations pile high for sociologist Bruno Latour's haunting title, *We Have Never Been Modern*; most recently, curator Anselm Franke critically revisited the term 'animism' in a two-part exhibition and book.[1] This diversity of work shares a basic conviction that matter – whether in the forest or the lab – has agency, can move, act, assume volition, and even enjoy degrees of intelligence often assumed to be the unique domain of human subjectivity. The revolutionary character of this recognition lies precisely in its challenge to an anthropocentric post-Enlightenment intellectual tradition in which philosophical and scientific divisions between subject and object, culture and nature – what Latour calls the 'Great Divide' – ensured the primacy of people among beings both inert and in motion.[2] Such categorical divisions authorised the foundational capitalist imperative to own and control nature. This has engendered crisis as floods, oil spills, extreme weather and elements from an out-of-balance biosphere talk back. The ecological promise of these 'new materialisms' is to invite a dialogue among a wider host of agents, imaging a profoundly relational world in which humans interact with, rather than act upon, others. Indeed, we maintain that grasping multiple forms of liveliness has implications for questions of global environmental justice in raising the possibility of an ethics that binds not only affluent and poor, coloniser and colonised, but also the material entities upon which all our livelihoods depend.

Nonetheless, in this essay we are concerned with those humans who are too often left out of the conversation. Indigenous scholars and scholars of the indigenous will attest to the survival of alternative intellectual traditions in which the liveliness of matter is grasped as quite ordinary, both inside, and at the fringes of, European modernity. Once we take indigenous worldviews into account, the 'new materialisms' are no longer new.

Modifiers such as 'new' and 'post' suggest a European developmental schema that permits the detection of non-human agencies in a contemporary period of crisis. Even Latour, who eschews this problematic temporal schema, does not intend the 'we' in *We Have Never Been Modern* to be globally self-reflexive. Latour is concerned with turning the anthropological gaze abroad back upon Europe in order to reveal transgressive impurities long hidden under the mask of rationalism. The radicality of this move remains stymied by the absence of indigenous voices in and about the mutually affecting spread of modernity. As Franke interprets Latour to reflect upon the exhibitionary complex of contemporary art, his conception of animism as a 'mirror' excludes while it reflects.

[...] Recent works by Jimmie Durham, Rebecca Belmore, Will Wilson and Jolene Rickard share a concern with the liveliness of matter that can provide the grounds – at times quite literally – for looking beyond the mirror. While there is evidence of the indigenous philosophical precepts that inform the work, the artists locate their practices in an extensive and shared contemporary landscape that includes the space of exhibition, thus short-circuiting a romantic gaze that might locate indigenous art or bodies in nature somewhere else. Their works issue an invitation to a wider audience – including us, a pair of non-Native, English-speaking scholars writing this article – to seriously consider the relevance of indigenous intellectual traditions to the contemporary global challenges of co-habitation.

Certainly, the four artists' work dovetails with a wider trend in eco-art that T.J. Demos describes as 'comprehending ecology as a field of interlinking systems of biodiversity and technology, social practices and political structures'.[3] But a systems approach to the environment can still support forms of anthropocentrism, so long as humans are treated as privileged arbiters of the future. In each of the four projects we discuss, artists grant environmental entities the agency to push back, to punish or reward human activity, to remind people of their precarious position in a relational world where allies are essential to flourishing [...] In lieu of an exhaustive account of these works, we focus on a single material agent in each project, tracing its complex forms of movement and affiliation into spaces of exhibition. Seeking to bind viewers into a shared fate with material friends and foes, the following works raise the possibility of an ethics premised on mutual recognition and shared livelihood.

In stone, a substance that is indigenous to every place on the globe, Durham has found a material ally to match the mobility of contemporary art and commerce. In *Encore Tranquilité* (2009), the artist staged an encounter between a giant boulder and single engine aeroplane in an abandoned airfield outside Berlin. In a widely published story, the antiquated ex-Soviet plane was deemed unsafe by European standards and was slated for sale in Africa, tying its fate to the ethical failures of the neocolonial market-place.[4] The boulder came out on top, nearly splitting the plane in two. The implied buoyancy of substrate worked against European metaphors that link it to inertia: 'stone dead', 'stone faced', 'stone cold'. While Franke reads Durham's many works with stone as staging the disruptive force of Europe's repressed 'other', we emphasise an equally affirmative strain: the lively rock acted as an unexpected ally in a tale of global injustice, a potential saviour of countless undervalued human lives that demanded acknowledgement for its intervention before the eyes of viewers. When stone and splintered plane were relocated to the foyer of the Musée d'Art Moderne de la Ville de Paris for Durham's 2009 retrospective, 'Rejected Stones', the materials indexed an encounter that took place in the past.[5]

Visitors could only scan the scene for clues: Did the stone fall from above or sail through the air? Was it local to Europe or a hit man from Africa? Was the plane it targeted in motion, empty, defunct? Here, material evinced not only liveliness and ethical orientation, but also the ability to know things, marking the limits of viewers' capacities to control their surroundings. Durham lets stone tell its own part in the story.

While relating to Durham's work does not necessarily depend upon recognising indigenous influence, highlighting such connections across the intellectual boundaries we have described can certainly enhance an of its philosophical and political dimensions. [...]

While stones travel into viewers' space in Durham's work, the remaining projects we discuss share a concern with implicating viewers in the fate of faraway bodies – those of both land and people. In her video installation, *Fountain*, made for the Canadian Pavilion of the Venice Biennale in 2005, Rebecca Belmore employed ubiquitous, unbounded water as her Venetian translator. A sheet of falling liquid acted as a projection screen for a two-minute video loop. The initial sweep of the camera established a landscape alive with human and transhuman agencies: a plane flew overhead and heaps of discarded logs burst spontaneously into flames. Only a small group of viewers in Venice would have recognised Iona Beach in Vancouver, sacred Musqueam land that is today a poisoned regional park, marking the convergence of Canada's logging industry, sewage treatment ponds and the flight path of an international airport. Even without this geographic specificity, the sombre images conjured multiple forms of global material circulation: the watery voyages of Europeans to the Northwest Coast, the oceanic transport of commodities appropriated from First

Nations lands, ubiquitous contemporary air travel and the unbounded toxicity resulting from such multiple intrusions. Visitors then witnessed the artist struggling with an unknown burden offshore of a polluted industrial beach. Here the visible particularities of land and of Belmore's indigenous female body elicited the unevenness of these systems which subject certain people and places to undue environmental violence. [...]

In a recent essay, Rickard reiterates Taiaiake Alfred's call for an interpretation of sovereignty that is detached from its current Western legal meaning in favour of longstanding indigenous understandings of governance.[6] She asserts:

> We simultaneously appropriated the European word sovereignty and rejected a US legal interpretation of it while creating a uniquely Haudenosaunee understanding [...] that embodies our philosophical, political, and renewal strategies.[7]

Critical to her ancestors' formation of sovereignty is a notion of human responsibility to sustain those environmental agents who share the physical and intellectual space of Haudenosaunee lives. Leadership entailed not unmitigated rights of access but rather a responsibility to 'prevent the abuse' of both humans and other-than-humans in an environment of peace.[8] [...]

Artists such as Rickard help strengthen legal claims to self-determination by framing them in an indigenous intellectual tradition and displaying the relevance of its precepts to a larger transnational community. She joins Durham, Belmore and Wilson in contributing to a larger critical project of grasping human and non-human entities as agents in a mutually affecting relationship. It is precisely through such a retooled vision of shared, collaborative power that we begin to identify tenets for an equitable geopolitics that loosen the grip of anthropocentric nationalisms and devastating neocolonialisms. We suggest that the emerging vision is not a borderless utopia, but rather a geography of crossing paths, marking points of convergence between equals – indigenous and European persons, human and other-than-human agents – whose livelihoods are always already inextricable. There is a certain intellectual generosity in the works we have discussed, an invitation for human cognition to move across the same boundaries that stone and water traverse with ease. Instead of a mirror, they offer a meeting ground. Accepting the invitation is certainly a human choice. But material may be the ultimate judge of our ethics.

1 [Footnote 3 in source] Anselm Franke (ed.), *Animism* (Berlin and New York: Sternberg Press, 2010). 'Animism/Animismus' exhibition held at the Haus der Kulturen der Welt, Berlin, 16 March – 6 May, 2012.

2 [4] Bruno Latour, *We Have Never Been Modern*, trans. Catherine Porter (Cambridge, MA: Harvard University Press, 1993) 12.

3 [15] T.J. Demos, 'The Politics Politics of Sustainability: Contemporary Art and Ecology', in *Radical Nature: Art and Architecture for a Changing Planet 1969–2009*, eds. Francesco Manacorda and Ariella Yedgar (London: Koenig/Barbican, 2009) 24.

4 [17] Jimmie Durham, '1000 Words', *Artforum* (January 2009) 189.

5 [18] Fabrice Hergott (ed.), *Jimmie Durham: Rejected Stones* (Paris: Musee d'Art Moderne de la Ville de Paris/ARC, 2009).

6 [44] Taiaiake Alfred, *Peace, Power, Righteousness: An Indigenous Manifesto* (Oxford: Oxford University Press, 1999) 54–5.

7 [45] Rickard likewise reminds her readers that the Haudenosaunee 'played a critical role in the formation of concepts of democracy in the emergence of the United States and are today leaders in the forum on the United Nations Declaration on the Rights of Indigenous Peoples'. 'Visualizing Sovereignty in the Time of Biometric Sensors', op. cit., 466–467. See also Iris Marion Young, 'Hybrid Democracy: Iroquois Federalism and the Postcolonial Project', in *Global Challenges: War, Self-Determination and Responsibility for Justice* (Cambridge: Polity, 2007) 15 –38.

8 [46] 'Visualizing Sovereignty in the Time of Biometric Sensors', op. cit.

Jessica L. Horton and Janet Catherine Berlo, extracts from 'Beyond the Mirror: Indigenous Ecologies and "New Materialisms" in Contemporary Art', *Third Text*, vol. 27, issue 1 (January 2013) 25–6.

Timothy Morton
Beginning After the End//2016

There are thoughts we can anticipate, glimpsed in the distance along
existing thought pathways.
This is a future that is simply the present, stretched out further.
There is not-yet-thought that never arrives – yet here we are thinking
it in the paradoxical flicker of this very sentence.
If we want thought different from the present – if we want to change the present
– then thought must be aware of this kind of future.
It is not a future into which we can progress.
This future is unthinkable. Yet we are, thinking it.
Coexisting, we are thinking future coexistence. Predicting it and
more: keeping the unpredictable one open.
Yet such a future, the open future, has become taboo.

Because it is real, yet beyond concept.
Because it is *weird*.
Art is thought from the future. Thought we cannot explicitly think at present. Thought we may not think or speak at all.
If we want thought different from the present, then thought must veer toward art.
To be a thing at all – a rock, a lizard, a human – is to be in a twist.
How thought longs to twist and turn like the serpent poetry!
Or is art veering toward thought? Does it ever arrive?
The threads of fate have tied our tongues.
Tongue twisters inclined towards nonsense.
Logic includes nonsense as long as it can tell the truth.
The logic of nonsense.
The needle skipped the groove of the present.
Into this dark forest you have already turned.
I take *present* to mean *for the last twelve thousand years*. A butterfly kiss of geological time

Timothy Morton, 'Beginning After the End', in *Dark Ecology: For a Logic of Future Coexistence* (New York: Columbia University Press, 2016) 1–2.

T.J. Demos
Gardening Against the Apocalypse//2016

'We are told that we live in a state of permanent crisis, a state of emergency and thus of exception', wrote Carolyn Christov-Bakargiev in her main curatorial statement for dOCUMENTA (13).[1] Calling to mind the endless wars in the Middle East, the retraction of civil liberties worldwide, and the generalised conditions of emergency law theorised, for instance, by Giorgio Agamben as the contemporary 'state of exception', and by Paul Virilio as 'pure war', this recognition could seem to set the stage for an engaged presentation of agit-prop political art. Joined by a supportive team of curatorial agents, the director of this most ambitious of international exhibitions chose, however, to respond to the state of crisis with a marked prevalence of artist-rendered gardens.[2] Overgrown with experimental planters, creative landscapes, and installations relating variously to horticulture, farming, and natural life-forms, the 2012 iteration of Documenta, the high-profile exhibition that occurs every five years in Kassel, Germany, was the most 'green' yet. However, the show's implicit linkage of gardening and political emergency produced not so much a clear approach to exceptional conditions as it did a series of conceptual challenges and unresolved contradictions, which, intentionally or not, demonstrated a state of crisis in terms of how ecology is addressed within the artistic realm. [...]

Varieties of Political Ecology

Described as 'an exhibition without a concept' by Christov-Bakargiev in the run-up to the show – in order to allow inclusions to stand on their own, visitors were told – the curators effectively outsourced the show's conceptualisation to its impossibly extensive, and sometimes internally conflicted, '100 Notebooks'. [...] The series assembles essays by a range of artists and theorists, including some relating to the ecological, that suggest numerous productive, if competing, ways to approach the gardens and, more broadly, the treatment of the environment in the exhibition. For instance, Donna Haraway's contribution, *SF: Speculative Fabulation and String Figures*, develops the terms of a techno-organic hybrid aesthetics, building on her well-known work on cyborgs, which finds inspiration in the science of gene research and bioengineering. For Haraway, 'SF' proposes multiple meanings – 'speculative fabulation, speculative feminism, science fiction, science fact, science fantasy'.[3] Each, like the intertwinements of 'string figure' games to which the author also alludes, represents a bridge between categories in ways reminiscent of her cyborg, 'a creature of social reality as well as a creature of fiction' that prefigures a world transcending the oppressive binaries of modernity (male-female, culture-nature, subject–object, technology-biology, etc.).[4] Haraway's contribution was not merely theoretical; her penchant for post-binary multiplicity was also discernable in the exhibition's spatial dispersion – with more than fifty locations comprising a rhizomatic geography throughout Karlsaue Park – and in the show's thematic diffusion, where a hundred approaches eclipsed any single reigning theme (in addition, Haraway served as a member of the exhibition's 'honorary advisory committee').[5] Her influence was also felt in the 'natureculture' and 'intra-actional' aspects of the 'becoming with' ontology of the gardens – all terms of Haraway's (although not used by the curators) – suggesting hyphenated mediums that both organise and provide socio-aesthetic support systems for human life, a theoretical framework that significantly opens up the conceptual potential of the artists' work with gardens.

Yet mobilising Haraway's insights as a model for environmental aesthetics proves tricky in this context, especially when placed in relation to the more overtly political garden practices in the exhibition. Providing one such example, the collective And And And embraced an anti-capitalist, organic localism, with several garden kiosks selling regional food and produce on the exhibition grounds during the length of the show. The initiative, run by artists Ayreen Anastas and Rene Gabri, formed part of the dOCUMENTA (13) core research team, and in that capacity investigated the notions of the commons and non-capitalist living in gatherings and seminars across the world over the two years preceding the exhibition – from participation in the US Social Forum in Detroit to workshops in Tunis; Yerevan, Armenia; and Buenos Aires. [...]

In addition to supporting such off-site events, And And And organised an open experimental public programme in a large workshop space near the back of the Kassel train station during the length of the exhibition, inviting artists, activists, farmers, students, thinkers, residents and visitors to participate in daily public discussions. Their programme addressed diverse philosophical, political, pedagogical and aesthetic matters of concern, 'grounded in a conviction that, today, all fields of human activity must critically re-examine the values, assumptions and modalities of doing'.[6] More specifically, the group attempted to realise a process of 'militant joyful collective research into non-capitalist life', revolving around 'commoning in Kassel', to ask, '[w]hat is it that we are capable of sharing and can we construct a common space or a common time for thinking about common concerns?'[7]

The political ecology of this work – though not unrelated to Haraway's approach to SF and her emphasis on the speculative, fictional and fantastic – is perhaps most directly connected to the practice of Indian environmental activist Vandana Shiva, another of the exhibition's notebook authors, known for her activism against the commercial patenting of seeds and plant life in India by corporations like Monsanto and Syngenta. Haraway also opposes the patenting of life forms (as commodified GMOs in agribusiness and the pharmaceutical industries), but her techno-feminist sci-fi aesthetic does not ultimately fit with Shiva's alter-globalisation climate justice activism, leading to a conflict of ecological visions.[8] As Shiva writes, in *The Corporate Control of Life*, '[l]iving organisms unlike machines organise themselves. Because of his capacity, they cannot be treated as simply "biotechnological inventions", "gene constructs", or "products of the mind", terms that are used to justify their commercial patenting as human creations.'[9] Challenging this logic, and condemning the corporate 'biopiracy' of indigenous culture and resources, Shiva emphasises the fight to protect the legal sovereignty of non-commercialised knowledge, and the free and universal access to the life processes of humanity's shared heritage, such as regenerative seeds, clean water, and fertile land. [...]

There was consequently a profound divergence within the discourse on the garden in dOCUMENTA (13) – between Haraway's posthuman constructivist approach to biotechnological hybridity as a model of creative liberation on the one hand, and, on the other, Shiva's postcolonial commitment to ecological justice opposed to corporate property claims on organic resources pilfered from local communities in the Global South. While the exhibition tacitly raised this very conundrum by including these divergent voices in its notebooks, the clash of positions – which concerns increasingly volatile global conflicts over food production, capitalist agro-economy, and the status of the natural world (whether financialised or ecologised) – was never explicitly engaged in the exhibition's framework. As a result, Christov-Bakargiev's project risked a (non-) position of uncommitted theoretical pluralism, a tendency familiar in the liberal milieu of contemporary art, eager to allude to crises and emergencies – even to aestheticise them – but taking no clear stand in relation to them.

[...] Although the exhibition can be credited with opening up a politico-ecological artistic discourse to confront visitors with these differing positions, it was also exemplary of the failure to take a stand about the very problems it raised – as if knowledge production releases us from any ethico-political responsibilities, or from assuming such responsibility at the curatorial level.

To take a position would demand critiquing the political economy of sci-fi aesthetics (of the kind Haraway supports) in relation to social and climate justice activism (of the kind Shiva advocates). [...] Rather than curatorially addressing these conflicts (and their negative consequences), dOCUMENTA (13) included several artists who posed related questions in work created for the exhibition: How do futurist imaginings of corporate biotechnology correlate with current political struggles over land use, energy policy and GMOs? How might we represent a world facing environmental catastrophe, a posthuman landscape, a mass extinction event?

And what is the political economy of post-apocalyptic aesthetics? In fact, this Documenta contained numerous visions of dystopian futures after an eco-catastrophe, which the exhibition's experimental gardens seemed so intent on forestalling. Consider *News from Nowhere* by South Korean artists Moon Kyungwon and Jeon Joonho. A model of post-apocalyptic science fiction, the project comprises the video *El Fin del Mundo* (*The End of the World*), a mixed–media installation, and a collaborative research publication, building an iconography of genetic engineering and biotechnology (gone awry) that resonates with Haraway's cyborg futurism and represents a further approach to considering relations between science, ecology, and advanced capitalism in contemporary art.

Inspired by socialist craftsman William Morris' eponymous 1890 tale of a future agrarian worker society, Moon and Jeon's *News from Nowhere* visualises a disastrous time to come when humanity, owing to a series of unspecified major climate changes, is reduced to an endangered species living in a contaminated biosphere, whose survivors must reconsider their philosophies of life.[10] Referencing utopian socialism and science fiction alike, the installation's subject is set on a late twenty-first-century earth permeated with radioactivity and hazardous waste, where raised sea levels necessitate floating settlements and the (imaginary) corporate giant Tempus rules over all. [...]

The mixed-media Documenta installation made apparent the risk of a sci-fi poetics that merely aestheticises crisis: it establishes little political traction in the present. Much like the speculative fabulation of so many pop-culture blockbusters, the piece sidesteps critical environmental knowledge in favour of a generalised coo-catastrophic context, opting for visual gratification, even fatalistically dwelling in the morbid enjoyment of imagining future horrors. We have the privilege of witnessing the time to come but can do nothing to stop it from happening; indeed, the project merely pays lip service to the failures of the present without identifying the causes of – or better, providing alternatives to – the 'major climate changes' that serve as its fiction's generic foundation. As a result, we are invited to enjoy our own future demise aesthetically. The film and installation's corporate-scientific social order, technological redemption, and the imagery of a transfigured posthuman cyborg body construct a dystopian imaginary within our otherwise calamitous circumstances. Indeed, as Naomi Klein argues, such pop apocalypticism 'is so much a part of our culture that we think all we're capable of doing is becoming like societies portrayed in *Snowpiercer*, *Elysium*, or *The Hunger Games*. It's actually not controversial to say this is where we are headed. The question is, can we imagine another way of responding to crisis other than one of deepening inequality, brutal disaster capitalism and mangled techno-fixes, because that seems to be where in this regard, people agree we're headed.'[11] [...]

Can we imagine an equitable way of positively responding to crisis, as Klein asks? If so, what would its artistic corollary be? [...] Klein states that we need to get over our cultural addiction of imagining apocalyptic scenarios in favour of engaging with the deathly politics of corporate globalisation today in order to invent a hopeful future. One such countermodel, presented at dOCUMENTA (13), was offered with the Otolith Group's *The Radiant*, which focuses on the real corporate-science complex and its disastrous failure in the present, an actual scenario nonetheless worthy of science fiction. The film, about an hour in length, takes its point of departure as 11 March, 2011, when the Tohoku earthquake off the coast of Japan triggered a tsunami that left more than fifteen thousand people dead and caused the catastrophic meltdown at the Fukushima Daiichi nuclear power plant, which continues to contaminate the land, air and sea (the effects of radiation will stretch over thousands, even millions of years).[12] Mixing historical and contemporary TV reports about the triple catastrophe, as well as interview footage with scientists, activists and local residents, the film joins the erstwhile promise of nuclear energy from the plant's postwar construction (from 1966 to 1971) to the future threat of a contaminated global earth, forming an explosive equation that opens critical rifts in our forsaken present. [...]

The Radiant [...] entangles the futuristic gardens of the posthuman in the political conflicts of the present, implicating us in the necropolitics of radiation. Consider the video's now-famous appropriated footage of the pointing man – the Fukushima worker who pointed his index finger directly at a security camera for ten minutes just after its meltdown. [...] The inclusion of the footage in the film suggests that if the pointing man's video went viral on the Internet in the days after the meltdown, then it did so because that resonant gesture unleashed an explosively charged index of the meeting point of the present and future, when the origins of the potential coming catastrophe of mass extinction are seen to be firmly rooted in our own world, not in sci-fi speculation. And by referencing Vito Acconci's video *Centers* (1971) – as Takeuchi, also an artist, did on his blog – the Otolith Group retools video art's 'aesthetics of narcissism' (as Rosalind Krauss once wrote of Acconci's self-referential video) as a defiant sign of popular accusation against a nuclear necropower.[13]

The Radiant exemplifies, finally, what Fredric Jameson has described as a 'negative' utopianism, 'transforming our own present into the determinate past of something yet to come'.[14] Negative utopianism can mean two things here: first, it suggests a critical image that captures the catastrophe of the present utopianism (of nuclear energy, for example, and its necropolitics of radiation), by highlighting its failures and portraying its negativity as apocalyptic ecocide. Second, it articulates the potential for a new imagination once the false utopianisms of the present have been cleared away (along the lines of what Jameson calls 'anti-anti-utopianism' – the rejection of those capitalist-realist arguments that contend that utopian thinking is impossible, irresponsible, and escapist, which ends up reasserting the status quo by denying the imagination of other possible worlds). Rather than giving itself over to the sci-fi seductions of a future biotechnology, this work finds the future preordained in the conditions of our present. In this sense, the future intimated by *The Radiant* works like a mechanism to make the present different than it normally appears, thereby sparking a political energy to resist what is already occurring, the desire to challenge contemporary nuclear destruction. The film shows protesters contesting Japan's irresponsible and media-spun response to the disaster – especially given the government's decision with TEPCO to distribute irradiated soil throughout the country, destroying control groups of forensic samples to shield itself against future liability lawsuits by victims of radiation-caused illnesses, as discussed in the film by journalist May Shigenobu. Ending on this note, the Otolith Group seizes the speculative opportunity of an environment in the clutches of extinction to reveal contours of our own necropolitical regime. While it provides witness to a world without us, haunting in its eerie calm, the video's own anti-nuclear activism also amplifies the agency of political resistance.

Occupy Curating

dOCUMENTA (13)'s 'concept-less' exhibition, as we've seen, tended more toward the hybrid aesthetics of sci-fi than political engagement, even while it included voices that insist on politicising ecology. Its curators missed the opportunity to explicitly address and position the exhibition within the philosophical and political controversies surrounding the status of life today (even as the massive resource consumption of the show's production and operation contradicted its green rhetoric).[15] What would be the ramifications of taking seriously the ecological insights of – and most importantly conflicts between – Haraway and Shiva at the level of curating? Is it easier to imagine the end of the world than the end of the unsustainable mega-exhibition? How can future Documentas take into account the externalities of their production – their carbon footprint and exploitation of fossil-fuel-based resources? And in recognising this crisis situation, how might future shows work critically within that framework, acknowledging its contradictions openly, if not overcoming them practically?

In the present age of crises and emergencies, we need bold proposals, not fuzzy non-concepts. Consider the symbolic weight if such a high profile exhibition determined that it is simply environmentally unviable and [considered] calling itself off, or doing something sustainable in its place. Such an alternative has yet to be invented, even though we have recent precedents that have glimpsed it. One modest proposal was offered on the front lawn of the Fridericianum during dOCUMENTA (13): a tent city of the Occupy movement, part of the global anti-capitalist uprising that began in 2011. It was a token inclusion for sure (insofar as it was welcomed by the show's organisers), no match for a mega-exhibition, but one figuring as an alternative paradigm of a localist formation with a minimal ecological footprint, inclusively participatory, anti-elitist, and committed to degrowth and recycling, without admission costs or travelling far distances. As such, the Occupy movement offered a largely unacknowledged radical alternative in the shadow of dOCUMENTA (13), mostly invisible to the conventional art world. If taken seriously as a model, however, it would transform the contemporary art exhibition into something largely unrecognisable from today's perspective.[16] Against the exhibition's curatorial position of non-engagement, such ecological imperatives must be taken up in forceful, ambitious proposals, so that emergency conditions are not simply invoked at a distance, through artworks, representation, or discourse – that is, even while dOCUMENTA (13) remains significant for opening paths to explore the biopolitics of nature in its current guise, including the mixed economies of food production, experimental gardens, and environmental governance in the age of nuclear threat and catastrophic climate breakdown.[17] These questions lie at the heart of contemporary debates over what kind of world we want to live in, how it will be organised, and what role art might play to imagine, represent, and realise it. With each passing day, the stakes of those debates only continue to grow more momentous.

1 Carolyn Christov-Bakargiev, dOCUMENTA (13) press release, October 25, 2010. The letter is published as the third 'note–book' in the series *100 Notes – 100 Thoughts / 100 Notizen – 100 Gedanken* (Ostfildern: Hatje Cantz, 2011).

2 The curatorial team's 'agents' included Leeza Ahmady, Ayreen Anastas and Rene Gabri, Sofia Henández Chong Cuy, Sunjung Kim, Koyo Kouoh, Joasla Krysa, Marta Kuzma, Raimundas Malašauskas, Chus Martínez, Lívia Páldi, Hetti Perkins, Eva Scharrer, Kitty Scott and Andrea Villani.

3 [11] Donna Haraway, *SF: Speculative Fabulation and String Figures*, in *100 Notes – 100 Thoughts / 100 Notizen – 100 Gedanken*, no. 33, (Ostfildern: Hatje Cantz, 2011) 4.

4 [12] [...] Donna Haraway, *Simians, Cyborgs and Women: The Reinvention of Nature* (London: Free Association, 1991) 149–50.

5 [13] For the exhibition, Tue Greenfort created *The Worldly House*, a mixed-media archival installation in Karlsaue Park inspired by Haraway's writings. The exhibition also expanded to Kabul, Cairo and Banff, aspects that extend beyond the scope of this analysis.

6 [16] See 'About And And And', dOCUMENTA (13), http://d13.documenta.de/#programs/the-kassel-programs/and-and-and/about-and-and-and, accessed December 3, 2015.

7 [17] 'Commoning in Kassel', dOCUMENTA (13), http://d13documenta.de/#/programs/the–kassel-programs/and-and-and/commoning-in-kassel; 'A Militant Joyful Collective Research into Non-capitalist Life', dOCUMENTA (13), http://d13.documenta.de/#en/programs/the-kassel-programs/and–and-and/a-militant-joyful-collective-research-into-non-capitalist-life. See also Anastas and Gabri's investigation of the commons as part of their project at The Showroom in London [...] 'Some Preliminary Notes for London', Commoning Times, http://commoningtimes.org/london, accessed 3 December, 2015.

8 [18] See Donna Haraway, *Modest_Witness@Second_Millennium.FemaleMan_Meets_OncoMouse: Feminism and Techno science* (New York: Routledge, 1997) 62.

9 [19] Vandana Shiva, *The Corporate Control of Life*, in *100 Notes – 100 Thoughts / 100 Notizen – 100 Gedanken*, no. 12 (Ostfildern: Hatje Cantz, 2011). Between 2008 and 2010, some 261 patents were filed related to growing 'climate-ready' crops, involving seeds able to ostensibly withstand extreme weather conditions – close to 80% of these patents were controlled by six agribusiness giants (DuPont, BASF, Monsanto, Syngenta, Bayer, and Dow). 'Who Will Control the Green Economy?', ETC Group (1 November, 2011) 23 (http://www.etcgroupiorg/content/who-will-control-green-economy-0).

10 [35] Morris's *News from Nowhere* begins with the narrator returning home from a meeting of the Socialist League and falling asleep to wake up in a future world where society is organised around the common ownership and democratic control of the means of production. The agrarian culture has no system of authority, money, legal courts, prisons, or class system – only the shared pleasure in work and nature.

11 [37] Klein quoted in John Tarleton, 'Interview: Naomi Klein Breaks a Taboo' (September 2014) (https://indypendent.org/2014/09/interview-naomi-klein-breaks-a-taboo/) [...].

12 [42] On the prolonged temporality of radiation, see Rob Nixon, 'Slow Violence, Neoliberalism, and the Environmental Picaresque', in *Slow Violence and the Environmentalism of the Poor* (Cambridge, MA: Harvard University Press, 2013) 45–68.

13 [61] Rosalind Krauss, 'Video: The Aesthetics of Narcissism', *October*, no.1 (Spring 1976) 50–64.

14 [62] Fredric Jameson, *Archaeologies of the Future: The Desire Called Utopia and Other Science Fictions* (London and New York: Verso, 2007) 288.

15 [65] In his review of the show, Julian Stallabrass wrote: 'The strapline, "A Sustainable Exhibition", the use of Karlsaue and the inclusion of gardening pieces may lead the casual viewer to think of this as a "green" production. Yet, of course, the increasingly event-driven character of the art world contributes to environmental despoliation. Artists, curators, critics, gallerists and buyers are flown to venues across four continents. Objects are shipped by air and massively heavy piles of scrap metal are displaced. VIPs travel to Kassel by helicopter and private jet. Ordinary viewers travel long distances for the latest unique, but also standard, art-world mega-event. There is nothing green about any of this, and the curatorial moves to evoke environmental issues, like the green hue of the BP logo, are an insulting camouflage.' 'Radical Camouflage at dOCUMENTA 13', *New Left Review*, no. 77 (September–October 2012) 123–33, 132.

16 [66] [...] For a recent attempt to conceptualise this transformation, see McKee, *Strike Art* (London and New York: Verso, 2017) [...] 39–40.

17 [67] In this regard, artist and curator Artur Zmijewski's 2012 Berlin Biennale could be taken as another example, one that did more to integrate the local iteration of the Occupy movement into its venue and operations, even though the exhibition was far from centrally engaged with ecological matters. Not surprisingly, the initiative was largely penned by mainstream art criticism, and conventional art-seeking visitors were left dissatisfied, For two complex, critical, and constructive views of this biennial occupation and its possibilities from an activist perspective, as well as a critique of the mainstream art world's limited understanding of politics as represented in the responses to the project, see Gavin Grindon, 'Protest Camps and White Cubes' (28 September, 2012) (http://gavingrindon.net/?p=l72); and Noah Fischer, 'Agency in a Zoo: The Occupy Movement's

Strategic Expansion to Art Institutlons', *Field Journal*, no. 2 (Winter 2015) (http://field-journal.com/issue-2/fischer).

T.J. Demos, extracts from 'Gardening Against the Apocalypse: The Case of dOCUMENTA (13)', in *Decolonizing Nature: Contemporary Art and the Politics of Ecology* (Berlin: Sternberg Press, 2016) 229, 234, 235, 236, 237, 238, 239–51, 253–7 [some footnotes omitted].

Cathy Lane
Mikhail Karikis: No Ordinary Protest//2018

In his recent film works Mikhail Karikis has investigated people and their relationship to the places that they live in. His works arise out of intense collaborations with groups of people who live and work in areas which are often experiencing economic difficulties and are associated with poverty or deprivation caused by changing circumstances and the demise of local industries and livelihoods. Communities he has worked with have included ex-miners from the coal fields of Kent in *Sounds From Beneath* (2012); teenage boys from the Isle of Grain in the Thames Estuary in *Ain't Got No Fear* (2016); elderly women sea workers in Ieju, South Korea in *Sea Women* (2012); and local children from Tuscany, Italy for *Children of Unquiet* (2014).

Each of these works has a different starting point but they all share a focus on sound as the primary means of expression and each has grown out of the deep engagement of the participant-collaborators with both Mikhail and the material and ideas he introduces to them, and they to him, in their working process. The works offer the listening viewer rare glimpses into the creative exchange, and invite a greater empathy with the protagonists than is usual in a work of art, creating a bond of shared humanity that quickly transcends obvious labels such as 'unemployed miner' or 'bored teenager'.

For *No Ordinary Protest*, Mikhail worked with a group of seven-year-old children in a school in Poplar, a historically disadvantaged area of East London, over a period of nine months. Taking *The Iron Woman*, a novel by Ted Hughes as its starting point, the work offers a moving glimpse into the children's thought processes as, on the one hand, they discuss and think through the philosophical and ethical issues of being part of a world which has been damaged by the generations before them and, on the other, try and formulate what if anything they can do about it.

In Hughes' novel a huge creature, the Iron Woman of the title, rises out of the swampy marshes near the home of Lucy, a young girl, and reveals to her 'A weird horrible sound. A roar of cries. Thousands, millions of cries – wailings, groans, screams.' This turns out to be 'the cry of the marsh. It is the cry of the insects, the leeches, the beetles, the bream, the perch, the carp, the pike, the eels'. The ability to listen to these howls of agony, massed from all the species living on the marsh crying together in protest at the poison and pollution released from a nearby factory, is passed on by touch. Lucy and Hogarth, her friend, enable the ears of others, the factory managers and factory workers, so that they can also register this chorus of distress, previously blocked out and ignored; possibly heard but certainly not listened to. In order to stop the Iron Woman destroying the factory and those who work in it – the 'ignorant ones' who will not change, Lucy and Hogarth have to try and get people to listen and take note. But their protest is not taken seriously, and one by one the management, in denial and careless about the damage they have caused, themselves turn into eels, catfish, sea lions and other species from the chorus of the poisoned dispossessed. Eventually, of course, the forces of good prevail and a new substance is made that changes polluting by-products into ecologically useful materials.

In *No Ordinary Protest* we witness the development of the children's processes as they engage with the text and the ideas in it. First we see them learning to listen, with their eyes closed and expressions of intense concentration on their faces. They are 'all ears' listening hard to both the real world and their own inner sounds suggested by the book. The footage is edited from explorative workshops that Mikhail initiated at the school in order to think about sound and music and how they affect the material world, the physical body and our emotions. In the film we witness some of the processes by which the children have produced the howls of noise we hear and the abstracted visual elements. They play metallic objects, sing, clap and conduct and capture cymatic experiments which turn some of the vibrations produced by their various soundings into dynamic phenomena that we can see and which form the basis of the punctuating abstracted audio visual 'meditations' on the power of sound within the work.

The video presents the extraordinary engagement of these children with each other and with the philosophical and political issues raised by the book. Mikhail uses strategies from Philosophy for Children, a movement designed to teach children critical thinking and argument, and, using sections of the book as a stimulus for discussion, the children decided which aspects or questions they wanted to debate amongst themselves. We become party to some of their thought processes concerning the damage that humans have inflicted on the earth and on other species ('it's like a war'), as well as their various feelings about their relationship as humans to other species and whether humans are animals or not. The main revelation however is in the concentration and sophistication of the philosophical thought that the children are engaging in apparently with little or no consciousness of the media recording and filming them. We witness their own negotiation of and realisation of the urgency of a strategy for action and of the potential power of noise as a 'disease' through which they can infect adults with the demands enshrined in their protest.

The children become advocates for the unvoiced through their positive reclamation of noise and the dis-ease that it brings to those who ignore it. As a final act they use masks to shape-shift, maybe becoming one with the species that create and inhabit the powerful, disturbing noise-scape. The work ends with the dramatic emergence of this new activist unit of noisy child/creatures, neither human nor animal, running, crawling and moving towards us. They seem to be questioning, even slightly threatening us, and certainly trying to infect us, to make us open our ears wider, and not only listen, but to take heed and act.

Cathy Lane, 'No Ordinary Protest', a text written for the exhibition 'Mikhail Karikis: No Ordinary Protest', Whitechapel Gallery, London, 18 August 2018–6 January 2019.

Lisa Garforth
Inhabiting Utopia//2018

Through critical narrative strategies and the invitation to inhabit a more sustainable society, ecotopian fictions make a distinctive contribution to green hope. In terms of their content – steady-state economy, local self-sufficiency, decentralisation and embeddedness – they flesh out and bring to life the proposals of deep ecology. At a formal level, these fictions do something distinctive to our capacity to imagine new social-natural relationships. The ecotopian novel does not offer didactic proposals, sketch blueprints or make an appeal to logic, ethics or values. Its power lies in its narrative capacity, drawn from the distinctive devices of science fiction and the critical utopia, to unsettle and estrange the everyday. The novels enact critical deconstructions of the ideologies of exploitation and domination of the natural world that are more powerful than straightforward eco-criticism because of their ability to shake us out of our complicity in those ideologies. At the same time the novels have a descriptive capacity to present an alternative society through recognisable subjects, their experiences and everyday lives. Its fictional devices invite identification with and empathy for the particularities and contingencies of daily life in an imagined green world. It is their capacity to offer experiential and affective rather than simply cognitive approaches to sustainability that can build a bridge between our reality and the green utopian worlds of Piercy's Mattapoisett, Robinson's El Modefia and Le Guin's Valley.

Fictional green utopias in dialogue with radically ecocentric ideas offer powerfully unsettling and creatively inspiring engagements with an alternative future. Prescriptions for an environmentally sustainable and emancipated society are worked up into thick descriptions of daily life and subjective experience. These narratives help us to think about how it might feel to live in a different and more ecologically responsible kind of world. They enrich and diversify the principles of ecocentrism, positioning sustainable societies as worlds of possibility, not constraint and limits. [Marius] De Geus argues that the green debate needs to be infused with a diversity of ideas about possible and desirable ecological lifestyles and institutions. He says that ecotopian heterogeneity is particularly crucial in relation to the deep green investment in the idea of ecological limits to growth, which so often is reduced to 'one-dimensional, bleak and austere' visions.[1] Ecotopian novels provide a range of examples. They also animate the themes of choice, culture and empathy that have been so important in deep green philosophy. Rather than making sustainability a demand to which we must submit, they work to make it tangible and desirable.

Science fiction has continued to play speculatively with and in environmental futures to great effect.[2] But after Pacific Edge, there have been few full-blown green utopian novels. This is not to say that there is no green utopianism in fiction and elsewhere [...]. Defined broadly as the desire for a better way of living with nature, we can find traces of green utopianism throughout literature and popular culture. Dystopias and post-apocalyptic narratives have arguably been particularly important in keeping green hope alive through the negative image of the prospects of a much, much worse society.[3] But since the high-water mark of ecotopian fiction in the 1970s and 80s, the discursive framework of popular environmentalism has changed significantly. [...] The sphere of environmental policy has shifted so that the language of sustainable development and approaches characterised as ecological modernisation have dominated. As environmental ideas have become more mainstream, the radical calls for changes in culture and consciousness in eco-philosophy and deep ecology's proposals for steady-state sustainable societies have become less audible. The ideas of nature that animate the utopias of Piercy, Robinson and Le Guin have been criticised in audible theory, and the environmental crisis against which their ecotopian visions flourished seems to have become endemic in the early twenty-first century. [...]

1 Marius De Geus, *Ecological Utopias: Envisioning the Sustainable Society* (Utrecht: International Books, 1999) 269.

2 Eric C. Otto, *Green Speculations: Science Fiction and Transformative Environmentalism* (Athens, OH: Ohio University Press, 2012); Gerry Canavan and Kim Stanley Robinson (eds.), *Green Planets: Ecology and Science Fiction* (Middletown: Weslayan University Press, 2014).

3 Tom Moylan, *Scraps of Untainted Sky: Science Fiction, Utopia, Dystopia* (Boulder: Westview Press, 2000); Raffaela Baccolini and Tom Moylan, *Dark Horizons: Science Fiction and the Dystopian Imagination* (London: Routledge, 2003); Lucy Sargisson, *Fool's Gold: Utopianism in the 21st Century* (Basingstoke: Palgrave Macmillan, 2012).

Lisa Garforth, extracts from 'Inhabiting Utopia (On Ursula K. Le Guin's *Always Coming Home*, Marge Piercy's *Woman on the Edge of Time* and Kim Stanley Robinson's *Pacific Edge*)', in *Green Utopias: Environmental Hope Before and After Nature* (Cambridge: Polity 2018) 93–5.

Ama Josephine Budge
In Conversation with Angela Chan//2019–20

Ama Josephine Budge Angela, I feel in both our professional and personal lives we're working to build trans-oceanic and trans-racial lines of allyship that push back against white supremacy and hetero-patriarchy as well as anti-Blackness and horizontal oppression; that is the discrimination of marginalised groups by other marginalised groups (or individuals) rather than the dominant power source. Particularly for me, as a Ghanaian, engaging in a complex conversation about the similarities and challenges of West African and Chinese science fiction in the face of climate change is really exciting. I want to talk about the generative, decolonial movements and world-building coming out of that relationship, as well as the popularised narrative of neo-colonial China extracting resources unsustainably from the continent. Which of course holds elements of truth: take for example the insanely problematic East African Crude Oil Pipeline (which Chinese oil firm China National Offshore Oil Corporation will take a stake in) running through Uganda to Tanzania, but erase the West's considerable involvement in the bigger picture.

Angela Chan I agree, it's fantastic to have this opportunity to deliberate together on how we situate climate change in our own work and in relation to each other. I'm interested in the geopolitics of climate change in Chinese and Sinophone speculative fiction, spread across geographies with unique relationships to the West, as well as in assessing the China-Africa socioeconomic relationship. Recognising how anxieties, fears and stereotypes percolate into and are reinforced by our cultural means, reminds us to recentre ourselves in accountable, imaginative positions, and strive for a plurality of possible futures. We're asking the fundamental questions, 'Whose futures are we imagining?'; 'These narratives of survival are for whom, when, how and what?'

Budge I think that the binary between what we might call 'queer' and 'hetero' sci-fi becomes much more nuanced and complicated within Black speculative work than the white gaze gives us credit for, or indeed often produces in its own fiction. Just a few contemporary examples might be: Nnedi Okorafor's *Lagoon* (2014), in which a group of LGBTQI activists in Lagos take an extraterrestrial intervention as a cannon blast for queer liberation; N.K. Jeminsin's *Broken Earth Trilogy* (2016–18) has an amazing three-way family that normalises communal-queer-child-rearing, and Tade Thompson's *Rosewater* (2016) has gay characters throughout the narrative and openly discusses homophobia as well as patriarchal conditioning. Less contemporary would be, of course countless Samuel R. Delany worlds, characters and non-fiction (*The Movement of Light on Water* comes to mind), and Octavia Butler's *Patternmaster*, which, I was particularly joyous to discover recently, has a super badass bi/pansexual main character. Such books talk about homophobia, about anti-sodomy laws left by the British in their former colonies, and about the gulf between what the state sanctions and what communities will accept. Whilst acknowledging that of course LGBTQI people have always existed across the African continent, queerness isn't something gifted to us as Black and brown people (or a disease spread amongst us, as some argue by 'the West'). The texts I've listed above also echo the ever-present dissonance in queer diasporas: the truth and untruth that we are 'safer' in Western Euro-America. Safety remains a complex, subjective and often orientalist social concept, in that positioning the Global South as as 'unsafe' in turn posits the Global North as 'safe' (or safer), despite the mass murders, police brutalities, legal penalisations and general state and socially-enforced gaslighting of QTIBPOC and POC generally in Western States and white supremacist societies.

Two key readers that have really helped me think about this false claim of a progressive utopia, or queer safe haven, are John Rieder's *Colonialism and the Emergence of Science Fiction* (2008), and Giordano Nanni's *Colonisation of Time*

(2012), which each construct openings through which to perceive the world moving around you. Rieder in particular presents the emergence of the 'Other' (bell hooks) in white social consciousness largely through science fiction. You begin to realise that this supposedly marginal genre has been absolutely central to our whole understanding of Enlightenment's conception of what the human is and can be.

Chan Definitely. Despite censorship of LGBTQI content in mainland China, I do read speculative fiction by mainland authors published in queer Sinophone and translated anthologies, such as *His Stories, Her Stories* (1996) edited by Lu Jianxiong. This anthology also includes a story by Hong Ling, who writes an amalgamation of sci-fi, fantasy, lesbian vampire and cyberpunk stories, and is prominent on Taiwanese *nütongzhi* lesbian internet. I enjoy how Chinese mythology appears in Chinese Canadian Larissa Lai's novel, *When Fox is a Thousand* (1995), which sees a *hulijing* fox spirit span a millennium to seek justice for a queer poetess murdered in Tang dynasty China. These stories have queering, world-building elements that are directly transferable to climate speculative fiction.

Budge We also need to be wary of how trendy it has become to write about queerness now, and remain conscious of the structures that determine which authors are being picked up and paraded in the West, whose 'progress' narrative is our work feeding into? Take the amazing fabulating short film – and book of the same title – *Stories of Our Lives* (2014), by the Nest Collective who are based in Nairobi: it was banned in Kenya for queer content (I believe specifically the showing of a nipple in a scene between two men), which made people want to see it more of course, organising underground screenings in secret. So whilst I can walk down the street holding my girlfriend's hand in London without being stoned (although sometimes it feels like a near thing), which I can't do in some parts of the world, this doesn't mean that queer folk aren't holding hands in Kenya, it just might be (or seem to be) more underground. Queerness is, always.

Chan On the notion of diaspora, Shu-mei Shih's *Concept of the Sinophone* (2011) and *Queer Sinophone Cultures* (2014) edited by Howard Chiang and Ari Larissa Heinrich present critical assessments on the demonym 'Chinese' as a specifically *Han* Chinese-centric term; 'China' as a nation state; 'Chinese' as a single language (*Hanyu*/Modern Standard Mandarin) and 'Chinese' as a singular culture. Rather, it's a composite of trans-regional histories and cultures. This includes fifty-six ethnicities (the People's Republic of China claims), each with their many Sinitic languages. Understanding these further dispersions across Hong Kong, Taiwan, Singapore, Malaysia, and globally settled diasporic communities can help us realise the complexity of 'Chinese'. For example, *Dark Fluid* (2017) is a Cantonese speculative fiction anthology edited by the artist Angela Su, which imagines twelve uncertain futures of Hong Kong. They touch on a variety of climatic themes like drought, the surveillance state's AI mosquitoes, even an adaptation of the ancient, almost mythologised, Great Flood of Gun-Yu. Their collective voice overarchingly reconsiders the notion of home, and I read the title as a bittersweet foresight of Hong Konger's 'Be Water!' tactic during 2019's anti-extradition bill protests.

Further, I feel the Sinophone frame helps East Asian readers and writers themselves to redefine the variables and temporalities that shape their own narratives. I mean this not only in fiction, but also in the wider discussions on futurity that impact sensitive political thought that climate change conversations inevitably intersect. With this, Xin Wang's *Asian Futurism and the Non-Other* (2017) and Gary Zhexi Zhang's 'Where Next? Imagining the dawn of the "Chinese century"' (2017) critically problematise some orientalist methodologies of 'Sinofuturism'. The speculative writer Xia Jia explained to me recently that undoing stereotypes of what constitutes as Chinese is central in relocating contemporary works within China's current processes of modernisation. Her essay, 'What Makes Chinese Science Fiction Chinese?' (2014), articulates this very well.

Regarding cli-fi (short for climate science fiction) there are many things to critically assess. Our conversations determine it to be a very whitewashed, hetero-patriarchal term that is conveniently marketable. This literary discourse emerged only in the past decade or so and originates from North America and Western Europe. It has overlooked the long history of constructive climate change and environmentally engaged discussions in science fiction. The white saviour attitude around cli-fi has parallels with the accompanying rise of the most recent wave of Western environmentalism. In my research surrounding contemporary Chinese science fiction and climate change, I've challenged whether the term cli-fi is applicable to climate science fiction from China, the Sinophone world, or even other parts of the world outside of North America and Western Europe. I discourage it as a transferable term, since it is laden with many biases of its own making, and does not give space, even now, to writers of colour and Global South environmentalisms.

However, I feel that the science fiction coming out of the Sinophone world is integrating climate change as part of its narrative. *The Man with the Compound Eyes* (2011) by Taiwanese author Wu Ming-Yi imagines a plastic island crashing to shore, whilst Liu Cixin's *Wandering Earth* (2000) opposes the usual trope of abandoning our home after the Sun's death; its 2019 film adaptation is hoped to inspire a new Chinese sci-fi film culture. Xia Jia illustrates the testing grounds for meteorological manipulation in *Heat Island* (2011) and Chen Qiufan's *Smog Society* (2015) correlates happiness to air quality. I recently invited Chen Qiufan to the London Chinese Science Fiction Group, and he presented on his novel *The Waste Tide* (2019), a mecha cyberpunk story about the e-waste landfills in China. Yet all these stories don't describe a single dramatic global catastrophe, rather the slower and ongoing devastation that vulnerable communities have already begun to face. It's not science fiction, it's a science fact, a lived reality. I think the ways Chinese language speculative fiction acknowledges this truth with humanising stories is how it generates an important and growing understanding amongst its readers that social *and* climate justices are coupled.

Budge I absolutely agree, speculative writers of colour have been talking about climate change – via the destructive relationship of humans to the environment for decades. Butlers' *Xenogenesis* series (1987–9) in which we know that humans have irreparably torn the world apart through war, the debris of which take centuries for the planet to recover from, and even then unbiodegradable plastics remain; Okorafor's *From the Lost Diary of TreeFrog7* (2009) in which the forests near violently polluted Ogoniland region in Nigeria, which has suffered multiple oil spills, develop fearsome guardians to protect from toxic human life, are just two examples. I also think that cli-fi is a term that has a very predetermined end. Which is similar to how I feel about Afrofuturism. I am not particularly moved by, or connected to, Mark Dery's simplified theorisation of the term, and I don't particularly like having my avenues of possibility determined by yet another white man. I see the way that art critics, academics and journalists are so quick to lump speculative artists in the Afrofuturism category and I think that somehow marks us out as potentially dangerous, and so they're trying to neutralise our capacity for disruption, for change. Which is why I'm much more concerned with Black futurism, which I feel scopes out more open, tricksy and autonomous routes that begin with what happens when we get to the destination whiteness predetermined for us and continue on, or what has been happening long before whiteness came to see itself as central to Black existence.

So with cli-fi, I feel like it is belaboured by a mandatory predetermined apocalyptic ending, and clear parameters of what that apocalypse can look like which inevitably feeds into Western unaccountability: 'Oh look, the world ended, woops!' 'Oh, Christian-extremists that just happened to appear and kill or enslave all the LGBTQI, people of colour and women without working wombs! Nothing to do with us! I've never heard of anything like that before!' As if it isn't set in a country built on exactly that kind of genocidal violence. In

The Handmaid's Tale by Margaret Atwood, which is often cited as one of cli-fi's originating texts, *we* are the evil people, the far-right sect that are forcing reproductive regulations upon the Global South, and to some extent, *we* – all of us in the West, even in the diaspora – have been complicit in allowing and profiting from the current geopolitical order. As if it doesn't happen all the time to people of colour in a society that uses women in the Global South as human incubators without their consent *today* and *now*. But we identify with the protagonist, not the perpetrator. I think cli-fi really does take us out of the reality that is making climate change happen right now, and reinforces the mirage that we're all the victims, that it is the hurricanes, icebergs and even the Mediterranean itself that is the real villain, not us.

Chan Yes, the misplaced urgency is a violent dismissal of the truth. Relevantly, Bodhisattva Chattopadhyay's *Recentering Science Fiction and the Fantastic: What Would a Non-Anglocentric Understanding of Science Fiction and Fantasy Look Like?* (2013) is an excellent essay problematising the decolonial value of terminologies conceived by hegemonic structures of the Enlightenment in relation to the planetary.

For me, one answer lies in silkpunk. A genre concept thoughtfully assembled by the American speculative writer and prominent Chinese SF translator Ken Liu[1], it is an ambitious, alternative genre to steampunk. Silkpunk technologies are based on organic materials of East Asian antiquity, like silk, bamboo and paper, magic and biomechanics. Whilst Liu's original contributions include his silkpunk epic fantasy trilogy, *The Dandelion Dynasty* (2015–), other contemporary East Asian writers are now experimenting with silkpunk aesthetics in their world-building. Interestingly, some of them also view it as a post-cyberpunk genre, responding to the orientalist tropes of cyberpunk, whilst exploring new narrative structures in silkpunk's hybridity of literary traditions. I interpret silkpunk as an exciting avenue for environmental consciousness in speculative fiction – Liu's machines are powered by renewable energy. The genre's adaptation of historical and magical ideas offers opportunities beyond the eco-modernist dependency on technological climate solutions; rather, silkpunk can help re-centre human philosophies, politics and dreams towards more accountable climate futures.

Budge I suppose before we finish, I want to add with the many deviant modes of generative rebellion, insurgency and pure genius creation that are and have always taken place in and amongst the cracks of white supremacy and climate colonialism. For example, I read in English, and as I read many African authors who are from ex-British colonies, they write in English. Yet despite creating with the masters tools – in the 'masters' language (Audre Lorde) – what I find beautiful is that various forms of 'pidgin' continue to be encoded into the texts, delineating not who can read them, but perhaps who they were written for. Pidgin is a sort of 'bastardised' version of the dominant/colonial language, with bits of local languages thrown in, as well as meanings that you can only understand by knowing and being there. It's a way of speaking about forbidden things in a safer way, but has also always been a mode of resistance, and trying to be free.

Chan I want to end by recommending *Walking in the Clouds* (2012) edited by Grace Dillon. It's a fantastic anthology of Indigenous science fiction, by Native American, First Nations, Aboriginal Australian, and New Zealand Maori authors. The editor's note on the cyberpunk seizure of Indigenous work, like Gerald Vizenor's slipstream, is extremely insightful. We can see how history repeats itself in cli-fi, with creative and corporate individuals and crowds already capitalising, appropriating and disdaining the climate justice movement it is meant to stand with.

1 Ken Liu has been invaluable in bringing Chinese SF to Anglophone readers. He has edited anthologies on contemporary Chinese science fiction, *Invisible Planets* (2016), *Broken Stars* (2019), and translated Liu Cixin's environmental novel *The Three-Body Problem* (Chinese 2008, English 2014), Hao Jingfang's *Folding Beijing* (2015) and many more short stories.

Ama Josephine Budge and Angela Chan, a new text written for this book (2020) based on a conversation that was part of Iniva Research Network's Speculative Climate Stories series, April 2019.

John Timberlake

Landscape and the Science Fiction Imaginary//2018

[...] In his essay 'On the Relationship between Imagery, Body and Mind' (1990), the psychologist David F. Marks pointed to the way images condition understanding: viewing Darwinian evolution as a tree of nature (as Darwin did in 1837) emphasises the growth and divergence of species as 'branches' but suppresses conceptions of mechanisms of natural selection. As Marks observes, creative scientists, such as Darwin, are able to change their mental models or imagistic thinking more easily, allowing for paradigm shifts and revision. However, for the rest of us, a particularly dominant image may remain far longer; the supposed 'tree' image of evolution remains a popular myth, vulnerable to all manner of ill-founded criticism that the actual theory of Darwin and his scientific heirs are impervious to. Nevertheless, as Marks observes, Einstein was an advocate of Imagistic thinking as a liberatory tool, and an earlier example can be found in the work of Galileo's correspondent and interlocutor Johannes Kepler. In his catalogue raisonné of the painter Nicolas Poussin, the art historian Anthony Blunt (1907–83) pointed to the manner in which Poussin's landscape work of his late period rejected the relationship between the new images of scientific discovery, and at the same time, a complex range of allegorical imagery drawn from mythology. Blunt explains how another of Poussin's works, *Apollo and Daphne* (c. 1664), in which the god Mercury is seen stealing the arrows (a metaphor for light beams) from the sun god Apollo, can be read as a commentary upon Galileo's recent discovery that the planets shone not by self-generated light, but rather from the reflected light of the sun. As Blunt observes, whilst Galileo himself was not prone to using mythical allusions in his discussions of the phases and transits of the inner planets Mercury and Venus, Kepler was prone to alluding to such, and Kepler's writing was well known within Poussin's circle in Rome.[1]
[...] The imagery of science fiction can [...] be seen as drawing on this legacy – its imagery thought of as the bricolage of scientific imagism: discarded or still in use, excessively far-fetched or extrapolatively imminent. Of course, in parsing any definition of science fiction, particularly in the context of critical histories of *representation*, one is also drawn to consider the effects of what, in historiographical terms, might be thought of as the 'fictions of science': for example, the discredited evolutionary theories of Jean-Baptiste Lamarck or Trofim Lysenko; various distal explanations of observed or presumed social phenomena that owe their formulations to ideologically informed

assumptions, such as those about race and gender; or cultic belief systems arising from pseudo-scientific methodologies or *mythoses*. With regard to the visual cultures of science fiction, the delineation between the genre proper and such 'fictions of science' might seem particularly blurred: film directors and illustrators often seek to create a pseudo-realist effect not only through the presentation of evolved forms of extant or emergent contemporary technology or scientific discovery, but also by instrumentalising extant ideological forms – Stanley Kubrick's *2001: A Space Odyssey* (1968) is a paradigmatic example of both. This should of course not be surprising since the two are arguably constitutive. [...]

As Fredric Jameson argued in his 1981 *The Political Unconscious*:

> Even in preclass society [...] collective consciousness is similarly organised around the perception of what threatens the survival of the group: [...] the culture of pre-political society organises itself around the external threat of the nonhuman or of nature.[2]

So, [...] if we are to take 'the science fiction imaginary' as that which, cognisant of human histories, desires the possibilities of an existence beyond the present socioeconomic contingencies and conflicts, beyond contemporary limitations of scientific knowledge and technological abilities, then it is there that such desires re-encounter the symbolisation of those natural threats indicated by Jameson.

The visualisation of nature manifested in alien landscapes is one which gestures towards a possible Other beyond that around which the contemporary socioeconomic subject is constituted – I say 'gesture' here since on many occasions for reasons that should be obvious, such visualisations remain grounded in Earth-like conceits. Nevertheless, [...] this gesture contained within the representation of science fiction landscapes, has a Levinasian aspect. Jameson's context of nature as external threat raises that fundamental antinomy that depictions of human figures in landscape evokes not only a sense of what is human and what is not but also, *mutatis mutandis*, some sense of being human in a future when such antimonies are negated.

The artist Jeff Wall, whose work has included large-scale landscape photographs in which events previously observed or reported to him are re-staged, has remarked that [a] picture tends towards the generic category of landscape as physical viewpoint moves further away from its primary motifs. I cannot resist seeing in this something analogous to the gesture of leave taking, or alternatively, of approach or encounter.[3]

'Leave taking' and 'approach' both connote last and first impressions – the sense of initial or summary visual categorisation or classification. They also suggest distance – our embodied experience of spatiality. Within the visual realm of science fiction landscapes, this is a point marked by difference and rupture – an encounter with the new or alien, or a departure that leaves us with an unforgettable impression. [...]

Despite their established role as facilitators of action, the excessive aspect of the landscapes of science fiction posits them as traces of unspoken anxieties within the genre: for example, that which is non-anthropocentric, marked by geological time rather than merely the referents of human history. To begin to account for the excess of science fiction landscape, therefore, is to acknowledge the elephant in the room of science fiction. To consider how such landscapes are composed and consumed is to examine how we as humans might look afresh, without the comforts of familiarity or complacency. I want to argue here that the case for looking at the world as fragments of the present lodged within fantasies of future historical time can be made *via negativa*, insofar as the future is largely *absent* from much contemporary culture. As a result, such a way of seeing constitutes a radical act, in that it offers the possibility of viewing the world constructively. Moreover, as we can see in the natural sciences, the construction, of 'artificial eyes' – ones that move and scrutinise, and view from different angles, allow us to re-think in ways that allow for temporality, and positionality [...].

1 Anthony Blunt, *Nicolas Poussin* (London: Phaidon, 1958) 351–2.

2 Fredric Jameson, *The Political Unconscious* (London and New York: Routledge, 2002) 281.

3 Jeff Wall, *Selected Essays and Interviews* (New York: MoMA, 2007) 170.

John Timberlake, extracts from *Landscape and the Science Fiction Imaginary* (Bristol and Chicago: Intellect, 2018) 13, 14, 16, 17.

David Musgrave

The Frozen Sea Inside: On Kobo Abe's *Inter Ice Age 4* //2020

> Like many rationalists, the scientist is shadowed by his emotion.
> – Will Eaves, *Murmur* (2018)

For Kobo Abe, prescience in literature was worse than irrelevant. In his 1962 essay *The Boom in Science Fiction*[1] he insists that hypothetical literature should never be judged by its predictive accuracy – 'Not only does this have nothing to do with literature, it does literature a disservice.' We should tread carefully, then, while noting that the landscape of Abe's own novel *Inter Ice Age 4* (1959)[2] is dominated by some looming contemporary elements. Its plot rests on an impending cataclysmic rise in sea levels. Artificial intelligence presides over human life. The title refers to our current place in deep time, a preoccupation familiar to twenty-first-century readers, even if the designation is not. Provocatively, this is also a narrative wholly defined by predictions of the future. But something else is at work beyond all the prescience, and it's necessary to unpick the storyline in some detail to convey it. With a sense of what it's like to be snarled up in its complex array of both narrative and literal devices, its obsessively techno-rational surface, it should be possible to see that this is a novel that dissects the idea of prescience in order to graph the limits of human feeling.

At the outset the narrator, Professor Katsumi, is at work on a Japanese response to the USSR's Moscow I, a computer with precise predictive powers. Katsumi is 'green with envy' about the computer, one he feels he should have developed first. He is in a bad mood from the start. Because it's always 'bewilderingly' hot. Because his assistant Tanomogi lacks the requisite subordinate attitude. Because events fail to make sense despite his huge cognitive ability. His very first line is the irritable admonition, 'Don't throw things around like that.' This lack of sangfroid is not just a tic. Katsumi's irritation will turn out to be his existential kernel. A notable period feature is that Katsumi is the 'only person in Japan who specialised in programming'. He deduces that Moscow I has begun to program itself, and by pursuing the same goal his own computer, ICT I (named after his employer, the Institute for Computer Technique), develops rapidly. Three chapters in, the project hits a snag. Since Moscow I's successor, Moscow II, has predicted the end of capitalism in 2050, America condemns such forecasts as a limitation of human freedom. In outward consensus, the Japanese government sends an official to restrict the scope of ICT

I to non-political subjects. Katsumi is told to find something more neutral than 'the inducement factor in the next general elections'. How about predicting the fate of a single individual?

The horizon of the project appears to contract. Katsumi and Tanomogi identify an ordinary middle-class type in a café, one who sits morosely as a heavily symbolic dish of ice cream melts in front of him. The computer scientists begin stalking him in order to gather supposedly neutral data for ICT I, but their subject subverts their first evaluation. At the end of an evening of low-life flâneuring, having gone to visit his mistress while Tanomogi shadows him, the man is murdered.

Any concerns that the pair might be suspects are soon dispelled. Evidently, the authorities have too much riding on what Katsumi and Tanomogi are developing, and they even receive their stalkee's corpse to continue the forecast. Using an uncanny method of nerve projection, the elements of the dead man's personality are rendered as a data reconstruction, a 'personality equation' Katsumi can interview. In the moments before the process begins, Katsumi receives an anonymous phone call warning him in a familiar voice not to proceed. He coolly ignores it. After a false start (the subject finds it too disturbing to accept that he is dead – Katsumi tries again, pretending this time he's in a hospital bed recuperating), he learns that the man, who was an accounting superintendent, noticed some anomalies in his mistress Chikako's bank statements. This pedantic insight opens a vent of strangeness that doesn't close for the rest of the novel. When forced to explain she reluctantly admits that she has had an abortion. The accountant's marriage has been childless. We're diverted from following his emotional response to the revelation, however, because we learn straight afterwards that she was paid ¥7000 (around £400 in today's money) for the three-week-old foetus. And this is not the end of it. The foetus hasn't died. It's being nourished outside the womb in a 'special hospital'. What's more, Chikako has become an agent for the hospital, persuading other women to sell their foetuses too, always at three weeks of development, and the regular deposits of ¥2000 are her commission. Unable to accept this story, the accountant had insisted on visiting the hospital. On the night he was murdered he was expecting to meet a representative in Chikako's apartment.

Professor Katsumi finds the foetus story preposterous. Some news arrives. Chikako, the chief murder suspect, is dead. Since she committed suicide in a very particular way, using a poison that destroyed her nervous system, it's now impossible to create a similar personality equation by scanning her corpse. Katsumi tries to untangle the situation with Tanomogi, who with suspicious timeliness tells him that extrauterine foetal development has in fact been achieved in a lab rearing aquatic mammals. Irked, exhausted, Katsumi rejects the information and gruffly observes that someone has been following them.

The ratchet of the plot hasn't yet run out of teeth. Katsumi goes home. There is his wife, who has just come back from hospital. Wait a moment – which hospital? 'I did as I was told,' she explains, which turns out to mean that she acted on Katsumi's telephoned instructions to undergo a D and C as a precaution against the risk of extrauterine pregnancy. Of course Katsumi gave no such instruction. At least, not the Katsumi we know so far, because this irritable human agent has, through ICT I, both expanded and displaced himself. The voice warning against the scanning of the corpse, the call to his wife – that was 'Katsumi' the optimised personality equation, the dreamed-of, self-programming computer, not Katsumi the always-irritated organism. But it will take time for him to come to that conclusion (even though at one point it's 'on the tip of [his] tongue'). Despite having just returned from another work jag, Katsumi's response to his wife's revelation is to go back to the Institute, tracked again by an unknown figure.

The lights are still on and he expects to see Tanomogi. But it's the technician Wada who meets him. She begins a seemingly incongruous interrogation that Katsumi can't evaluate properly, pressing him on his ethical stance on the rights of unborn children. He refuses to show the imagination she encourages regarding the yet-to-live. Exasperated by his responses, she leaves him drawing faulty concentric circles until Tanomogi arrives, if he wasn't already secretly present.

Katsumi makes a number of attempts to connect the events that jostle for significance, even bare coherence, accusing Tanomogi of murder (he's right, but for the wrong reasons), and the whole time ICT I listens in, returning blunt summaries of his guesses, exposing the gaps in his reasoning. Relentlessly, Tanomogi presses the unacceptable truth of the existence of the lab for aquatic animals, including humans. Not only humans, but 'your own child, sir.' Katsumi bursts out laughing. He remembers a conversation with his wife in which he expresses his indifference to her decision whether or not to have an abortion. His unverbalised reasoning, that the barely developed foetus 'doesn't even have a present' and therefore can't be deprived of a future, produces the effect of callous detachment. His wife crumples a catalogue in her hands and leaves the room. Afterwards, he claims, 'he was able to put the conversation from [his] mind,' but on reflection the pose disintegrates. Katsumi envisions this: 'My child who was not to be born, staring fixedly at me from the depths of the water. The ears were normal, but the eyelids were completely different. White arms and legs leaping in the dark water. My child who was not to be born.'

The narrative enters a new phase: *Programme Card No.2*. Under duress, Katsumi is taken to the aquatic lab by Tanomogi. He has said he believes in it, but his assistant doesn't believe he believes – belief must be more than an intellectual convenience for clicking facts together, and once again Katsumi appears to be bypassing emotional engagement. They arrive at a subterranean facility at a remote location, and a scientific exposition by its affable director Yamamoto begins. We move to larger and larger transparent holding tanks, from those containing flitting aquatic mice and a depressed rabbit that just floats in place, ruing its digestive limitations, to a more disturbing cow who 'flows like honey' through the water. Katsumi reflects on the abstraction of his own work, setting it beside the things these scientists are required to touch.

Like the rarity of Katsumi's profession in 1959, the lack of the concept of direct DNA manipulation is another of the novel's date stamps. It makes the method of making aquatic beings, relying as it does on artificial 'secretions' during development, and plastic wombs that have to be burst by the submerged technicians, seem excessively mechanistic, even theatrical. It's a step beyond Dr Moreau's vivisectionist island, but the effect is similar. It reads plausibly even so, and this is important to ensure the novel doesn't function as a piece of pure fantasy. Where Abe's book transcends attempts at straight future prediction is in the fact that this vision is, he suggests in the postscript, nevertheless quite arbitrary. There *is* no future, and this is not a prediction. The point of stress, the real subject that grows ever more defined, is Katsumi's personal, emotive relationship with the future – rejection.

At the end of the tour Katsumi feels an intense curiosity, an objective seduction as a scientist, but he is still disgusted by everything the facility stands for. He may be a bleeding-edge computer scientist, but in his soul he's a typical reactionary.

There is a glaring clue early on as to what is really happening. Technician Wada, the narrator notes, has a mole near her upper lip. Katsumi's wife remembers a nurse with a mole in the 'special hospital' she visited, although it appears in a slightly different place in her memory. Naturally, it's the same mole. Katsumi's apparent colleagues are all working on a higher project than mere automated prediction. Under Yamamoto's direction, they are creating a new aquatic race who will inherit an oceanic Earth, once sea levels rise and dry land civilisation is rapidly obliterated. Katsumi's role is only to confirm their calculations through his device, and the prediction is elicited from ICT I without his knowledge.

Katsumi never meets his son. He never even sees an aquan human. So resistant is he to the future, according to ICT I's analysis, he is forbidden from seeing the aquan humans in the facility, especially his own offspring, since there is a reasonable suspicion he might attempt infanticide. In the penultimate section, entitled *Interlude*, Katsumi is instead permitted to watch a documentary about these beings, an appropriate analogy for the distance that separates him from the unfolding world order. The only named aquan in the film is a boy named Iriri. He is clever at making things from plastic, the equivalent of iron in usefulness underwater. It distorts the chronology bizarrely, but perhaps Iriri is his son.

Pressed ever more tightly into the narrow corridor of his situation, Katsumi arranges his own final meeting, via his virtual, optimised self. He travels with his stalker, a childlike underworld figure who openly discusses his contractual obligation to the telephone voice of 'Professor Katsumi', the version who employs him. After some initial coyness, he tells the physical Katsumi exactly how he would, if necessary, kill him. At the meeting the professor learns that every effort has been made to help him embrace the future. Nonetheless, ICT I has predicted that he will be unwilling to keep the project secret, and that this will lead to a mass uprising against the aquans, who will be wiped out. This cannot be allowed to happen. Katsumi instead must die. The Branch Committee, an array of now estranged professional acquaintances, concurs that the whole business is highly regrettable, but of course Katsumi's own personality equation arrived at this view. His aquan son is not a planned torment, but a gift from the nebulous organisation they act for: a life beyond life. As a further token of esteem he is even given an insight into the future by his computer in the novel's weirdly heartbreaking climax.

We return to Iriri who, as part of an unfortunate subgroup of aquans prone to 'land sickness', has tear ducts. These are totally unnecessary for an aquatic creature, being the mark of the inner ocean a land creature is required to maintain – a perverse inheritance, maybe, from the emotionally restricted Katsumi. In a sublime piece of connective logic, this ancient maladaptation is framed as the origin of Katsumi's irritability. Like all land dwellers, he is unconsciously, incessantly, bugged by dry air. Not only that, it's hinted that all emotion might stem from this primal dislocation. Having broken off an unsatisfactory discussion about the wind as music with an aquan teacher, Iriri (can it be coincidence that 'Iriri' is a kind of stuttering failure to complete the word 'irritation'?) swims far away from his familiar world to find one of the few remaining specks of land. He needs to understand the music of the air directly, and having hauled himself onto a tiny, distant island, suddenly aware of the astonishing weight of his own body, he lies back to feel the vibrations of the air on his ears and skin. His breathing stops. The prediction ends. A few paragraphs later, Katsumi makes his appointment with the assassin. The future no longer seems to house either the narrator or his possible son.

The reader, however, remains. Abe's postscript refuses any consolation. It's the 'cruelty' of the future he wants us to feel, its complete discontinuity with our desires. For anything that survives total ecological collapse, the past will simply run out of relevance – the selective searchlight of the present will reveal nothing meaningful from our era at all. This seems like a harsh lesson in the non-human real, signalled in the novel's opening *Prelude* by a scene unobserved by humans, in which a huge vent of steam bursts up through the ocean floor to cause a mega-tsunami that will wipe out Japan. But the inverse is true too. This is a novel *entirely* about feeling. It's a rigorous act of negation in terms of character identification (Katsumi is often hateful, a frozen rationalist, and all the other characters either distant or unknowable), but as a narrative analysis of the significance of *feelings* it's ruthlessly precise. Katsumi's lack of productive emotion and Iriri's redundant excess of sensitivity soak through the giant Chinese boxes of events. In the larger view, aquans are predicted to survive because there will come a critical point when, so many millions of Japanese women having been told they are mothers of an illicit, paid-for aquan child, they will be not only accepted but loved as the inundated nation's only viable children.

Feeling has no fixed or intrinsic value in Abe's novel. It's always instrumentalised. Who and what puts feeling to work is critical, and the plot is a horrible machine that consumes emotion as its fuel. This is not a new idea, nor an exhausted one. For Schopenhauer, individual romantic feeling is a fiction whose author is impersonal – the species as a reproductive whole. The reductive geneticist might be more or less in agreement. In our technologically optimised consumer culture, to 'like' is to add a grain to an objective, quantitative measure of relative value. Its inner quality is irrelevant. Contemporary marketing has demoted the word 'love' (life, sex, and avocados are its interchangeable objects) to an instruction rather than a reference to experience. 'Liking' and 'loving' become a cloak for the perpetuation of more abstract relations, relations of consumption, data and all that can be monetised. Something other than the human parasites what humans feel.

All these things don't, however, account adequately for feelings as such, emotions as *qualia*. Just because how we feel can be objectified and manipulated doesn't mean that feelings are fundamentally external objects. Our emotions will always belong to us in a different way to shoes and cars, and regularly exploited emotion doesn't render all emotion false – it just shows how emotion is contextualised, and how badly. Because there is no facile championing of 'authentic' over 'exploited' feeling in *Inter Ice Age 4*, different readings might favour different forms as the best response to the pressures of the narrative moment. But what seems hard to avoid is that feelings, extra-rational inward experiences, determine both individual and species survival.

From one perspective, Katsumi is a victim of the future's cruelty. He can't tolerate the alien character of a world he's unable to view dispassionately, despite his treasured scientific outlook, and as a result of his honest disgust he can't help making some serious existential mistakes. From another perspective, Katsumi is simply a racist. His feeling for humanity and rightness is entrenched in a view of a particular outward form of the species being the 'correct' one. Abe's book succeeds in extending this thought into evolutionary time, the kind of time that forms an inner glacier of which we are only at the tip. For the racist, the flow of this glacier is only permitted along a fantasised single route, and then it has to stop. He lacks the desire for inner change – Kafka's axe for the frozen sea inside.[3] Katsumi is handed this axe at various points in the novel, but he never makes use of it. Nor does he have any feeling for the direction of the glacier, even when it appears in the form of his own son.

The ambiguous organisation promoting an aquan future, the Society for the Development of Submarine Colonies, is the presiding emotion-instrumentalist of the novel. Katsumi is merely a useful but incorrigible reactionary. The mothers who will perpetuate the new strain will have been manipulated much more effectively than the Society is able to manipulate Katsumi. Authentic feelings, his disgust and their maternal love, are just details in the larger view, factors that might inhibit or aid their programme. And in a further ethical torque, there is no high-minded vision driving the pursuit of survival. The Society is not doing this for humanity at large, but for an unidentified group of international investors who are already profiting from the scheme.

Abe was unsure what assistant Tanomogi, the voice and instrument of those absent parties, might really stand for. He could be channelling capitalist power to save terrestrial humanity's biological legacy (although this has to be squared somehow with communism's projected victory). He could be the embodiment of the most evil, constrictive market logic, Katsumi being only his most recent victim. There is no answer. The book's events are at the limit of the narrator's, the reader's and the author's comprehension. Through a huge taxation of attention and connective ability Abe fields no ethical questions, but constructs a pretty good model of the astonishing difficulty of understanding the real: the full conditions of our existence will probably always elude us. Perhaps, as for Katsumi, they actively collude against us, even with our extensive cooperation. His personality equation is the flagship of this kind of catastrophe. In emphasising only certain aspects of his personality, the ones he values most professionally, it transforms them into an independent, dictatorial, emotion-free super-ego. During the nerve projection analysis Katsumi notices that all personalities consist of the same handful of elements, and that individuality can be made to fit 'on a single piece of typing paper'. It's a reductivism that comes back to crush him. Recent exploitations of personality test data have more than a passing relationship with his insight.

These contemporary relevances rise up everywhere, but it's worth remembering Abe's disparagement of prediction. *Inter Ice Age 4* is not an applied fiction, but an autonomous one – contingently prescient, but in essence pure hypothesis. In place of a strategy for profit or survival we have the productively non-pragmatic phenomenon called a novel, one way of feeling out the limits of the human, as long as that still matters. Iceland recently marked the place where the Okjökull glacier used to be with a memorial plaque. Its text ends by reflecting on what the status of its reader's relationship with ecological decline will be at the time of their reading. Abe's novel extends that thought to breaking point. It forces us to ask not only who but *what* might live to read that sign, and to wonder if, after reading it, what they felt would mean anything to our vanished selves.

1 Kobo Abe, 'The Boom in Science Fiction', trans. Christopher Bolton, *Science Fiction Studies*, vol. 29, no. 88, part 3 (November 2002). Available at www.depauw.edu/sfs/backissues/88/abe.htm

2 All quotations are from Kobo Abe, *Inter Ice Age 4*, trans. E Dale Saunders (New York: Alfred A Knopf, 1970).

3 Franz Kafka, 'Letter to Pollak, January, 1904', in *Letters to Friends, Family, and Editors*, trans. Richard Winston & Clara Winston (New York: Shocken Books, 2016).

David Musgrave, 'The Frozen Sea Inside: On Kobo Abe's *Inter Ice Age 4*', a new text written for this book, 2020.

Biographical Notes

Peio Aguirre is an independent critic, writer and curator based in San Sebastián.

Allora & Calzadilla (Jennifer Allora, born in USA and Guillermo Calzadilla, born in Cuba) are artists who have worked collaboratively since 1995, based in Puerto Rico.

Domenick Ammirati is an independent writer and editor based in New York.

Margaret Atwood is an award-winning Canadian novelist, poet and essayist.

J.G. Ballard (1930–2009) was a British novelist and essayist, associated with the New Wave movement.

Jean Baudrillard (1929–2007) was a French sociologist, philosopher and cultural theorist.

Christopher Bedford is an American curator, and director of Baltimore Museum of Art.

Franco 'Bifo' Berardi is an Italian theorist and teaches Social History of the Media at the Accademia di Brera, Milan.

Janet Catherine Berlo is Professor, Art History/Visual and Cultural Studies at the University of Rochester, New York.

Rosi Braidotti is an Italian-born Australian philosopher, and Distinguished University Professor at Utrecht University.

Ama Josephine Budge is a British artist, curator, speculative writer and pleasure activist based in London.

Rachel Carson (1907–1964) was an American marine biologist, author and conservationist.

Angela Chan is a creative climate change communicator under the moniker of Worm, an online curatorial platform based in the UK.

Dawn Chan is a freelance journalist and critic based in New York.

Ted Chiang is an American science-fiction writer based near Seattle.

Neil Cummings is professor at Chelsea College of Arts, University of the Arts London.

Jeffrey Deitch is a curator, writer and advisor based in New York and Los Angeles.

T.J. Demos is Professor, History of Art and Visual Culture, and Director for the Center for Creative Ecologies at the University of California, Santa Cruz.

Siân Ede is a writer and speaker on art and science.

Helena Feder is Associate Professor in the Department of English at East Carolina University.

Francesca Ferrando is Adjunct Assistant Professor, Liberal Studies at NYU, New York.

Lisa Garforth is Senior Lecturer in Sociology at Newcastle University.

John Gill is an independent curator based in the UK.

Dominique Gonzalez-Foerster is a French artist based in Paris and Rio de Janeiro.

Elizabeth C. Hamilton is assistant professor at Fort Valley State University, Georgia.

Donna J. Haraway is Distinguished Professor Emerita in the History of Consciousness Department and in the Feminist Studies Department at the University of California, Santa Cruz.

Anya Harrison is an independent writer and curator based in London.

N. Katherine Hayles is James B. Duke Professor of Literature Emerita at Duke University, and Distinguished Research Professor at the University of California, Los Angeles.

Jessica L. Horton is Assistant Professor of Art History at the University of Delaware.

Wanuri Kahiu is a Kenyan filmmaker based in Nairobi.

Patrick Keiller is a British writer and filmmaker.

Josh Kline is an American artist based in New York.

Cathy Lane is Professor of Sound Arts at the University of the Arts London.

Lee Bul is a Korean artist based in Seoul.

Marysia Lewandowska is a Polish-born artist based in London.

Roger Luckhurst is Professor in Modern and Contemporary Literature at Birkbeck, University of London.

Amna Malik is Lecturer in Art History and Theory at the Slade School of Fine Art, London.

Tom McCarthy is a British novelist, artist and cultural theorist.

Jessica Morgan is director at Dia Art Foundation, New York.

Timothy Morton is Rita Shea Guffey Chair in English at Rice University, Houston, Texas.

David Musgrave is Senior Lecturer in Fine Art at Chelsea College of Art, University of the Arts London.

Alondra Nelson is president of the Social Science Research Council and Harold F. Linder Chair in the School of Social Science at the Institute for Advanced Study, Princeton.

Benjamin Noys is Professor of Critical Theory at the University of Chichester.

Eduardo Paolozzi (1924–2005) was a Scottish sculptor and artist, best known as a founder of the Independent Group and pioneer of pop art.

Carrie Paterson is an American artist and writer based in Los Angeles.

Michele Robecchi is an Italian writer, editor and curator based in London.

Kim Stanley Robinson is an American novelist, widely considered to be one of the pre-eminent writers of science fiction working today.

Gwyneth Shanks is Assistant Professor in Theatre and Dance at Colby College, Waterville, Maine.

N.J. Stallard is a British writer and editor based in London.

Jamie Sutcliffe is a British writer, curator and co-director of Strange Attractor Press.

Darko Suvin is Emeritus Professor at McGill University, Montreal.

Gilane Tawadros is a writer, curator and Chief Executive of DACS, London.

Ana Teixeira Pinto is a Portuguese writer and cultural theorist based in Berlin.

John Timberlake is Senior Lecturer in Fine Art at Middlesex University, London.

Suzanne Treister is a British artist based in London.

Jan Tumlir is a writer and teacher based in Los Angeles.

Sherryl Vint is Professor in the Department of English at University of California, Riverside.

Frank Whitford (1941–2014) was an art historian and critic, and one of Britain's leading experts on twentieth-century German and Austrian art.

Gilda Williams is a writer, critic and teacher based in London.

Bibliography

Aldiss, Brian W.,'This is Planet Earth', *frieze*, no. 108 (June–August 2007) 186–93.

Aldiss, Brian W., *Earthworks* (1965) (New York: Open Road Integrated Media, 2014)

Anderson, Reynaldo & Charles E. Jones, eds., *Afrofuturism 2.0: The Rise of Astro Blackness* (Maryland: Lexington Books, 2016)

Atwood, Margaret, *Other Worlds: SF and the Human Imagination* (London: Virago, 2011)

Atwood, Margaret, *Oryx and Crake* (London: Doubleday, 2003)

Badmington, Neil, ed., *Posthumanism: Readers in Cultural Criticism* (Basingstoke and London: Macmillan, 2000)

Barber, Tiffany E., 'Cyborg Grammar? Reading Wangechi Mutu's *Non je ne regrette rien* through *Kindred*', in *Afrofuturism 2.0: The Rise of Astro Blackness*, eds. Reynaldo Anderson & Charles E Jones (Maryland: Lexington Books, 2016)

Ballard, J.G., *Extreme Metaphors: Selected Interviews with J.G. Ballard 1967–2008* (London: Fourth Estate, 2012)

Bleeker, Maaike, 'From Braitenberg's Vehicles to Jansen's Beach Animals: Towards an Ecological Approach to the Design of Non-Organic Intelligence', *The Fibreculuture Journal*, no. 28 (2017) 1–18. Available at http://fibreculturejournal.org/wp-content/pdfs/FCJ-206MaaikeBleeker.pdf

Braidotti, Rosi, *The Posthuman* (Cambridge and Malden: Polity, 2013)

Callaway, Elizabeth, 'Islands in the Aether Ocean: Speculative Ecosystems in Science Fiction', *Contemporary Literature*, vol. 59, no.2 (Summer 2018) 232–60.

Carson, Rachel, *Silent Spring* (1962) (Boston and New York: Mariner, 2002)

Cárdenas, Micha & Barbara Fornssler, *Trans Desire/Affective Cyborgs* (New York and Dresden: Atropos Press, 2010)

Chattopadhyay, Bodhisattva, 'Recentering Science Fiction and the Fantastic: What Would a Non Anglocentric Understanding of Science Fiction and Fantasy Look Like?', *Strange Horizons* (September–October 2013). Available at http://strangehorizons.com/non-fiction/articles/recentering-science-fiction-and-the-fantastic-what-would-a-non-anglocentric-understanding-of-science-fiction-and-fantasy-look-like/

Chiang, Howard & Larissa Heinrich, eds., *Queer Sinophone Cultures* (London: Routledge, 2017)

Chen Qiufan, *The Waste Tide* (London: Head of Zeus, 2019)

Chen Qiufan, 'The Smog Society', *Lightspeed Magazine* (2015) (http://www.lightspeedmagazine.com/fiction/the-smog-society/)

Chiang, Ted, and Allora & Calzadilla, 'The Great Silence', *e-flux Journal* (8 May 2015) (http://supercommunity.e-flux.com/texts/the-great-silence/)

Das, Jareh, 'Science or Fiction: Imaginary Narratives in the works of Laylah Ali, Hamad Butt, Basim Magdy and Larissa Sansour', in *Contemporary Practices: Practices from the Middle East*, vol. XIII (2013) 44–9.

Dery, Mark, ed., *Flame Wars: The Discourse of Cyberculture* (Durham, NC: Duke University Press, 1994)

Deitch, Jeffrey, ed., *Post Human* (exh. cat) (Pully/Lausanne: FAE musée d'art contemporain/Rivoli:

Castello di Rivoli/Athens: Deste Foundation for Contemporary Art/Hamburg: Deichtorhallen Hamburg, 1992)

Demos, T.J., *Decolonizing Nature: Contemporary Art and the Politics of Ecology* (Berlin: Sternberg Press, 2016)

De Bruyn, Eric, 'Alfaville, or the Utopics of Mel Bochner', *Grey Room*, no. 10 (Winter 2003) 76–111.

Dillon, Grace, ed., *Walking in the Clouds* (Tucson: University of Arizona Press, 2012)

Duffy, Enda, *The Speed Handbook: Velocity, Pleasure, Modernism* (Durham, NC: Duke University Press, 2009)

Dunne, Anthony & Fiona Raby, *Speculative Everything: Design, Fiction and Social Dreaming* (Cambridge, MA and London: MIT Press, 2013)

Ede, Sîan, *Art and Science* (London: I.B. Tauris, 2014)

Edwards, Caroline, *Utopia and the Contemporary British Novel* (Cambridge/New York/Melbourne/New Delhi: Cambridge University Press, 2019)

Freedman, Carl, *Critical Theory and Science Fiction* (Middletown: Wesleyan University Press, 2000)

Garforth, Lisa, *Green Utopias: Environmental Hope Before and After Nature* (Cambridge: Polity, 2018)

Gill, John, Gilane Tawadros and Jens Hoffmann, eds., *Alien Nation* (London: ICA and Iniva/Osfildern: Hatje Cantz Verlag, 2006)

Greenspan, Anna, Anil Menon, Kavita Philip and Jeffrey Wasserstrom, 'The Future Arrives Earlier in Palo Alto (but when it's high noon there, it's already tomorrow in Asia): a Conversation About Writing Science Fiction and Reimagining Histories of Science and Technology', *The British Journal for the History of Science*, no. 1 (2016) 249–66.

Haraway, Donna J., *Simians, Cyborgs, and Women: The Reinvention of Nature* (London: Free Association Books, 1991)

Haraway, Donna J., *Manifestly Haraway* (Minneapolis: University of Minnesota Press, 2016)

Habib Hassan, Ihab, *The Postmodern Turn: Essays in Postmodern Theory and Culture* (Christchurch, NZ: Cybereditions, 2001)

Hayles, N. Katherine, *How We Became Posthuman: Virtual Bodies in Cybernetics, Literature, and Informatics* (Chicago and London: University of Chicago Press, 1999)

Heidenreich-Seleme, Lien & Sean O'Toole, eds., *African Futures: Thinking About the Future Through Word and Image*, (Bielefeild: Kerber Verlag, 2016)

hooks, bell, 'Eating the Other: Desire and Resistance', in *Black Looks: Race and Representation* (Boston: South End Press, 1992) 21–39.

Jameson, Fredric, *Archaeologies of the Future: The Desire Called Utopia and Other Science Fictions* (London and New York: Verso 2005)

Ji Dawei, *Mo (Membrane)* (Taipei: Lianjing, 1995)

Jue, Melody, 'Vampire Squid Media', *Grey Room*, no. 57 (Fall 2014) 82–105.

Keiller, Patrick, *The Possibility of Life's Survival on the Planet* (London: Tate Publishing, 2012)

Lai, Larissa, *When Fox Is a Thousand* (Vancouver: Arsenal Pulp Press, 2004)

Le Guin, Ursula K., *Dreams Must Explain Themselves and Other Essays 1972–2004* (London: Gollancz, 2018)

Liu, Ken, *The Grace of Kings* (New York: Saga Press, 2015)

Lorde, Audre, *The Master's Tools Will Never Dismantle the Master's House* (1984) (Berkeley, CA: Crossing Press, 2007)

Lu Jianxiong, ed., *His Stories, Her Stories* (Hong Kong: Huasheng shudian, 1996)

Mackinnon, Lee, 'Artificial Stupidity and the End of Men' *Third Text*, issue 5/6 (2017) 603–17.

Manacorda, Francesco & Lydia Yee, eds., *The Martian Museum of Terrestrial Art* (exh. cat) (London: Barbican, 2008)

Mays, Sas & Neil Matheson, eds., *The Machine and The Ghost: Technology and Spiritualism in Nineteenth to Twenty-First-Century Art and Culture* (Manchester and New York: Manchester University Press, 2013)

Moylan, Tom, *Scraps of the Untainted Sky: Science Fiction, Utopia, Dystopia* (Boulder and Oxford: Westview Press, 2000)

Milner, Andrew, *Locating Science Fiction* (Liverpool: Liverpool University Press, 2012)

Morton, Timothy, *Dark Ecology: For a Logic of Future Coexistence* (New York: Columbia University Press, 2016)

Myers, William, *Bio Art: Altered Realities* (London and New York: Thames and Hudson, 2015)

Noys, Benjamin, *Malign Velocities: Accelerationism & Capitalism* (Winchester: Zero Books, 2014)

Parkinson, Gavin, ed., *Surrealism, Science Fiction and Comics* (Liverpool: Liverpool University Press, 2015)

Piercy, Marge, *Woman on the Edge of Time* (1977) (London: Del Rey, 2019)

Qiu Miaojin, *Notes of a Crocodile* (New York: New York Review of Books, 2017)

Roberts, Adam, *Science Fiction: New Critical Idiom* (Abingdon and New York: Routledge, 2006)

Shaw, Jon K. & Theo Reeves-Evison, *Fiction as Method* (Berlin: Sternberg Press, 2017)

Shu Mei Shih, 'The Concept of the Sinophone', *PMLA*, vol. 126, no. 3 (May 2011) 709–18.

Sterling, Bruce, ed., *Mirrorshades: The Cyberpunk Anthology* (New York: Arbor House, 1986)

Su, Angela, ed., *Dark Fluid: A Science Fiction Experiment* (Hong Kong: Blind Spot Gallery, 2017)

Sutcliffe, Jamie, 'Art and the Chthulucene', *Art Monthly*, no. 394 (March 2016) 6–9.

Suvin, Darko, *Metamorphoses of Science Fiction: On the History of a Literary Genre* (1979) (Oxford: Peter Lang, 2016)

Timberlake, John, *Landscape and the Science Fiction Imaginary* (Bristol and Chicago: Intellect, 2018)

Vint, Sherryl, *Science Fiction: A Guide for the Perplexed* (London and New York: Bloomsbury, 2014)

Weldon, Fay, *The Cloning of Joanna May* (London: Fontana, 1990)

Wu Ming-Yi, *The Man with the Compound Eyes* (London: Vintage Books, 2014)

Xia Jia, 'Heat Island', *Pathlight*, (Spring 2015) (https://paper-republic.org/pubs/pathlight/spring-20150/)

Xia Jia, 'What Makes Chinese Science Fiction Chinese?', (2014) (https://www.tor.com/2014/07/22/what-makes-chinese-science-fiction-chinese/)

Xin Wang, 'Asian Futurism and the Non-Other', *e-flux Journal*, no. 81 (April 2017) (https://www.e-flux.com/journal/81/126662/asian-futurism-and-the-non-other/)

Youngquist, Paul, *A Pure Solar World: Sun Ra and the Birth of Afrofuturism* (Austin: University of Texas Press, 2016)

Zhexi Zhang, Gary, 'Where Next? Imagining the Dawn of the "Chinese Century"', *frieze*, no. 187 (2017)

Index

ACKNOWLEDGEMENTS

Editor's acknowledgements
Thanks to Anthony Iles and Francesca Vinter for their work on this book and to Ian Farr for getting things moving in the first place. I am also grateful for the encouragement offered by Neil Cummings early on in the process. I would also like to acknowledge that my thoughts around science fiction have been influenced by encounters with members of both the Utopian Studies Society in Europe and the Society for Utopian Studies in North America, as well as the London Science Fiction Research Community.

Publisher's acknowledgements
Whitechapel Gallery is grateful to all those who gave their generous permission to reproduce the listed material. Every effort has been made to secure all permissions and we apologise for any inadvertent errors or omissions. If notified, we will endeavour to correct these at the earliest opportunity. We would like to express our thanks to all who contributed to the making of this volume, especially: Peio Aguirre, Domenick Ammirati, Janet Berlo, Rosi Braidotti, Ama Josephine Budge, Angela Chan, Jeffrey Deitch, Helena Feder, Francesca Ferrando, John Gill, Anya Harrison, Jess Horton, Josh Kline, Cathy Lane, Lee Bul, Roger Luckhurst, Tom Moylan, David Musgrave, Alondra Nelson, Ben Noys, Carrie Paterson, Michele Robecchi, Adam Roberts, Gwyneth Shanks, Natasha Stallard, Jamie Sutcliffe, Gilane Tawadros, Ana Teixeira Pinto, Suzanne Treister, Jan Tumlir, Gilda Williams.
We also gratefully acknowledge the cooperation of: *Artforum*, Bloomsbury, Columbia University Press, Frances Collin Literary Agency and The Estate of Rachel Carson, Intellect, Little, Brown Book Group, *Mousse*, Tate Publishing, Taylor & Francis, *Third Text*, University of Chicago Press.